T0318285

Economic Growth and Convergence

There are many different types of convergence within economics, as well as several methods to analyse each of them. This book addresses the concept of real economic convergence or the gradual levelling-off of GDP (gross domestic product) per capita rates across economies.

In addition to a detailed, holistic overview of the history and theory, the authors include a description of two modern methods of assessing the occurrence and rate of convergence, BMA-based and HMM-based, as well as the results of the empirical analysis. Readers will have access not only to the conventional econometric approach of β convergence but also to an alternative one, allowing for the convergence issue to be expressed in the context of automatic pattern recognition. This approach is universal as it can be adapted to a variety of input data. The lowest aggregation level study investigates regional convergence through the case of Polish voivodships, where convergence towards the leader is tested. On a higher level of aggregation, the authors examine the existence of GDP convergence in such groups as the EU28, North Africa and the Middle East, sub-Saharan Africa, South America, Caribbean, South-East Asia, Australia and Oceania, or post-socialist countries. For each group, the real β convergence is tested using the two above-mentioned approaches. The results are widely discussed, broadly illustrated, interpreted, and compared. The analysis allows readers to draw interesting conclusions about the causes of convergence or the drivers behind divergence. The book will stimulate further research in the field, but the research was conducted from the point of view of individual countries.

Michał Bernardelli is Associate Professor and Vice-Dean of Graduate Studies at the SGH Warsaw School of Economics. He is a Doctor of mathematics with habilitation in the field of economic sciences. The interdisciplinarity of his scientific works is based mainly on the use of the IT and mathematical apparatus to solve problems in areas related to data analysis and exploration, in particular in Big Data issues, predictive methods, and optimization. For almost 20 years, he was a lecturer at courses related to studies in quantitative methods, as well as a consultant and contractor of many scientific and commercial projects.

Mariusz Próchniak is Associate Professor, Head of Department of Economics II, and Dean of Collegium of World Economy at SGH Warsaw School of Economics. He is the author or co-author of many books and journal articles on macroeconomics, including economic growth, real economic convergence, and quantitative studies in macroeconomics. He teaches both micro- and macroeconomics at undergraduate, graduate, and postgraduate (including MBA) courses.

Bartosz Witkowski is Full Professor, Head of the Institute of Econometrics, and Dean of Undergraduate Studies at SGH Warsaw School of Economics. He is the author and co-author of about 100 journal articles and books dedicated to the use of econometrics, particularly panel data, in economics and finance. His main research area is microeconometrics. For 20 years, he has been teaching various courses on econometrics and the use of quantitative methods at each level of studies as well as co-operating with numerous institutions such as the National Bank of Poland or the World Bank for providing training and expertise in this area.

Routledge Studies in the Modern World Economy

For more information about this series, please visit: www.routledge.com/
Routledge-Studies-in-the-Modern-World-Economy/book-series/SE0432

Economic Growth and Convergence

Global Analysis through Econometric and Hidden Markov Models

**Michał Bernardelli,
Mariusz Próchniak and
Bartosz Witkowski**

LONDON AND NEW YORK

First published 2021
by Routledge
2 Park Square, Milton Park, Abingdon, Oxon OX14 4RN

and by Routledge
605 Third Avenue, New York, NY 10158

Routledge is an imprint of the Taylor & Francis Group, an informa business

The research project has been financed by the National Science Centre, Poland (project number 2015/19/B/HS4/00362).

British Library Cataloguing-in-Publication Data
A catalogue record for this book is available from the British Library

Library of Congress Cataloging-in-Publication Data
Names: Bernardelli, Michał, author. | Próchniak, Mariusz, author. | Witkowski, Bartosz, author.
Title: Economic growth and convergence : global analysis through econometric and hidden Markov models / Michał Bernardelli, Mariusz Próchniak, Bartosz Witkowski. Description: Abingdon, Oxon ; New York, NY : Routledge, 2021. |
Series: Routledge studies in the modern world economy | Includes bibliographical references and index.
Identifiers: LCCN 2021001437 (print) | LCCN 2021001438 (ebook)
Subjects: LCSH: Economic development—Econometric models. | Econometrics. | Markov processes.
Classification: LCC HD75.5 .B47 2021 (print) |
LCC HD75.5 (ebook) | DDC 338.9001/5195—dc23
LC record available at https://lccn.loc.gov/2021001437
LC ebook record available at https://lccn.loc.gov/2021001438

ISBN: 978-0-367-77488-2 (hbk)
ISBN: 978-0-367-77490-5 (pbk)
ISBN: 978-1-003-17164-5 (ebk)

Typeset in Times New Roman
by codeMantra

Contents

Figures

Maps

Tables

Preface

A number of different concepts of convergence in economics and many more methods to analyse each of them can be found in the literature. This book concerns the concept of real convergence, which stands for the gradual levelling up of the GDP per capita across economies on different levels of their aggregation. The intention of the authors is to provide the readers with a holistic overview of the history and theory, but most of all the detailed description focuses on selected innovative approaches to assess the occurrence and the rate of convergence. While we do not intend to describe and analyse all the approaches that can be found in the literature, we focus on the most popular and historically best established idea of the β convergence as well as on the less popular, and different in terms of its meaning, stochastic convergence and the innovative use of the hidden Markov models to the analysis of convergence. While the starting method for validation of the convergence hypothesis is the conventional econometric regression based on the approach proposed merely 30 years ago by Barro, we extend this approach by applying the newer concept of the Bayesian model averaging. While it has existed in the literature for some time now (it seems reasonable to treat the milestone paper of Sala-i-Martin, Doppelhofer, and Miller from 2004 as its initials), it still should be considered innovative and developing. Furthermore, its importance is undoubtful either as a baseline solution or as an element of the robustness analysis. The next considered approach is based on the hidden Markov model (HMM) idea. While the HMMs have been well known for decades, the concept of their application to the convergence analysis is new – to the best of our knowledge, this is the first book where such an approach is adopted. We provide the reader not only with the necessary definitions, theory, and examples of the HMM usage but also with the detailed description of the whole procedure based on this tool, which involves *inter alia* sophisticated Baum-Welch and Viterbi algorithms, Monte Carlo simulations, and various criteria of optimization. This approach, which is an alternative to the conventional methods, allows for expressing the convergence issue in the context of automatic pattern recognition. Moreover, the HMM procedure is universal in the sense of input data, which is proved by the empirical examples of regional convergence and the worldwide perspective.

A major part of this book's value added refers to the empirical analysis of different levels of aggregation based on real-life data. The lowest aggregation level study investigates the regional convergence for US states, Chinese provinces, and Polish voivodships with different approaches involved: β convergence, stochastic convergence, and HMM convergence. On a higher level of aggregation, we examine the existence of the GDP convergence in various groups of countries: the European Union (EU28), Europe, North Africa and the Middle East, sub-Saharan Africa, South America, Caribbean, South-East Asia, Australia and Oceania, post-socialist countries, and OECD. For each group, the β convergence is tested (in both absolute and conditional terms) based on single regression models and using the BMA-based method. For each group, the HMM convergence is also verified. The research covers the period from 1995 to 2019 including the global financial crisis of 2007–2009 – so far the macroeconomic data covering the COVID period are not available. The calculations are conducted for the whole period as well as for two shorter subperiods: before the global crisis (i.e. till 2008) and after it (from 2009 onwards). Based on the results, a multidimensional comparative analysis is presented, including similarities and differences between groups of countries, before and after the global crisis, and across different methods applied. Considering the structural break at the time of the global financial crisis seems particularly important and – in some cases – yielding original results.

The results of the β convergence analysis can be interpreted as giving the average picture of the behaviour of individual economies. In the HMM approach, the countries are treated individually, and the results are valid for a given pair of countries. Therefore, the results are complementary to those from single regression models and the BMA method. Hence, the analysis allows us to draw interesting conclusions about the causes and mechanisms of convergence and divergence. It may also be an inspiration for further research in this field conducted from the point of view of individual countries.

The book is composed of five chapters. The first chapter provides the theoretical background as it describes in detail selected models of economic growth, focusing on their implications regarding convergence and divergence. Chapter 2 concentrates on hidden Markov models and shows the possibilities of applying this tool to the studies on convergence. The details of the procedure are described with the emphasis put on the technical aspects. The third chapter presents the results of the analysis of the regional convergence for three countries: Poland, the USA, and China. The convergence concepts that are applied at the regional level include the β convergence, stochastic convergence, and HMM convergence. Chapters 4 and 5 present the results of β convergence and the HMM convergence, respectively, for various worldwide groups of countries. The approach adopted in Chapters 4 and 5 allows for an easy comparison of the results obtained from different methods and an observation of the differences across the different approaches and the conclusions that they yield.

We hope that the presented combination of theory and empirical results will make this book an interesting material not only for the master and doctoral students of economics all over the world, but also for theorists and practitioners dealing with the theory of economic growth and quantitative studies in macroeconomics. We hope that the extensive descriptions of the procedures – in most cases from scratch – as well as the references will simplify the reception of the analysis. Referring to such issues as the hidden Markov models, Bayesian averaging, and the theory of economic growth, a part of this book can be treated as a textbook. In the more methodologically advanced parts of the chapters, we assume only the very basic knowledge of mathematics. We believe that the variety of countries, numerous graphs supplemented with a substantive description make this book excellent literature for a wide range of researchers and people interested in contemporary macroeconomic issues related to economic growth and the phenomenon of convergence.

The research project has been financed by the National Science Centre, Poland (project number 2015/19/B/HS4/00362).

1 Real income-level convergence

The theoretical background

There exist many definitions of convergence in economics (Bernardelli, Próchniak and Witkowski, 2017). In general, we distinguish between nominal convergence and real convergence. The former means the levelling up of the nominal variables between countries, like price levels (inflation rates), interest rates, or exchange rates. The latter refers to the real variables – primarily gross domestic product (GDP).

Real convergence can be divided into two categories: cyclical and income-level convergence. Cyclical convergence means the tendency towards the equalization of business or growth cycles between economies. The term "growth cycle" was popularized by V. Zarnowitz. We deal with a growth cycle in which the expansionary phase means an acceleration of the economic growth rate. On the other hand, in the contractionary period, there is a decline in the growth rate (as opposed to the classical business cycle, in which the recession means a decrease in the GDP level).[1] Income-level convergence means the equalization of GDP per capita levels between the economies (countries or regions).

The theoretical background of the concept of income-level (or real) convergence (catching-up) is embodied in the models of economic growth. The models of economic growth are the theoretical models that describe the behaviour of the economy in a simplified way to find the answers to various questions related to the process of economic growth. They often are very advanced and complicated mathematical constructions that require very good mathematical knowledge.[2] The models of economic growth are generally divided into two broad categories: neoclassical models and endogenous models, belonging to the so-called new growth theory. In this book, we describe selected models of economic growth focusing on their explanation of the concept of convergence. For a detailed analysis of these and many other models of economic growth, see, e.g., Barro and Sala-i-Martin (2003) and Romer (2019).

1.1 The neoclassical growth theory

The first works related to economic growth date back to the 18th and 19th centuries. During this period, Adam Smith, Thomas Malthus, and David

Ricardo, and many years later, Frank Ramsey, Allyn Young, Joseph Schumpeter, and Frank Knight provided many elements used in modern growth models (Barro and Sala-i-Martin, 2003, p. 16).

Here, we will not explore the old history but will focus on contemporary models of economic growth. Robert Solow (1956) was the first economist who formalized the analysis of economic growth. His model included the neoclassical production function and initiated an era of neoclassical models of economic growth. Neoclassical production function assumes, *inter alia*, constant returns to scale and diminishing marginal product of capital. To this day, the Solow model constitutes the basis for the contemporary theory of economic growth. But important works in this field appeared earlier.

Harrod (1939) and Domar (1946) tried to combine the Keynesian analysis with the elements of economic growth. According to the Harrod-Domar model, the pace of economic growth is proportional to the investment rate (equal to the savings rate) and inversely depends on the marginal capital intensity of production. The growth rate of GDP is described by the following equation:

$$g_y = \frac{s}{k}, \tag{1.1}$$

where g_y is a real GDP growth rate, s the investment rate (the savings rate), and k the capital intensity of production (investment outlays per unit increase in national income).

In 1928, Frank Ramsey published the article on the optimal level of savings among nations (Ramsey, 1928). Currently, the Ramsey model is widely recognized as the neoclassical approach. But the Ramsey model gained significant acceptance among economists in the early 1960s, following the Solow model, so about 30 years after its development. The neoclassical group also includes the Diamond model (Diamond, 1965).

Neoclassical models share a common disadvantage. They do not explain well the long-run economic growth. According to neoclassical theories, the long-run economic growth depends on technological progress which is assumed to be exogenous. The desired property of the model would be to endogenize technical progress so that economic growth could be explained within the model. Moreover, neoclassical models (in their basic forms) do not cope well with the explanation of differences in income levels between countries. Differences in physical capital stock are too small to explain the differences in income.

We present here in detail two neoclassical models: the Solow model (in basic and extended versions) and the Ramsey model.[3]

1.1.1 The Solow model

1.1.1.1 Basic Solow model

The Solow model, also called the Solow-Swan model, was developed by Robert Solow (1956) and Trevor Swan (1956). We present here the Solow model with labour-augmenting technological progress.

Let F be the production function. Inputs to production are physical capital $K(t)$ and effective labour $A(t)L(t)$. The latter is the product of the level of technology $A(t)$ and the population (labour force) $L(t)$:[4]

$$F\big(K(t), A(t)L(t)\big).$$ (1.2)

The production function exhibits constant returns to both inputs (capital and effective labour) and the diminishing marginal product of capital. One of the functions satisfying these assumptions is the Cobb-Douglas production function:

$$F\big(K(t), A(t)L(t)\big) = K(t)^{\alpha}\big[A(t)L(t)\big]^{1-\alpha},$$ (1.3)

where $0 < \alpha < 1$. Technology and population both grow at constant exogenous rates, which are equal to a and n, respectively:[5]

$$\frac{\dot{A}(t)}{A(t)} = a \quad \text{and} \quad \frac{\dot{L}(t)}{L(t)} = n.$$ (1.4)

Equations (1.4) imply that $A(t) = A(0)e^{at}$ and $L(t) = L(0)e^{nt}$.

The increase in capital stock equals investment (savings) minus depreciation:

$$\dot{K}(t) = sF\big(K(t), A(t)L(t)\big) - \delta K(t),$$ (1.5)

where s is the exogenous savings rate and δ is the capital depreciation rate.

The dynamics of the economy is analysed in terms of capital and output per unit of effective labour, which are denoted by $k(t)$ and $f(k(t))$, respectively:[6]

$$k \equiv \frac{K}{AL} \quad \text{and} \quad f(k) \equiv \frac{F(K, AL)}{AL} \left\{= F\left(\frac{K}{AL}, \frac{AL}{AL}\right) = F(k,1) = f(k)\right\}.$$ (1.6)

To find the equation describing the dynamics of the economy, we differentiate the definition of k (equation 1.6) with respect to time, and then we use formulas (1.4)–(1.6). As a result, we obtain

$$\dot{k} = sf(k) - (n + a + \delta)k.$$ (1.7)

The above equation is the basic formula describing the dynamics of the economy in the Solow model. The increase in capital per unit of effective labour equals actual investment $sf(k)$ minus replacement investment $(n + a + \delta)k$.

Given that,

- marginal product of capital is positive and diminishing ($f'(k) > 0$ and $f''(k) < 0$),

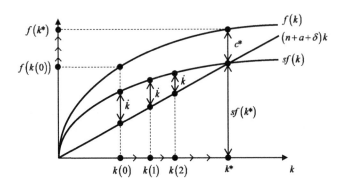

Figure 1.1 The transition period and the steady state in the Solow model.

- zero inputs yield zero outputs ($f(0) = 0$),
- the production function satisfies Inada (1963) conditions ($\lim_{k \to \infty} f'(k) = 0$; $\lim_{k \to 0} f'(k) = \infty$),

The dynamics of the economy and the steady state can be illustrated graphically as in Figure 1.1.

The long-run equilibrium (steady state) occurs at the point of intersection between $sf(k)$ and $(n + a + \delta)k$ functions. At this point, output and capital per unit of effective labour are constant over time (equation (1.7) implies that if $sf(k) = (n + a + \delta)k$, then $dk/dt = 0$).

Assuming that the production function is of the Cobb-Douglas type $y = k^\alpha$, by setting $dk/dt = 0$ in equation (1.7), we can calculate the volume of capital and output per unit of effective labour in the steady state:

$$k^* = \left(\frac{s}{n+a+\delta}\right)^{\frac{1}{1-\alpha}}, \quad y^* = k^{*\alpha} = \left(\frac{s}{n+a+\delta}\right)^{\frac{\alpha}{1-\alpha}}. \tag{1.8}$$

What is the growth rate of total GDP ($Y = F(K, AL)$) and GDP per capita (Y/L) in the steady state? In order to answer this question, we have to differentiate between $Y \equiv f(k)AL$ and $Y/L \equiv f(k)A$ with respect to time (see equation (1.6)). This yields

$$\frac{\dot{Y}}{Y} = \frac{\dot{f}(k)}{f(k)} + \frac{\dot{A}}{A} + \frac{\dot{L}}{L} \quad \text{and} \quad \frac{\dot{Y/L}}{Y/L} = \frac{\dot{f}(k)}{f(k)} + \frac{\dot{A}}{A}. \tag{1.9}$$

In the steady state, output per unit of effective labour is constant ($df/dt/f = 0$), while technology and population both grow at constant rates equal to a and n, respectively. Thus, we have obtained two important implications of the Solow model. In the steady state (long-run equilibrium),

- the growth rate of GDP equals technological progress plus population growth,
- the growth rate of per capita GDP equals technological progress.

These findings also confirm the weaknesses of neoclassical theories discussed earlier, i.e. economic growth depends on exogenous variables formed outside the model.

The steady state in the Solow model is stable. This means that regardless of the initial capital stock (except for $k(0) = 0$), the economy always tends towards the steady state and, eventually, approaches it. If $k(0) < k^*$, then $sf(k) > (n + a + \delta)k$ (see Figure 1.1); k will grow over time and eventually reaches k^*. During the transition period, the growth rate of total and per capita GDP is higher than in the steady state because capital and output per unit of effective labour both increase ($df/dt/f > 0$ in equation (1.9)).

The above property of the Solow model, indicating a faster pace of economic growth during the transition period, has very important implications. The Solow model confirms the existence of conditional β convergence.[7] Convergence (β-type) means that less developed countries (with lower GDP per capita) grow faster than more developed ones. The catching-up process confirmed by the Solow model is conditional because it only occurs if the economies tend to reach the same steady state.

The convergence is conditional because it is limited to a situation in which both economies tend to reach the same steady state. The conditional character of convergence is explained in Figure 1.2. The vertical distance between the two curves in Figure 1.2 measures the growth rate of capital. The curves on the graph are obtained by dividing both sides of equation (1.7) by k and assuming that the production function is of the Cobb-Douglas type: $f(k) = k^{\alpha}$.

Let us consider two countries – a poor one and a rich one – with different savings rates. Since the savings rate in the rich country is higher, the steady-state value of capital in the rich country is also higher than in the poor

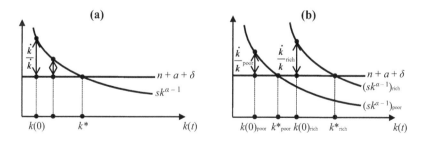

Figure 1.2 Economic growth in the Solow model under the same and different steady states.

country. This is shown in part (b) of Figure 1.2. Although the rich country starts from a higher capital level, it reveals a more rapid growth because it approaches a different steady state than the poor country. In this case, both economies will not converge.

The existence of convergence can also be proved mathematically. To show the existence of convergence, we divide equation (1.7) by k and then we differentiate it with respect to k:

$$\frac{d\left(\dot{k}/k\right)}{dk} = \frac{d}{dk}\left(s\,\frac{f(k)}{k}-(n+a+\delta)\right) = s\,\frac{f'(k)\cdot k-f(k)}{k^2} = -s\,\frac{dF\,/\,d(AL)}{k^2} < 0.$$

(1.10)

Equation (1.10) informs that the growth rate of capital per unit of effective labour decreases with k (negative derivative with respect to k). This means that the higher the level of capital and output, the lower the growth rate of these variables, which indicates the occurrence of convergence.

The existence of catching-up can also be demonstrated by the log-linearization of the accumulation equation of capital per capita given by formula (1.7). This method allows us to calculate the rate of convergence coefficient, which informs what percentage of the distance towards the steady state the economy covers during one period. Assuming that the production function is of the Cobb-Douglas type $f(k) = Bk^\alpha$ $(B > 0)$, equation (1.7) can be written as

$$\dot{\ln}\,k = sBe^{\ln k^{\alpha-1}}-(n+a+\delta) = sBe^{(\alpha-1)\ln k}-(n+a+\delta).$$

(1.11)

We then apply a first-order Taylor expansion around a steady state to find the approximate time path for $\ln k$:

$$\dot{\ln}\,k \approx \dot{\ln}\,k^* + \left.\frac{d\,\dot{\ln}\,k}{d\,\ln k}\right|_{\text{in the steady-state}} \times (\ln k-\ln k^*) = (\alpha-1)(n+a+\delta)(\ln k-\ln k^*).$$

(1.12)

The solution of differential equation (1.12) is as follows:

$$\ln k = \ln k^* + \left(\ln k\,(0)-\ln k^*\right)e^{-(1-\alpha)(n+a+\delta)t},$$

(1.13)

which in terms of output per unit of effective labour can be written as

$$\ln y = \ln y^* + \left(\ln y\,(0)-\ln y^*\right)e^{-(1-\alpha)(n+a+\delta)t}.$$

(1.14)

By defining

$$\beta = (1-\alpha)(n+a+\delta) > 0$$

(1.15)

and differentiating equation (1.14) with respect to time, we obtain

$$\frac{\dot{y}}{y} = \beta \left(\ln y^* - \ln y \right).$$ (1.16)

Equation (1.16) informs that the rate of economic growth depends on the distance from the steady state. The parameter β measures the speed of convergence. The β coefficient determines what percentage of the distance to the steady state the economy covers during one period.

By subtracting $\ln y(0)$ from both sides of equation (1.14), we have

$$\ln y - \ln y(0) = \left(1 - e^{-\beta t}\right) \ln y^* - \left(1 - e^{-\beta t}\right) \ln y(0).$$ (1.17)

The above equation shows that the rate of economic growth depends on the initial GDP per capita and the steady-state level of income. A negative relationship between the economic growth and the initial income level indicates the existence of real convergence. However, the convergence is conditional because it also depends on the other variables determining the long-run equilibrium. This is clearly visible when $\ln y^*$ is replaced with the logarithmized y^* given by formula (1.8):

$$\ln y - \ln y(0) = \left(1 - e^{-\beta t}\right)\frac{\alpha}{1-\alpha}\ln s - \left(1 - e^{-\beta t}\right)\frac{\alpha}{1-\alpha}\ln (n + a + \delta)$$
$$- \left(1 - e^{-\beta t}\right)\ln y(0)$$ (1.18)

Estimating the above equation using the linear regression method allows us to verify the existence of conditional β convergence. In contrast, to test for the absolute convergence, it is enough to estimate the model where the dependent variable is $\ln y - \ln y(0)$ and the only independent variable is $\ln y(0)$.

In the empirical part of the book, we will estimate the various types of convergence equations given by formula (1.18) with different specifications of economic growth factors. The theoretical model presented here focuses on only a selected number of economic growth determinants. In empirical studies, it is necessary to test more variables than equation (1.18) indicates.

1.1.1.2 The Solow model with human capital (the Mankiw-Romer-Weil model)

We present now the augmented Solow model developed by Mankiw, Romer, and Weil (1992). The augmented Solow model is a continuation of the neoclassical growth theory, although it was developed during the era of endogenous models. The Mankiw-Romer-Weil (MRW) model shows, *inter alia*, that the neoclassical growth theory explains correctly the differences in income levels between countries and the phenomenon of conditional convergence. The development of the augmented Solow model and its rising popularity is called "neoclassical revival".

The main difference between the basic and augmented Solow models is that the MRW model includes human capital. Human capital (H) is the third input, in addition to physical capital (K) and effective labour (AL). The production function is given as follows:[8]

$$Y = K^\alpha H^\beta (AL)^{1-\alpha-\beta}, \tag{1.19}$$

where $\alpha > 0$, $\beta > 0$, and $\alpha + \beta < 1$. As we can see, the production function still shares all the neoclassical features, namely, the diminishing marginal product of each input, constant returns to scale, and Inada conditions. In the MRW model, the output may be devoted to consumption, accumulation of physical capital, or accumulation of human capital.

The level of technology and the labour force both grow at constant exogenous rates equal to a and n, respectively (see equation (1.4)). Both types of capital depreciate at the same rate δ. Let s_K be the income share spent on physical capital accumulation (i.e. the savings rate), and s_H be the income share spent on human capital accumulation. Thus, the accumulation equations for physical capital and human capital are as follows:

$$\dot{K} = s_K Y - \delta K, \tag{1.20}$$

$$\dot{H} = s_H Y - \delta H. \tag{1.21}$$

The dynamics of the model is analysed for capital and output per unit of effective labour, denoted as k, h, and y:

$$k = \frac{K}{AL}; \quad h = \frac{H}{AL}; \quad y = \frac{Y}{AL} = \frac{K^\alpha H^\beta (AL)^{1-\alpha-\beta}}{AL} = k^\alpha h^\beta. \tag{1.22}$$

To find equations describing the dynamics of the economy, we differentiate the definitions of k and h with respect to time. The result is

$$\dot{k} = s_K y - (n+a+\delta)k = s_K k^\alpha h^\beta - (n+a+\delta)k, \tag{1.23}$$

$$\dot{h} = s_H y - (n+a+\delta)h = s_H k^\alpha h^\beta - (n+a+\delta)h. \tag{1.24}$$

The above equations describe the dynamics of the economy in the MRW model. They are analogous to equation (1.7) in the basic Solow model. The increase in human and physical capital per unit of effective labour is equal to the actual investment in a given type of capital net of replacement investment.

In the steady state, the capital per unit of effective labour is constant. Thus, setting equations (1.23) and (1.24) to zero, we obtain the stock of physical and human capital in the long-run equilibrium:

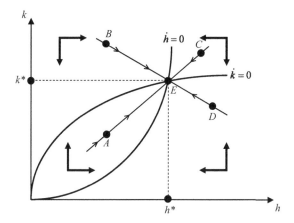

Figure 1.3 The transition period and the steady state in the Solow model with human capital (the Mankiw-Romer-Weil model).

$$k^* = \left(\frac{s_K^{1-\beta} s_H^{\beta}}{n+a+\delta} \right)^{\frac{1}{1-\alpha-\beta}}, \tag{1.25}$$

$$h^* = \left(\frac{s_K^{\alpha} s_H^{1-\alpha}}{n+a+\delta} \right)^{\frac{1}{1-\alpha-\beta}}. \tag{1.26}$$

Figure 1.3 illustrates the steady state and the transition period in the MRW model.

The dynamics of the augmented Solow model is considered in a two-dimensional space (k, h). The curves $dk/dt = 0$ and $dh/dt = 0$ in Figure 1.3 are determined by setting equations (1.23) and (1.24) to zero. These curves have the following functional forms:

$$\text{the curve } \dot{k} = 0 : k = \left(\frac{s_K}{n+a+\delta} \right)^{\frac{1}{1-\alpha}} h^{\frac{\beta}{1-\alpha}}, \tag{1.27}$$

$$\text{the curve } \dot{h} = 0 : k = \left(\frac{n+a+\delta}{s_H} \right)^{\frac{1}{\alpha}} h^{\frac{1-\beta}{\alpha}}. \tag{1.28}$$

Since $\beta < 1 - \alpha$ and $1 - \beta > \alpha$, the curve $dk/dt = 0$ is concave, while the curve $dh/dt = 0$ is convex. The steady state is at the point of intersection between $dk/dt = 0$ and $dh/dt = 0$ functions (point E). As in the basic Solow model, the long-run equilibrium is stable. From any starting point (e.g. A, B, C, or D), depending on the initial stock of physical and human capital, the economy is moving towards the steady state according to equations (1.23) and (1.24).

In the steady state, physical capital, human capital, consumption, and output per unit of effective labour are all constant. This means that GDP growth rate equals the sum of technological progress and population growth (i.e. the variables exogenously given), while the growth rate of per capita GDP equals technological progress. Thus, the augmented Solow model gives the same answer as the basic Solow model and other neoclassical theories to a question about the determinants of long-run economic growth.

In the MRW model, the investment rates in physical and human capital are exogenously given. Hence, the model – like the standard Solow approach – reveals dynamic inefficiency.

The MRW model, like the basic Solow model and the other neoclassical theories, confirms the existence of conditional β convergence. To formally demonstrate the prevalence of convergence and to calculate its speed, the equation describing the dynamics of the economy should be log-linearized. By logarithmizing and differentiating with respect to time the production function $y = k\alpha h\beta$ and using formulas (1.23) and (1.24), we obtain the equation describing the growth rate of output per unit of effective work in the augmented Solow model:

$$\dot{\ln} y = \alpha s_K k^{\alpha-1} h^\beta + \beta s_H k^\alpha h^{\beta-1} - (\alpha+\beta)(n+a+\delta). \tag{1.29}$$

We then apply a first-order Taylor expansion around the steady state to find the approximate time path for $\ln y$:

$$\dot{\ln} y \approx \dot{\ln} y^* + \frac{d \dot{\ln} y}{d \ln k}\bigg|_{\text{in the steady-state}} \times (\ln k - \ln k^*) + \frac{d \dot{\ln} y}{d \ln h}\bigg|_{\text{in the steady-state}} \times (\ln h - \ln h^*). \tag{1.30}$$

Calculating the appropriate derivatives and using the fact that in the steady state, the variables k and h are determined by formulas (1.25) and (1.26), from equation (1.30), we obtain

$$\dot{\ln} y = -\alpha(1-\alpha-\beta)(n+a+\delta)(\ln k - \ln k^*) - \beta(1-\alpha-\beta)(n+a+\delta)(\ln h - \ln h^*). \tag{1.31}$$

By defining

$$\lambda = (1-\alpha-\beta)(n+a+\delta) > 0, \tag{1.32}$$

equation (1.31) can be written as

$$\frac{\dot{y}}{y} = \lambda(\ln y^* - \ln y). \tag{1.33}$$

Equation (1.33) is identical to equation (1.16), proper for the basic Solow model.[9] Both formulas indicate that the rate of economic growth is proportional to the distance separating the economy from its steady state. The greater this distance, i.e. the more $\ln y$ is less than $\ln y^*$, the faster the pace of economic growth. This means that there is a convergence phenomenon.

Equation (1.32) shows the value of the coefficient determining the convergence rate in the MRW model. The analogous coefficient for the Solow model is given by equation (1.15). Based on equations (1.32) and (1.15), it can be seen that in the MRW model, the convergence is slower than in the basic Solow model.

The Solow model (both basic and augmented) does not explain well differences in economic growth rates between countries, but it can be used to explain differences in income levels. According to the Solow model, the savings rate (in the augmented version – also the percentage of income allocated to the accumulation of human capital) and the rate of population growth are the basic factors determining the level of income per capita. An increase in the savings rates and/or a decline in population growth lead to higher levels of per capita income in the steady state (and a temporarily higher rate of economic growth).

In order to formally demonstrate the impact of s_K, s_H, and n on the level of GDP per capita in the steady state, the production function $y^* \equiv (Y/AL)^* = k^{*\alpha}h^{*\beta}$ should be logarithmized using equations (1.25) and (1.26). As a result, we obtain

$$\ln\left(\frac{Y^*}{L^*}\right) = \ln A(0) + at + \frac{\alpha}{1-\alpha-\beta}\ln s_K + \frac{\beta}{1-\alpha-\beta}\ln s_H - \frac{\alpha+\beta}{1-\alpha-\beta}\ln(n+a+\delta).$$

(1.34)

The above equation shows that an increase in s_K and s_H, and a decrease in n contribute to an increase in GDP per capita in the steady state in the augmented Solow model, while $\alpha/(1-\alpha-\beta)$ and $\beta/(1-\alpha-\beta)$ are the elasticities of income with respect to s_K and s_H. The analogous equation for the basic Solow model is the following ($\beta = 0$):

$$\ln\left(\frac{Y^*}{L^*}\right) = \ln A(0) + at + \frac{\alpha}{1-\alpha}\ln s - \frac{\alpha}{1-\alpha}\ln(n+a+\delta). \qquad (1.35)$$

Equations (1.34) and (1.35) – obtained from the augmented and basic Solow models – show the most important factors determining the level of income in individual countries. At this point, the question arises whether the savings rate, investment in human capital, and population growth are indeed the variables responsible for differences in income levels between countries. The empirical part of this book will partially answer this question.

1.1.1.3 The Solow model with many factors of production

Nonneman and Vanhoudt (1996) further augmented the Solow model. They analyse a model with many factors of production, each of which is treated as some kind of capital. The production function is as follows:

$$Y = K_1^{\alpha 1} K_2^{\alpha 2} \ldots K_m^{\alpha m} (AL)^{1- \sum\limits_{i=1}^{m} \alpha_i}, \tag{1.36}$$

where m is the number of capital goods treated as factors of production. In the basic Solow model, taking into account only physical capital, $m = 1$. The MRW model with human capital assumes $m = 2$. Nonneman and Vanhoudt in empirical research analyse the model with three inputs ($m = 3$): physical capital, human capital, and technological know-how.

The analysis of the dynamics of the model with many factors of production is the same as the basic variant or the variant with human capital. Assuming the same assumptions, the accumulation equation of the ith type of capital is as follows (cf. equations (1.7), (1.23), and (1.24)):

$$\dot{k_i} = s_i y - (n + a + \delta) k_i, \tag{1.37}$$

where s_i is the rate of investment in the given type of capital. In steady state, capital per unit of effective labour is constant; therefore, $dk_i/dt = 0$. Given this and the fact that the production function per unit of effective labour is $y = k_1^{\alpha 1} k_2^{\alpha 2} \ldots k_m^{\alpha m}$, formula (1.37) allows us to calculate the steady-state level of capital:

$$k_i^* = \left[s_i^{\left(1- \sum\limits_{j=1}^{i-1} \alpha_j + \sum\limits_{j=i+1}^{m} \alpha_j \right)} \cdot \left(\prod\limits_{j=1}^{i-1} s_j^{\alpha j} \right) \cdot \left(\prod\limits_{j=i+1}^{m} s_j^{\alpha j} \right) \cdot (n + a + \delta)^{-1} \right]^{\frac{1}{1 - \sum_{j=1}^{m} \alpha_j}}. \tag{1.38}$$

After the appropriate substitution into the production function $y = k_1^{\alpha 1} k_2^{\alpha 2} \ldots k_m^{\alpha m}$, we obtain

$$y^* = \prod\limits_{i=1}^{m} \left[\left(\frac{s_i}{n + a + \delta} \right)^{\frac{\alpha_i}{1 - \sum_{i=1}^{m} \alpha_i}} \right]. \tag{1.39}$$

The Solow model with m inputs explains the convergence in an analogous way to the models presented earlier. The relationship between the economic growth rate and both the initial GDP per capita and steady-state level of income is the same in all variants of the Solow model and described by equation (1.17). Differences between the various variants of the

Solow model emerge when trying to expand this equation. In the Solow model with m factors of production, we substitute $\ln y^*$ with the logarithmized level of income y^* determined by formula (1.39). As a result, we obtain

$$
\ln y - \ln y(0) = \sum_{i=1}^{m} \left[\left(1 - e^{-\beta t}\right) \frac{\alpha_i}{1 - \sum_{i=1}^{m} \alpha_i} \ln s_i \right]
$$
$$
- \left(1 - e^{-\beta t}\right) \frac{\sum_{i=1}^{m} \alpha_i}{1 - \sum_{i=1}^{m} \alpha_i} \ln(n + a + \delta) - \left(1 - e^{-\beta t}\right) \ln y(0) \quad (1.40)
$$

Equation (1.40) is analogous to equation (1.18), appropriate for the basic Solow model. Both equations indicate the prevalence of convergence. It is conditional because it depends on the variables determining the level of income in long-run equilibrium. The parameter β indicates the speed of convergence.

Nonneman and Vanhoudt analyse the Solow model with three factors: physical capital K, human capital H, and technological know-how T. For such a model specification, the production function (1.36) is as follows:

$$
Y = K^{\alpha_1} H^{\alpha_2} T^{\alpha_3} \tag{1.41}
$$

or in terms of per unit of effective labour:

$$
y = k^{\alpha_1} h^{\alpha_2} \tau^{\alpha_3}. \tag{1.42}
$$

For three types of capital, expression (1.40) takes the form

$$
\ln y - \ln y(0) = \left(1 - e^{-\beta t}\right) \frac{\alpha_1}{1 - \alpha_1 - \alpha_2 - \alpha_3} \ln s_K
$$
$$
+ \left(1 - e^{-\beta t}\right) \frac{\alpha_2}{1 - \alpha_1 - \alpha_2 - \alpha_3} \ln s_H
$$
$$
+ \left(1 - e^{-\beta t}\right) \frac{\alpha_3}{1 - \alpha_1 - \alpha_2 - \alpha_3} \ln s_\tau
$$
$$
- \left(1 - e^{-\beta t}\right) \frac{\alpha_1 + \alpha_2 + \alpha_3}{1 - \alpha_1 - \alpha_2 - \alpha_3} \ln(n + a + \delta)
$$
$$
- \left(1 - e^{-\beta t}\right) \ln y(0). \tag{1.43}
$$

The β convergence models estimated in the next chapters of the book are extensions and modifications of formula (1.43).

1.1.2 The Ramsey model

The Ramsey model was developed by Frank Ramsey, the British economist, who in 1928 published an article on the optimal level of saving (Ramsey, 1928). The Ramsey approach was extended by David Cass and Tjalling
Koopmans (Cass, 1965; Koopmans, 1965), and the Ramsey model is also
known as the Ramsey-Cass-Koopmans model.

The main difference between the Ramsey model and the Solow model
is in their savings rates. The savings rate in the Solow theory is exogenous,
while in the Ramsey approach, it is endogenously given and results from
optimal decisions made by utility-maximizing individuals.

The Ramsey model may be analysed for the perfectly competitive economy or the centrally planned economy. In this book, the analysis is carried
out for a perfectly competitive economy. We begin with the description of
the behaviour of firms and households. Then, we switch to the analysis of
the steady state and the transition period. Finally, we discuss some implications in terms of the β convergence process.

1.1.2.1 Firms

As in the Solow model, $F(K, AL)$ is the production function. The inputs to
production are physical capital, K, and effective labour, AL. The production function is neoclassical, so it exhibits constant returns to both inputs
(physical capital and effective labour), diminishing marginal productivity of
capital, and satisfies Inada conditions.[10]

Technology and population both grow at the constant exogenous rates
equal to a and n respectively, as in the case of the Solow model.

Firms are producing a homogenous product according to the production
function $F(K, AL)$. The factors of production (physical capital and labour)
are purchased from households at the prices of $(r + \delta)$ and w, respectively,
where r stands for the interest rate (the price of capital), δ is the depreciation
rate, and w represents the wage rate (the price of labour).

The firms aim at maximizing their profits. Profit is the total revenue
minus the total cost. This yields

$$\pi = F(K, AL) - (r + \delta)K - wL \quad \rightarrow \quad \max. \tag{1.44}$$

The above expression is maximized with respect to capital and labour. The
profit-maximization conditions are as follows:

$$\frac{d\pi}{dK} = 0, \tag{1.45}$$

$$\frac{d\pi}{dL} = 0. \tag{1.46}$$

Before solving these conditions, let us introduce – as in the case of the Solow model – the variables per unit of effective labour. We do it because the analysis of the dynamics of the economy will be carried out for capital and output per unit of effective labour, which are denoted as $k(t)$ and $f(k(t))$, respectively:

$$k \equiv \frac{K}{AL} \quad \text{and} \quad f(k) \equiv \frac{F(K,AL)}{AL}. \tag{1.47}$$

Given equation (1.47), profit defined by equation (1.44) can be expressed as

$$\pi = f(k)AL - (r+\delta)kAL - wL \to \max. \tag{1.48}$$

The first of the two profit-maximization conditions, equation (1.45), applied to the objective function (1.48) yields

$$\frac{d\pi}{dK} = f'(k)\frac{dk}{dK}AL - (r+\delta)\frac{dk}{dK}AL - 0 = 0. \tag{1.49}$$

In equation (1.49), the term dk/dK appears several times. It is equal to

$$\frac{dk}{dK} = \frac{d\left(\dfrac{K}{AL}\right)}{dK} = \frac{1}{AL}. \tag{1.50}$$

Applying equation (1.50) to equation (1.49) yields

$$r = f'(k) - \delta. \tag{1.51}$$

Equation (1.51) shows that in equilibrium, the interest rate is equal to the marginal product of capital (in "per unit of effective labour" terms) minus depreciation rate.

Similarly, the second profit-maximization condition, equation (1.46), applied to the objective function (1.48) yields

$$\frac{d\pi}{dL} = A\left[f'(k)\frac{dk}{dL}L + f(k)\frac{dL}{dL}\right] - (r+\delta)A\left[\frac{dk}{dL}L + k\frac{dL}{dL}\right] - w = 0. \tag{1.52}$$

In equation (1.52), the term dk/dL appears several times. It is equal to

$$\frac{dk}{dL} = \frac{d\left(\dfrac{K}{AL}\right)}{dL} = \frac{d\left(KA^{-1}L^{-1}\right)}{dL} = -\frac{K}{AL^2}. \tag{1.53}$$

Applying equation (1.53) to equation (1.52) yields

$$w = A\left[f(k) - kf'(k)\right]. \tag{1.54}$$

Equation (1.54) shows the equilibrium wage rate.

In summation, the firms' optimization yields two equations for input prices: the equation for the interest rate, equation (1.51), and the equation for the wage rate, equation (1.54). From the economic point of view, both of them are profit-maximization conditions implying that each of them represents the equality between the marginal factor product and the input price.

1.1.2.2 Households

Suppose that people live infinitely long. Each adult supplies to the market one unit of labour regardless of the wage rate. In the economy, there are N households (N = const.), which grow (i.e. increase the number of their members) at the rate n. Consumers aim at maximizing utility of consumption over the whole life. Thus, the utility function of a household can be expressed as follows:

$$U = \int_0^\infty e^{-\rho t} u(c_{pc}) \frac{L}{N} dt, \tag{1.55}$$

where $u(c_{pc})$ stands for the utility of consumption achieved by one individual,[11] L/N is the number of members of a single household, and ρ is the rate of time preference ($\rho > 0$). The higher the ρ, the higher the value of current consumption for households. We assume that marginal utility is positive and diminishing ($u'(c) > 0$; $u''(c) < 0$) and that the utility function satisfies Inada conditions ($\lim_{c \to \infty} u'(c) = 0$; $\lim_{c \to 0} u'(c) = \infty$). Substituting $L(t) = L(0)e^{nt}$, dividing utility by a constant number of $L(0)/N$, and assuming that the utility function is of the CRRA type,[12] the consumer utility function can be expressed in the following way:

$$U = \int_0^\infty e^{(n-\rho)t} \frac{c_{pc}^{1-\sigma} - 1}{1-\sigma} dt. \tag{1.56}$$

To formulate the utility-maximization problem, the budget constraint is needed. Let us start from the general relationship that an increase in physical capital stock amounts to investment (equal to saving) minus depreciation of that physical capital stock:

$$\dot{K} = I - \delta K. \tag{1.57}$$

From equation (1.57), we obtain the volume of investment, I:

$$I = \dot{K} + \delta K. \tag{1.58}$$

Moreover, we know that

$$Y = C + I = C + \dot{K} + \delta K \tag{1.59}$$

and

$$Y = (r+\delta)K + wL. \tag{1.60}$$

Equation (1.59) is the standard GDP equation. In a closed economy without government, according to the expenditure approach, GDP equals consumption plus investment. Equation (1.60) is a zero-profit condition. As we assume the perfectly competitive economy, firms make exactly zero profit in the long run.

Equalizing equations (1.59) and (1.60) yields

$$C + \dot{K} + \delta K = (r+\delta)K + wL. \tag{1.61}$$

Since

$$K = k_{pc}L \Rightarrow \dot{K} = \dot{k}_{pc}L + k_{pc}\dot{L}, \tag{1.62}$$

equation (1.61) may be expressed as follows:

$$C + \dot{k}_{pc}L + k_{pc}\dot{L} = rK + wL. \tag{1.63}$$

Dividing equation (1.63) by L yields

$$\dot{k}_{pc} = w + rk_{pc} - c_{pc} - nk_{pc}. \tag{1.64}$$

Equation (1.64) is the budget constraint. It states that an increase in capital per capita equals income (from labour and capital) net of consumption and a term representing the change of the country's population.

Now, we can formulate the consumer's optimization problem. It is given in the following:

$$U = \int_0^\infty e^{(n-\rho)t} \frac{c_{pc}^{1-\sigma} - 1}{1-\sigma} dt \quad \rightarrow \quad \max, \tag{1.65}$$

such that $\dot{k}_{pc} = w + rk_{pc} - c_{pc} - nk_{pc}$ and $k(0) > 0$ where the value of $k(0)$ is given.

Moreover, for the integral to be finite, we additionally assume $\rho > n$.

In order to solve equation (1.65), we build the current-value Hamiltonian:

$$H = \frac{c_{pc}^{1-\sigma} - 1}{1-\sigma} + \theta\left(w + rk_{pc} - c_{pc} - nk_{pc}\right). \tag{1.66}$$

The first-order conditions (FOCs) are the following:

$$\frac{\partial H}{\partial c_{pc}} = 0, \tag{1.67}$$

$$\dot{\theta} = \theta(\rho - n) - \frac{\partial H}{\partial k_{pc}}, \tag{1.68}$$

$$\dot{k}_{pc} = \frac{\partial H}{\partial \theta}, \tag{1.69}$$

$$\lim_{t \to \infty} e^{(n-\rho)t} k_{pc} \theta = 0. \tag{1.70}$$

The variable θ, appearing in equation (1.66), is the shadow variable associated with the accumulation equation for capital. This variable evaluates households' saving, i.e. it indicates how much current saving contributes to the increase in the future utility (via its impact on the increase of future consumption).

Equation (1.70) is a transversality condition. It states that at the end of the period (i.e. when $t \to \infty$), a household should get rid of its whole capital or the capital left should be worthless.

The FOCs are solved in the following way. From equation (1.67), we obtain

$$\frac{\partial H}{\partial c_{pc}} = \frac{1}{1-\sigma}(1-\sigma)c_{pc}^{1-\sigma-1} - \theta = 0 \Rightarrow \dot{\theta} = -\sigma c_{pc}^{-\sigma-1}\dot{c}_{pc}. \tag{1.71}$$

From equation (1.68), we have

$$\dot{\theta} = \theta(\rho - n) - r\theta + n\theta \Rightarrow \dot{\theta} = \theta(\rho - r). \tag{1.72}$$

Substituting equations (1.71) into (1.72) yields

$$\frac{\dot{c}_{pc}}{c_{pc}} = \frac{r-\rho}{\sigma}. \tag{1.73}$$

From equation (1.69), we obtain

$$\dot{k}_{pc} = w + rk_{pc} - c_{pc} - nk_{pc}. \tag{1.74}$$

Transversality condition (1.70) can be written as

$$\lim_{t \to \infty} \theta(0) k_{pc} e^{(n-r)t} = 0. \tag{1.75}$$

Summing up, equations (1.73)–(1.75) are the final equations characterizing the dynamics of a household on the optimal path. The first one is the Euler equation which states that consumption increases over time if the interest rate exceeds the rate of time preference, i.e. if benefits from net saving exceed a fall in utility due to switching consumption to the next period. The elasticity of substitution, $1/\sigma$, measures the strength of this relationship.

1.1.2.3 Combining firms and households

Let us now combine the results for firms and households to obtain equations describing the whole economy. The dynamics of the economy are analysed in terms of the variables per unit of effective labour. Hence, we have to change per capita variables obtained from the examination of households into per unit of effective labour terms. To do it, the following relationships will be useful:

$$c_{pc} = cA \Rightarrow \frac{\dot{c}_{pc}}{c_{pc}} = \frac{\dot{c}}{c} + \frac{\dot{A}}{A} = \frac{\dot{c}}{c} + a \tag{1.76}$$

and

$$k_{pc} = kA \Rightarrow \dot{k}_{pc} = \dot{k}A + k\dot{A}. \tag{1.77}$$

Now let us substitute the interest rate equation obtained from the firms' profit-maximization problem, equation (1.51), into the growth rate of per capita consumption obtained from the consumers' utility-maximization problem, equation (1.73). Making use of equation (1.76) yields

$$\frac{\dot{c}}{c} = \frac{f'(k) - \delta - \rho - a\sigma}{\sigma}. \tag{1.78}$$

Similarly, let us substitute the interest rate and wage rate equations obtained from the firms' profit-maximization problem, equations (1.51) and (1.54), into the growth equation of capital per capita obtained from the consumers' utility-maximization problem, equation (1.74). Making use of equations (1.76) and (1.77) yields

$$\dot{k} = f(k) - c - (n + a + \delta)k. \tag{1.79}$$

Equations (1.78) and (1.79), augmented by the transversality condition, are the final equations describing the dynamics of the economy on the optimal growth path.

1.1.2.4 Steady state

In the steady state, the variables per unit of effective labour are constant over time. Therefore, to determine the steady state, we have to equalize the growth of consumption per unit of effective labour and the growth of capital per unit of effective labour to zero, i.e.

$$\dot{c} = 0, \tag{1.80}$$

$$\dot{k} = 0. \tag{1.81}$$

Let k^* be the steady-state value of capital per unit of effective labour and c^* be the steady-state value of consumption per unit of effective labour. Applying equations (1.80) and (1.81) to equations (1.78) and (1.79), we obtain the properties of the steady state in the Ramsey model. The steady state is described by the following equations:

$$f'(k^*) = \delta + \rho + a\sigma, \tag{1.82}$$

$$c^* = f(k^*) - (n + a + \delta)k^*. \tag{1.83}$$

The graphical illustration of the transitional dynamics and the steady state in the Ramsey model is presented in Figure 1.4. The steady state occurs at the point of intersection between the $dc/dt = 0$ and $dk/dt = 0$ functions. It is the saddle point located on one stable and one unstable trajectory. The economy starting from the initial capital stock $k(0)$ achieves the steady state under the condition that in the initial period, the level of consumption $c(0)^S$ chosen implies that the economy enters the stable trajectory T_2T_2. If the consumption level is too low (e.g. $c(0)^M$), the economy will tend towards the point on the horizontal axis, while if the consumption level is excessively high (e.g. $c(0)^D$), the economy will approach the point on the vertical axis and will jump to the origin. We exclude both these cases because they do not satisfy the model equilibrium conditions.

What are the implications of the Ramsey model for the economic growth rate? In the steady state, physical capital, consumption, and output per unit of effective labour are all constant. This means that GDP growth rate equals the sum of technological progress and population growth (i.e. the variables exogenously given), while the growth rate of per capita GDP equals the technological progress. Thus, the Ramsey model gives the same answer as the Solow model to a question about the determinants of long-run economic growth.

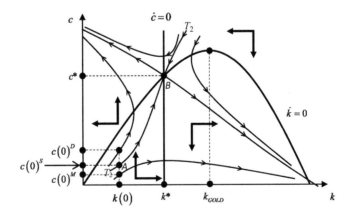

Figure 1.4 The transition period and the steady state in the Ramsey model.

The Ramsey model – like the Solow model – confirms the existence of conditional β convergence. It means that less developed countries (with lower GDP per capita) grow faster than more developed ones given that all the economies tend to reach the same steady state.

In order to determine the speed of convergence, equations (1.78) and (1.79) should be log-linearized with the simplifying assumption that the production function is of the Cobb-Douglas type: $f(k) = k^{\alpha}$. Accumulation equations for capital and consumption per unit of effective labour will therefore be given as follows:

$$\ln k = e^{(\alpha-1)\ln k} - e^{\ln c}e^{-\ln k} - (n+a+\delta); \ln c = \frac{1}{\sigma}\left(\alpha e^{(\alpha-1)\ln k} - \delta - \rho - a\sigma\right). \quad (1.84)$$

Applying the first-order Taylor expansion around the steady state to the above system of differential equations, we obtain the eigenvalues of the characteristic matrix with different signs ($\lambda_1 > 0$, $\lambda_2 < 0$), which means that the steady state is a saddle path:

$$\lambda_{1,2} = \frac{(\rho-n-a(1-\sigma)) \pm \sqrt{(\rho-n-a(1-\sigma))^2 - 4\left[\alpha^{-1}(\delta+\rho+\sigma a) - (n+a+\delta)\right]\frac{\alpha-1}{\sigma}(\delta+\rho+\sigma a)}}{2} \begin{array}{c} > \\ < \end{array} 0.$$
$$(1.85)$$

To find the strength of convergence, the general solution of the system of equations (1.84) for $\ln k$, $\ln k = \ln k^* + A_1 e^{\lambda_1 t} + A_2 e^{\lambda_2 t}$, is transformed into the defined form, substituting $A_1 = 0$ (because otherwise the transversality condition or the accumulation equation for the variable c are not satisfied) and computing A_2 from the initial condition. Then using the fact that $y = k^{\alpha}$, we obtain

$$\ln y^* - \ln y = \left(\ln y^* - \ln y(0)\right)e^{-\beta t}, \quad (1.86)$$

where $\beta \equiv -\lambda_2 > 0$ is the rate of convergence to the steady state:

$$\beta = \frac{1}{2}\sqrt{(\rho-n-a(1-\sigma))^2 - 4\left[\alpha^{-1}(\delta+\rho+\sigma a) - (n+a+\delta)\right]\frac{\alpha-1}{\sigma}(\delta+\rho+\sigma a)} - \frac{1}{2}(\rho-n-a(1-\sigma)).$$
$$(1.87)$$

After differentiating equation (1.86) with respect to time, the rate of economic growth can be written as

$$\frac{\dot{y}}{y} = \beta(\ln y^* - \ln y). \quad (1.88)$$

Equations (1.87) and (1.88) are analogous to equations (1.15) and (1.16), which characterize the convergence process explained by the Solow model. Equation (1.88) indicates that the rate of economic growth decreases as the economy approaches the steady state, and the parameter β, defined by equation (1.87), determines the speed of convergence.

1.2 Endogenous models of economic growth

In the early 1970s – along with the oil crisis that changed dramatically the current trends of economic development of many Western countries – the growth theory left the main area of interest among economists. The breakthrough came only in 1986 with the article by Paul Romer (1986), initiating an era of endogenous growth models.[13]

Endogenous models – as the name suggests – explain the economic growth in an endogenous manner, i.e. within the model. This feature contrasts with neoclassical growth theory where long-run growth depended on exogenous technological progress introduced into the model along with other assumptions. Achieving endogenous growth is possible due to not including the neoclassical production function which assumes diminishing returns to accumulable inputs and constant returns to scale. Endogenous models assume that there are at least constant returns to accumulable inputs.

The mechanism of endogenous growth can be explained by introducing the following production function into the Solow model:

$$Y(t) = AK(t). \tag{1.89}$$

The above function exhibits constant returns to capital – the only accumulable factor of production. Given the income identity $Y = C + I = C + dK/dt$ and the equality of investment and savings $I = sY$ (where s is the exogenous savings rate), the economic growth rate in such a model is given as follows:

$$\frac{\dot{Y}}{Y} = sA. \tag{1.90}$$

The above equation shows that endogenous growth is achievable without exogenous technical progress. Equation (1.90) implies that the economy is continuously growing at a rate of sA. It also indicates that the increase in the savings rate is sufficient to accelerate permanently the long-run rate of economic growth. Since the production function is of the form $Y = AK$, this simple growth approach is known as "the AK model".

Endogenous growth occurs – in general – by eliminating the assumption of diminishing returns to accumulable inputs. In particular models, however, the introduction of constant returns takes various forms.

The Romer learning-by-doing model is a one-sector model, in which long-run growth is achieved due to increasing returns to accumulable factors at the whole economy level. In the Rebelo (1991) and Lucas models, endogenous growth is possible due to the existence of two sectors, each of which exhibiting constant returns. Models with an expanding variety of products (Romer, 1990) and models with an improving quality of products (Grossman and Helpman, 1991; Aghion and Howitt, 1992) are known as R&D models. In these models, the long-run economic growth is obtained by endogenizing technical progress, which is the output of the R&D sector.

Here, we will briefly discuss two basic models of endogenous growth: the Romer learning-by-doing model and the Lucas two-sector model. We present only the main assumptions and implications of these models. A more detailed analysis of these models was conducted by Próchniak and Witkowski (2016, pp. 45–56).

1.2.1 The Romer learning-by-doing model

The Romer model differs from the neoclassical models in that it does not assume diminishing returns to accumulable inputs. On the contrary, knowledge, which is the only accumulable factor of production, exhibits increasing returns at the social (whole economy) level. The rationale for adopting this assumption is that knowledge, being created through an investment of individual firms, can spread freely throughout the economy, and thus it can be used by all firms without incurring additional costs. Such a mechanism of knowledge diffusion is called "learning-by-doing" which means learning (i.e. acquisition of knowledge) through practice. The concept of learning-by-doing and the assumption of increasing returns both refer to the work of Arrow (1962). Due to increasing returns, the Romer model reveals an accelerating and permanent economic growth without introducing exogenous variables.

The assumptions that lead to endogenous growth are the following. Let f_i be the production function of an individual firm:

$$f_i(a_i, k_i, A),\tag{1.91}$$

where a_i is the level of knowledge of an individual firm, k_i represents other factors of production (capital, labour, etc.), and A is the general level of knowledge in the economy (the sum of knowledge possessed by N firms: $A = \sum_{i=1}^{N} a_i$). To simplify the analysis, we assume that other inputs are constant (k_i = const.), which means that knowledge is the only accumulable factor of production. Since all firms are identical, we have $f_i(a_i, k_i, A) = f(a, k, A)$ and $A = Na$. The production function exhibits increasing returns with respect to all inputs (a, k, A) and constant returns with respect to a and k:

$$f(\lambda a, \lambda k, \lambda A) > \lambda f(a, k, A) \text{ and } f(\lambda a, \lambda k, A) = \lambda f(a, k, A).\tag{1.92}$$

Since all other factors of production except knowledge are constant ($k = $ const.), production functions can be written as follows:

– at the individual firm's level: $f(a,k,A) = f(a,A)$,   (1.93)

– at the social (whole economy) level: $f(a,k,A) = f(a,k,Na) = F(a)$.   (1.94)

Differences in the production function lead to differences in the marginal product of knowledge. We assume that the marginal product of knowledge at the social level is increasing, while from the firm's point of view, it is decreasing or constant:

$$\frac{d^2 f(a,A)}{da^2} \le 0 \text{ and } \frac{d^2 F(a)}{da^2} > 0.$$ (1.95)

The dynamics of the economy in the Romer learning-by-doing model differ from the dynamics of the economy in the neoclassical theory especially because there is no steady state in the Romer model. At the optimal trajectory, a perfectly competitive economy reveals a permanent and accelerating economic growth. The pace of knowledge accumulation is increasing and asymptotically approaches its upper growth limit. Therefore, the growth rates of GDP and consumption increase as well.

The Romer model does not confirm the existence of convergence between countries. Moreover, it suggests rather divergence trends. According to the Romer approach, the rate of economic growth increases with income, meaning that more developed countries grow faster than less developed ones. Although GDP growth rates tend asymptotically towards the same upper limit, poor countries will grow more slowly because at any given point they have less knowledge. Thus, differences in income levels between countries are permanently increasing.

A perfectly competitive economy in the Romer model is not Pareto optimal. This is because investments in knowledge made by a single firm lead to the increase of the overall level of knowledge which is a common input. But a single company in its investment decisions does not take into account these positive externalities. The marginal product of knowledge from the point of view of a single firm is less than the marginal product of knowledge at the social level. This means that a perfectly competitive economy accumulates too little knowledge and reveals lower growth than a centrally planned economy.

The latter conclusion is a bit shocking at first glance. It results from the fact that the Romer model includes positive externalities. The concept of learning-by-doing suggests that there is a need for government intervention to ensure a level of knowledge accumulation being optimal from the whole economy's perspective. Without government involvement, individual firms will take into account only private costs and benefits. As a result, in a perfectly competitive economy, both the level of knowledge and the pace of economic growth will be lower than in an economy with government intervention.

1.2.2 The Lucas model

The Lucas (1988) model is a two-sector model of economic growth that includes – in addition to physical capital –human capital. The concept of the economy consisting of two sectors refers to the work of Uzawa (1964, 1965). Therefore, the Lucas model is also called the Uzawa-Lucas model. Endogenous growth is achieved due to the existence of two sectors that both exhibit constant returns.

The Lucas model explains very well the differences in income levels between countries. The economies, which initially are capital scarce, achieve a long-run equilibrium with a low level of capital. The economies that are initially richer tend to steady state characterized by higher capital level. However, the growth rate of GDP is the same in each steady state. Thus, differences in income levels between countries will not disappear: the poor countries remain poor, while the rich countries are still rich.

The Lucas model, therefore, does not explain the phenomenon of convergence – in terms of both the comparison of various steady states and the comparison of transition periods for the economies tending to reach the same steady state. In the first case, it appears that in the long-run equilibrium, the rate of economic growth does not depend on the level of capital and output. This means that countries grow at the same rate regardless of the income level reached. In the second case, when we consider the transition period for economies striving for the same steady state, it turns out that less developed countries may grow faster or slower than more developed ones. It depends on whether the low level of development results from the lack of physical capital (poorer countries would grow faster) or the lack of human capital (then poorer countries would record slower growth).

Notes

1 See Zarnowitz and Ozyildirim (2006) for details.
2 The description of the mathematical procedures used in economic modelling is clearly explained in Chiang and Wainwright (2004) and Chiang (1992).
3 The Diamond model is described, among others, by Próchniak and Witkowski (2016, pp. 39–45).
4 The technological progress may be introduced to the production function three-fold. First, we may deal with Hicks-neutral technological progress when the variable representing the state of technology is multiplied with the production function depending on only two variables (labour and capital): $A(t) \cdot F(K(t), L(t))$. The Harrod-neutral technological progress or – in other words – the labour-augmenting technological progress occurs when the variable measuring the level of technology is multiplied with the labour input: $F(K(t), A(t)L(t))$. Such a production function is usually included in the analysis (as in our case) because it yields slightly better properties for the dynamics of the model. It is also possible

to consider the capital-augmenting technological progress when the production function is given as follows: $F(A(t)K(t), L(t))$.

5 The dot over a variable means its time derivative.

6 In the rest of the analysis, we omit the time index t in order to preserve the transparency of the formulas.

7 The concept of β convergence is described in detail from the theoretical and empirical perspective by Próchniak and Witkowski (2016).

8 The Solow model with human capital (the MRW model) and its augmentation for institutions is described by Próchniak (2013a, 2013b).

9 In the augmented Solow model, the convergence coefficient, previously denoted by the symbol β, is defined by λ because β has already been used in the description of the production function.

10 Apart from the assumptions that marginal product of capital is positive and decreasing ($f'(k) > 0$ and $f''(k) < 0$) and that zero inputs produce zero output ($f(0) = 0$), the neoclassical production function is characterized by the Inada conditions that are given as follows: $\lim_{k\to\infty} f'(k) = 0$ and $\lim_{k\to 0} f'(k) = \infty$.

11 We have to distinguish between variables expressed in "per capita" terms and those expressed in "per unit of effective labour" terms. The former ones are denoted by a subscript "cp" and are obtained by dividing total aggregates by the population number, L. The latter ones are calculated by dividing total aggregates by the stock of effective labour, AL.

12 In optimization models, two types of the utility function are most often used: CRRA (constant relative risk aversion) and CARA (constant absolute risk aversion). These functions are given as follows:

$$\text{CRRA:}\quad u(c)=\frac{c^{1-\sigma}-1}{1-\sigma} \text{ for } \sigma>0, \sigma\neq 1 \quad\text{and}\quad u(c)=\log c \text{ for } \sigma=1; \quad \text{CARA:}$$

$$u(c)=-\frac{1}{\gamma}e^{-\gamma c} \text{ for } \gamma>0,$$

where log stands for the natural logarithm. For the CRRA function, the elasticity of substitution $(-u'(c)/u''(c)c)$ equals $1/\sigma$, while the elasticity of marginal utility to consumption $(u''(c)c/u'(c))$ amounts to $-\sigma$. For the CARA function, these measures are equal to $(\gamma c)^{-1}$ and $-\gamma c$, respectively. The names of both functions result from the fact that in the case of the CRRA function, the Arrow-Pratt measure of relative risk aversion $(-u''(c)c/u'(c))$ is constant and equal to σ, while in the case of the CARA function, the Arrow-Pratt measure of absolute risk aversion $(-u''(c)/u'(c))$ is constant and equal to γ.

13 The first works containing elements of contemporary endogenous models were published, however, much earlier – already in the 1960s (see, e.g., Arrow, 1962; Kaldor and Mirrlees, 1962; Uzawa, 1964, 1965; Shell, 1966; Sheshinski, 1967).

References

Aghion, P. and Howitt, P. (1992). A Model of Growth through Creative Destruction. *Econometrica*, 60(2), pp. 323–351, doi: 10.2307/2951599.

Arrow, K. (1962). The Economic Implications of Learning by Doing. *Review of Economic Studies*, 29(3), pp. 155–173, doi: 10.2307/2295952.

Barro, R. and Sala-i-Martin, X. (2003). *Economic Growth*. 2nd ed. Cambridge, MA: The MIT Press.

Bernardelli, M., Próchniak, M. and Witkowski, B. (2017). Konwergencja dochodowa: mocne i słabe strony istniejących podejść. *Kwartalnik Kolegium Ekonomiczno-Społecznego. Studia i Prace*, 3, pp. 71–86, doi: 10.33119/kkessip.2017.3.4.

Cass, D. (1965). Optimum Growth in an Aggregative Model of Capital Accumulation. *Review of Economic Studies*, 32(3), pp. 233–240, doi: 10.2307/2295827.

Chiang, A.C. (1992). *Elements of Dynamic Optimization*. New York: McGraw-Hill.

Chiang, A.C. and Wainwright, K. (2004). *Fundamental Methods of Mathematical Economics*. 4th ed. New York: McGraw-Hill.

Diamond, P.A. (1965). National Debt in a Neoclassical Growth Model. *American Economic Review*, 55, pp. 1126–1150.

Domar, E.D. (1946). Capital Expansion, Rate of Growth, and Employment. *Econometrica*, 14(2), pp. 137–147, doi: 10.2307/1905364.

Grossman, G.M. and Helpman, E. (1991). Quality Ladders in the Theory of Growth. *Review of Economic Studies*, 58(1), pp. 43–61, doi: 10.2307/2298044.

Harrod, R. (1939). An Essay in Dynamic Theory. *Economic Journal*, 49, pp. 14–33.

Inada, K.-I. (1963). On a Two-Sector Model of Economic Growth: Comments and a Generalization. *Review of Economic Studies*, 30(2), pp. 119–127, doi: 10.2307/2295809.

Kaldor, N. and Mirrlees, J.A. (1962). A New Model of Economic Growth. *Review of Economic Studies*, 29(3), pp. 174–192, doi: 10.2307/2295953.

Koopmans, T.C. (1965). On the Concept of Optimal Economic Growth. In: J. Johansen, ed., *The Econometric Approach to Development Planning*. Amsterdam: North Holland, pp. 225–300.

Lucas, R.E. (1988). On the Mechanics of Economic Development. *Journal of Monetary Economics*, 22(1), pp. 3–42, doi: 10.1016/0304-3932(88)90168-7.

Mankiw, N.G., Romer, D. and Weil, D.N. (1992). A Contribution to the Empirics of Economic Growth. *Quarterly Journal of Economics*, 107(2), pp. 407–437, doi: 10.2307/2118477.

Nonneman, W. and Vanhoudt, P. (1996). A Further Augmentation of the Solow Model and the Empirics of Economic Growth for OECD Countries. *Quarterly Journal of Economics*, 111(3), pp. 943–953, doi: 10.2307/2946677.

Próchniak, M. (2013a). To What Extent Is the Institutional Environment Responsible for Worldwide Differences in Economic Development. *Contemporary Economics*, 7(3), pp. 17–38, doi: 10.5709/ce.1897-9254.87.

Próchniak, M. (2013b). An Attempt to Assess the Quantitative Impact of Institutions on Economic Growth and Economic Development. *International Journal of Management and Economics*, 38(1), pp. 7–30, doi: 10.2478/ijme-2014-0012.

Próchniak, M. and Witkowski, B. (2016). *Konwergencja dochodowa typu beta w ujęciu teoretycznym i empirycznym*. Warszawa: Szkoła Główna Handlowa w Warszawie.

Ramsey, F.P. (1928). A Mathematical Theory of Saving. *Economic Journal*, 38(152), pp. 543–559, doi: 10.2307/2224098.

Rebelo, S. (1991). Long-Run Policy Analysis and Long-Run Growth. *Journal of Political Economy*, 99(3), pp. 500–521, doi: 10.1086/261764.

Romer, D. (2019). *Advanced Macroeconomics*. 5th ed. New York: McGraw Hill.

Romer, P.M. (1986). Increasing Returns and Long-Run Growth. *Journal of Political Economy*, 94(5), pp. 1002–1037, doi: 10.1086/261420.

Romer, P.M. (1990). Endogenous Technological Change. *Journal of Political Economy*, 98(5), pp. S71–S102, doi: 10.1086/261725.

Shell, K. (1966). Toward a Theory of Inventive Activity and Capital Accumulation. *American Economic Review*, 56(1/2), pp. 62–68.

Sheshinski, E. (1967). Optimal Accumulation with Learning by Doing. In: K. Shell, ed., *Essays on the Theory of Optimal Economic Growth*. Cambridge, MA: The MIT Press, pp. 31–52.

Solow, R.M. (1956). A Contribution to the Theory of Economic Growth. *Quarterly Journal of Economics*, 70(1), pp. 65–94, doi: 10.2307/1884513.

Swan, T.W. (1956). Economic Growth and Capital Accumulation. *Economic Record*, 32(2), pp. 334–361, doi: 10.1111/j.1475–4932.1956.tb00434.x.

Uzawa, H. (1964). Optimal Growth in a Two-Sector Model of Capital Accumulation. *Review of Economic Studies*, 31(1), pp. 1–24, doi: 10.2307/2295932.

Uzawa, H. (1965). Optimal Technical Change in an Aggregative Model of Economic Growth. *International Economic Review*, 6(1), pp. 18–31, doi: 10.2307/2525621.

Zarnowitz, V. and Ozyildirim, A. (2006). Time Series Decomposition and Measurement of Business Cycles, Trends and Growth Cycles. *Journal of Monetary Economics*, 53(7), pp. 1717–1739, doi: 10.1016/j.jmoneco.2005.03.015.

2 Hidden Markov models as an example of an alternative approach to convergence

There exist plenty of approaches to the general issue of convergence in the literature. While the β convergence is surely the most popular one, others shed light on the different aspects of the phenomenon. In this chapter, we introduce a proposal of a novel approach to the convergence studies based on the use of the hidden Markov models and describe the key steps of the procedure.

2.1 Applicability of hidden Markov models

The generalization of Markov models, known as HMMs or Markov-switching models, has been known in literature since the 1960s (Cappé, Moulines and Rydén, 2005). For decades, this class of models has played a prominent role in the analysis of many phenomena (Podgórska et al., 2002) of natural, technical, or economic character. With the development of computer technology, the popularity of this kind of automatic pattern recognition has increased. A comprehensive description of applications of HMM is given, e.g., in the study by Mor, Garhwal, and Kumar (2020). This method was used, among others, in speech recognition (Rabiner, 1989), natural language processing including part of speech tagging (Charniak, 1993), and engineering of non-stationary signal processes such as voice signals, image sequences, and time-varying noise (Vaseghi, 2000, pp. 143–177). Recent years have brought a rapid increase in the popularity of HMM in feature engineering for modelling purposes (Lucas et al., 2019), and in bioinformatics, especially in gene prediction (Munch and Krogh, 2006), sequence alignment (Pachter, Alexandersson and Cawley, 2002), structure prediction (Yoon and Vaidyanathan, 2008), or modelling DNA sequencing errors (Lottaz et al., 2003). Compared to engineering and bioinformatics, relatively little space has been devoted to the applications of HMM in economic sciences. Meanwhile, this method is the basis for tackling the problems such as turning point identification (Chauvet and Hamilton, 2005; Bernardelli, 2015), business cycle synchronization analysis (Smith and Summers, 2005; Dufrénot and Keddad, 2014), early warning signalling (Abberger and Nierhaus, 2010), and even similarity between time series issue (Bernardelli, 2018).

One of the most promising applications of HMM in economics is the convergence analysis. The concept of Markov models with a hidden layer of observations, which corresponds to the periods of a better or worse situation in the economy, has been proposed by Bernardelli, Próchniak, and Witkowski (2017). This chapter is devoted to the presentation of basic theory and terminology behind HMM, and most of all the detailed description of the HMM approach, which can be used to determine the rate of convergence.

2.2 HMM – definitions and theory

There are a few possibilities for defining the HMMs. They are used to a different extent depending on the field of science. It is possible to give a definition that uses the terminology from the field of a finite-state probabilistic machine or a finite-state probabilistic automaton (Rabin, 1963). HMM could be also considered as the simplest dynamic Bayesian network (Ghahramani, 2001). However, probably the most popular approach in economic science is to define HMM as a stochastic process (Cappé, Moulines and Rydén, 2005). Below we give one of many possible definitions with its interpretation and some exemplary usage.

Let $S = \{s_1, s_2, ..., s_N\}$ be the finite N-element state space. States are not visible but are related to the visible M-element set of observations $V = \{v_1, v_2, ..., v_M\}$. Instead of each state, we observe randomly generated observations. The hidden Markov chain is the sequence of states $\{X_t\}_{t=1}^n$, where $X_t \in S$, which fulfils the so-called Markov chain property that says that the probability of each subsequent state depends only on what was the previous state, that is for $t > 1$:

$$P\left(X_t = x_t | X_1 = x_1, X_2 = x_2, ..., X_{t-1} = x_{t-1}\right) = P. \tag{2.1}$$

A HMM is defined by the three sets of probabilities (A, B, π):

- matrix of transition probabilities $A = \{P(s_i|s_j)\}_{i, j=1}^N$,
- matrix of observation probabilities $B = \{P(v_i|s_j)\}$ for $i = 1, ..., M$, $j = 1, ..., N$,
- vector of initial probabilities $\pi = \{P(s_i)\}_{i=1}^N$.

The simplest type of HMM is the one with observable components being conditionally independent Gaussian variables. This class of models is called a normal HMM. The N-state normal HMM is a model with $N^2 + 3N$ parameters which include:

- transition probabilities of an unobserved Markov chain (N^2 parameters),
- means and covariances of the conditional distribution of an observed variable in the given state ($2N$ parameters),
- distribution of an unobserved Markov chain (N parameters).

There are at least two major challenges with the HMM. The first one is the learning problem of the HMM. Given some training observation sequences and general structure of HMM (numbers of hidden states and elements of the set of observations), we want to find the probabilities (A, B, π) which fit the HMM best ($N^2 + 3N$ parameters). For the estimation of those parameters, the Baum-Welch algorithm may be used (Yang, Balakrishnan and Wainwright, 2017). The Baum-Welch algorithm is an iterative process that follows the idea of the expectation-maximization (EM). Although it gives a deterministic output for each set of input values, the result may vary depending on the initial values of probabilities, and thus, the given solution may be far from optimal. The often-used remedy for this problem is repeating calculations several times for the same set of data and different initial values. This approach is a Monte Carlo simulation and it increases the chances of finding the optimal solution.

There are many criteria for choosing the best solution (Bernardelli, 2013). The most common are given as follows:

- Akaike's information criterion (AIC),
- Bayesian information criterion (BIC),
- the log-likelihood value,
- frequency of obtaining a certain solution of the Baum-Welch algorithm.

Depending on many factors, including the numerical stability of results, generally, thousands of simulations have to be performed. Therefore, the whole procedure combining the Baum-Welch algorithm with Monte Carlo simulations can be quite time-consuming. The detailed procedure of estimation HMM parameters used in the convergence analysis is given at the end of this section.

The second issue with the HMM refers to the so-called decoding problem, which comes down to calculate the most likely sequence of hidden states that generates this observation sequence for the particular HMM and the observation sequence $\{Y_t\}_{t=1}^{n}$, where $Y_t \in V$. A classic example of this kind of task is to determine the weather (three states: snow, rain, and sunshine) based on two possible observations: hot and cold. Another one is to uncover the letters based on handwriting. An identification of the states of the economy based on business tendency surveys or any other macroeconomic time series can be given as economic examples (see Bernardelli, 2015). In each case, we have a Markov chain $\{X_t\}_{t=1}^{n}$, which we cannot observe, and the observation sequence $\{Y_t\}_{t=1}^{n}$, which is visible to us. For normal HMM, we add an extra assumption that for $i = 1, 2, \ldots, N$,

$$Y_t \mid_{X_t = s_i} \sim N(\mu_i, \sigma_i). \tag{2.2}$$

Assume that we have information about the realization of an observable variable in the period from 1 to T. Mainly due to the big computational complexity, the most common approaches to the decoding problem over the years were the smoothed probability

$$w_t(s_i) = P \tag{2.3}$$

or the filtered probability

$$f_t(s_i) = P(X_t = s_i | Y_1 = y_1, Y_2 = y_2,.., Y_n = y_n). \tag{2.4}$$

The simplest assessment (Chauvet and Hamilton, 2005) of the state at time t is to use $\underset{i \in \{1,2, ..., N\}}{\mathrm{argmax}} \ w_t(s_i)$ or $\underset{i \in \{1,2, ..., N\}}{\mathrm{argmax}} \ f_t(s_i)$. This kind of "step-by-step decoding" cannot be accurate, especially in the case of larger state space. An alternative is to find a sequence of hidden states, which corresponds to the observation sequence and is the most probable realization of it in the whole period covered by the analysis, not only locally. Formally speaking, we determine the path $(\tilde{x}_1, \tilde{x}_2, ..., \tilde{x}_T) \in S^T$ such that

$$P(X_1 = \tilde{x}_1, X_2 = \tilde{x}_2, ..., X_T = \tilde{x}_T | Y_1 = y_1, Y_2 = y_2,.., Y_T = y_T) =$$

$$\underset{(x_1, x_2, ..., x_T) \in S^T}{\max} \{P(X_1 = x_1, X_2 = x_2, ..., X_T = x_T | Y_1 = y_1, Y_2 = y_2, ..., Y_T = y_T)\}. \tag{2.5}$$

Computation using brute force would take exponential time, but a more efficient approach exists and it is known as the Viterbi algorithm (Viterbi, 1967). This most likely sequence resulting from the Viterbi algorithm is called the Viterbi path. The resulting states can be renumerated to give a proper interpretation. For instance, in the case of turning point identification in macroeconomic analysis and two-state normal HMM, state 0 corresponds to the periods of contraction and state 1 relates to the periods of expansion. To ensure the same order of states in each considered case, we additionally assume that state 1 is associated with the greater mean value (within the meaning of the parameter of the normal distribution) and state 0 with the smaller mean value, that is, $\mu_0 < \mu_1$, with notation provided in formula (2.2).

Knowing the Baum-Welch algorithm (complemented with Monte Carlo simulation) and the Viterbi algorithm, we can tackle the two mentioned problems of learning and decoding HMM. The main advantage of the method based on Viterbi paths, calculated from the probabilities connected with the hidden Markov chains, is the minimal set of assumptions about the input data compared to the classical econometric models, where usually problems with the potential presence of unspecified variables or restrictive assumptions about the model, input data, and irregular (random) component are present. Although HMMs can be considered as an example of a statistically restrictive method, the definition and exemplary application of HMM given in this chapter are limited to the purely automatic pattern recognition – if there is some hidden regularity, then this approach helps to find it.

Another advantage of using the HMM approach is the ease of interpretation. Depending on the studied phenomenon, each state has its unique interpretation. For instance, in the case of turning point identification, state 1 is associated with periods of relatively good conditions and state 0 is associated with a worse situation. If we expand the state space from two to three states, the interpretation of states 0 and 1 will be the same and the state ½ will correspond to uncertain, transient periods.

As an illustration of the HMM approach revealing its potential, in Figure 2.1 the cyclical component of the Research Institute for Economic Development industrial confidence indicator (RIED ICI, see Adamowicz et al., 2019) and associated turning points identified by the two-state HMM are given. In Figure 2.2, the analogous graphs are drawn, but for the three-state Viterbi path.

In the case of two-state HMM, two troughs (in May 2005 and December 2015) are missed, but in the three-state model, all turning points are captured. In both cases, the automatic procedure in the form of the HMM gives similar results to the time series decomposition. In the case of HMM, however, there is no ambiguity in the interpretation of the phases in the economy – they are given explicitly by the states of the hidden Markov chain. Thanks to the use of decomposition, the cyclical component of time series is extracted, but the interpretation of the phases is up to the researcher because not all amplitudes at the turning points are comparable over time.

Adding an extra state ½ may give more accurate results; however, the more the states, the greater the computational complexity and the more unstable the results. With every new state, the number of model parameters is increasing, and not only time series must be longer, but also the number of Monte Carlo simulations will probably increase.

The Baum-Welch and Viterbi algorithms can be found in many modern programming languages such as R and Python. However, combining them both with the Monte Carlo simulations and proper optimization criteria in one consistent procedure must be implemented individually. The details of the procedure of estimation HMM parameters, which is the basis of the convergence analysis tool, are described in the following steps:

1   Choose M sets of initial probabilities (A, B, π) for the HMM. One set of initial values for the N-state normal HMM consists of $N^2 + 3N$ parameters. Initial values may be chosen randomly.
2   Perform the Baum-Welch algorithm for every set of initial values to estimate the parameters of the HMM. Based on the expected values of conditional distributions, find the correct order of states.

The computation time of the whole procedure depends mainly on this step and is proportional to the number of sets M. The multiple repetitions of

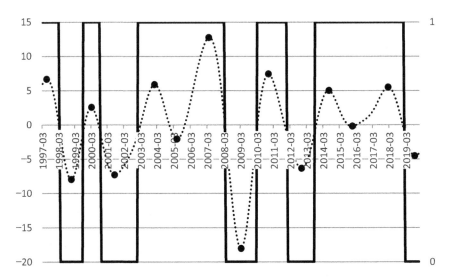

Figure 2.1 The cyclical component of the RIED ICI (dotted line) and associated turning points (points) along with the two-state Viterbi path (solid line) from March 1997 to December 2019.

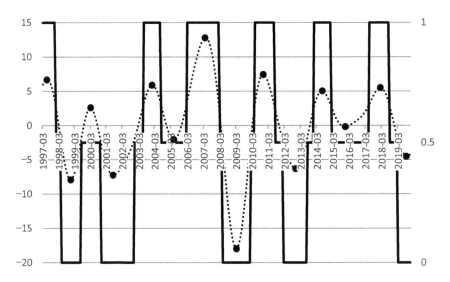

Figure 2.2 The cyclical component of the RIED ICI (dotted line) and associated turning points (points) along with the three-state Viterbi path (solid line) from March 1997 to December 2019.

the parameter estimation are needed to increase the chance of finding a good approximation of the global, and not only local, solution. One has to, however, balance the number of Monte Carlo iterations with the overall calculation time. Theoretically, it is possible to discretize parameter values and perform calculations for discretization mesh nodes. The finer the mesh step, the more the number of nodes, and the greater the M value. Given the number of parameters for the N-state normal HMM, and assuming the discretization size equal m for each parameter, the number of nodes of the mesh grid would be $\left(N^2 + 3N\right)^m$. To obtain the result in a reasonable time, the mesh used in the procedure would have to be rather thick. For example, for the simplest two-state HMM and $m = 10$, we get a 10 billion initial set of values, which is unacceptable in terms of the time of calculations. This is the reason why instead of a mesh grid, some random initial points are chosen.

As the output of this step of the procedure, we get M sets of HMM parameters. Due to different initial points and numerical rounding, those parameters are almost always unique. However, the differences between parameters of the two models could be small; for example, they can differ on the eighth or tenth decimal place.

3   Group the parameters of all M calculated models based on – rounded to one decimal place – expected values of conditional distributions. Depending on the number M of an initial set of values and characteristics of input data, we can get only a few or even several dozen groups. For each group, define a representative model with parameters being averages of the respective parameters of all models from this group. From the fourth step, the only representative model of each group is considered.

4   For representative models, calculate the most probable sequence of hidden states using the Viterbi algorithm. The calculations are not so costly as it was in the second step because only one Viterbi path per group is computed.

5   Choose the most suitable HMM and the Viterbi path from the Viterbi paths computed in the fourth step. This selection is the final output of the whole procedure. The choice could be made based on various optimization criteria as well as on comparison with the reference time series. In the procedure, we take into consideration the Akaike information criterion and size of each group, which corresponds to the frequency of obtaining a given set of parameters in the Baum-Welch algorithm (with an accuracy of one decimal place).

The presented procedure is the basis of the convergence analysis. For a set of data, it was used many times for different pairs of countries or regions. A description of the HMM approach to the convergence problem is given in the following section.

2.3 HMM convergence

In the remaining part of the chapter, the application of the HMM to the analysis of real convergence is presented. This kind of application is almost absent in the literature. Due to the length of the considered time series, in the description we restrict ourselves to the two-element state space only. All the computation related to the HMM was inspired by the article by Bernardelli, Próchniak, and Witkowski (2017), in which HMMs and the Viterbi path are employed to analyse the process of real convergence of 28 EU countries in the 1995–2016 period. The procedure presented in the cited article computes the Viterbi paths for the variables being the differences of particular macro-economic time series of two countries. State 0 on that path identifies a year of greater similarity in terms of the variable under analysis, whereas state 1 indicates a divergence between countries (e.g. Poland and country *C*). For each year, averages of the states of Viterbi paths for all countries for the given variable are calculated. The resulting values vary from 0 to 1, where the value of 0 means perfect similarity interpreted as a convergence. Analogously, the average equals 1 means the period of undisputable divergence between the countries. We will call this convergence HMM convergence to distinguish it from other measures of convergence.

This kind of approach joins the simplicity of concept and elasticity if it comes to input data. It allows to analyse a pair of countries separately, as well as the HMM convergence of the chosen country towards the group of other countries or the HMM convergence of the certain subgroups of countries towards the reference time series like the leader country. The HMM convergence was also the basic technique of examining the similarity of countries in terms of the tax system (Felis et al., 2020). A similar technique was used in the computations conducted in the research described in this book. It will be given in detail in the next paragraphs.

Following the idea of the HMM convergence, we adapt the method to verify the degree of similarity of the selected group of regions (Chapter 3) as well as countries (Chapter 5). In the case of the Polish voivodships, US states, and provinces in China, the convergence towards the leader is analysed. Considering the GDP per capita, the mazowieckie voivodship in Poland, the District of Columbia in the USA, and Beijing in China have been chosen as leaders.

Let V be the set of all regions except the leader. The procedure of HMM convergence analysis can be split into three steps.

In the first step, for each of the considered regions from the V set, time series of differences are created as

$$\tilde{v}_t^{\text{region}} = v_t^{\text{reference region}} - v_t^{\text{region}}, \tag{2.6}$$

where $t = 1,\ldots, T$, region $\in V$.

In the second step, parameters of the HMM using the Baum-Welch algorithm and a large number of Monte Carlo simulations are estimated for each of the series $\tilde{v}_t^{\text{region}}$, and then the Viterbi paths VP_t^{region} are calculated. State 0 on this path is the year in which the regions were similar in terms of the GDP per capita, while state 1 indicates a discrepancy between the regions (the leader against every other region). In this step, parameters of as many models as the cardinality of V set is are estimated.

In the third step, for each year the averages of the states of the Viterbi paths for all regions are calculated:

$$r_t = \frac{1}{|V|} \sum_{\text{region} \in V} VP_t^{\text{region}}, \tag{2.7}$$

for $t = 1,\ldots, T$, where $|V|$ stands for the number of considered regions. In this context, an average equal to 0 means perfect similarity (convergence) while the year in which the average is equal to 1 is the period of a complete lack of similarity (divergence) between the leader and the remaining regions.

While it is tempting to expand the approach to the global (worldwide) case, a problem arises: in most groups of countries there exists no single leader in terms of the GDP per capita who would not change during the analysed period. In those cases, instead of a leader, we explore the convergence towards the artificially constructed reference time series. This reference is created by choosing the leader in the last year of the considered period and shifting it by multiplication transformation. The multiplier for this transformation is the minimal real number such that, after multiplication, the resulting reference time series (GDP per capita of the leader) is not smaller than all other time series (GDP per capita in the remaining countries) in the entire period.

Depending on the value of the multiplier, we deal with the actual leader or just the hypothetical time series which is calculated as the product of the multiplier and GDP per capita of the country being the leader in the last considered year of analysis. In both cases in the description of the procedure, we will be using the "reference time series" nomenclature. As in the case of the regional HMM convergence, we denote V as the set of all countries except the reference country. The procedure of HMM convergence analysis in the selected group of countries is given in the following three steps:

1   For each of the country C from the V set create the time series of differences:

$$\tilde{v}_t^C = v_t^{\text{reference}} - v_t^C, \tag{2.8}$$

where $t = 1,\ldots, T, C \in V$.

2 Estimate parameters of the HMM using the combination of Baum-Welch algorithm and Monte Carlo simulations for each of the time series $\tilde{v}_t^C$, and then calculate the Viterbi paths VP_t^C. Use many different initial values for the Monte Carlo simulations to ensure solution stability and a high probability of finding the close approximation of the globally optimal solution.

3 Calculate the year-by-year averages of the states on the Viterbi paths for all countries:

$$r_t = \frac{1}{n} \sum_{C \in V} VP_t^C, \tag{2.9}$$

for $t = 1,..., T$, where n is the size of the V set.

The results of the procedure described above, which exploits the HMM convergence, are given in Chapters 3 for the regional convergence and Chapter 5 for the country convergence. In the analysis, we restrict ourselves to the two- and three-state hidden Markov chains, due to the limited length of available time series and clarity of interpretation. Theoretically, the concept could be easily generalized to more than three states. In practice, however, long enough time series should be used to ensure proper parameter estimation. Also, computation time resulting mainly from the increased number of Monte Carlo simulations would be much longer. The last, but not least aspect of the greater state space is the interpretability of the results. In the case of convergence, states 0, 1, and 0.5 have quite obvious economic meaning. For a dozen possible states, this economic interpretation would be blurred. The main drawback of this method is its relativity concerning the studied period. Changing the period would change the states associated with a given point in time, and thus the interpretation. In fact, however, this is also a feature of econometric models. In Chapter 4, there is a discussion about the parameters of models estimated in the whole period and two shorter subperiods. From this perspective, the HMM approach gives the opportunity to identify periods with a different pace of the convergence process and thus is not inferior to the panel econometric methods.

In the HMM convergence, the countries or regions are treated individually; therefore, it is possible to give a meaningful interpretation for an analysed pair of time series. This is not the case with the BMA method. This is one of the reasons why those two approaches should be treated as complementary, not substitutional. Actually, those two methods could have different results in terms of convergence, but there is no contradiction here. In both cases, a different type of convergence is investigated. β convergence tells us about the convergence process in the whole group of countries or regions. In turn, by HMM convergence, the comparison of the group of time series with one selected (richest) region or country is meant. Therefore, convergence should be tested using different methods to get a complete picture of the catching-up process.

References

Abberger, K. and Nierhaus, W. (2010). Markov-Switching and the Ifo Business Climate: the Ifo Business Cycle Traffic Lights. *OECD Journal: Journal of Business Cycle Measurement and Analysis*, 2, pp. 1–13, doi: 10.1787/jbcma-2010–5km4gzqtx248.

Adamowicz, E., Dudek, S., Kluza, S., Ratuszny, E. and Walczyk, K. (2019). Koniunktura gospodarcza i bankowa w Europie Środkowo-Wschodniej. In: M. Strojny, ed., *Europa Środkowo-Wschodnia wobec globalnych trendów: gospodarka, społeczeństwo i biznes.* Warszawa: Szkoła Główna Handlowa w Warszawie, pp. 353–383.

Bernardelli, M. (2013). Nieklasyczne modele Markowa w analizie cykli koniunktury gospodarczej w Polsce. *Roczniki Kolegium Analiz Ekonomicznych SGH*, 30, pp. 59–74.

Bernardelli, M. (2015). The Procedure of Business Cycle Turning Points Identification Based on Hidden Markov Models. Analyzing and Forecasting Economic Fluctuations. *Prace i Materiały Instytutu Rozwoju Gospodarczego SGH*, 96, pp. 5–23.

Bernardelli, M. (2018). Hidden Markov Models as a Tool for the Assessment of Dependence of Phenomena of Economic Nature. *Acta Universitatis Lodziensis. Folia Oeconomica*, 5(338), pp. 7–20, doi: 10.18778/0208–6018.338.01.

Bernardelli, M., Próchniak, M. and Witkowski, B. (2017). The Application of Hidden Markov Models to the Analysis of Real Convergence. *Dynamic Econometric Models*, 17, pp. 59–80, doi: 10.12775/DEM.2017.004.

Cappé, O, Moulines, E. and Rydén, T. (2005). *Inference in Hidden Markov Models.* New York: Springer.

Charniak, E. (1993). *Statistical Language Learning.* Cambridge, MA: MIT Press.

Chauvet, M. and Hamilton, J.D. (2005). Dating Business Cycle Turning Points. *NBER Working Paper*, 11422, doi: 10.3386/w11422.

Dufrénot, G. and Keddad, B. (2014). Business Cycle Synchronization in East Asia: A Markov Switching Approach. *Economic Modelling*, 42, pp. 186–197, doi: 10.1016/j.econmod.2014.07.001.

Felis, P., Bernardelli, M., Jamroży, M., Lipiec, J., Malinowska-Misiąg, E., Szlęzak-Matusewicz, J. and Otczyk, G. (2020). Tendencje w polityce podatkowej w krajach Europy Środkowo-Wschodniej: opodatkowanie dochodów przedsiębiorstw. In: M. Strojny, ed., *Raport SGH i Forum Ekonomicznego 2020.* Warszawa: Szkoła Główna Handlowa w Warszawie, pp. 427–480, doi: 10.33119/978-83-8030-386-7.2020.

Ghahramani, Z. (2001). An Introduction to Hidden Markov Models and Bayesian Networks. *International Journal of Pattern Recognition and Artificial Intelligence*, 15(1), pp. 9–42, doi: 10.1142/S0218001401000836.

Lottaz, C., Iseli, C., Jongeneel, C.V. and Bucher, P. (2003). Modeling Sequencing Errors by Combining Hidden Markov Models. *Bioinformatics*, 19 (Suppl 2), pp. ii103–ii112, doi: 10.1093/bioinformatics/btg1067.

Lucas, Y., Portier, P.-E., Laporte, L., Calabretto, S., Caelen, O., He-Guelton, L. and Granitzer, M. (2019). Multiple Perspectives HMM-Based Feature Engineering for Credit Card Fraud Detection. *SAC '19: Proceedings of the 34th ACM/SIGAPP Symposium on Applied Computing*, pp. 1359–1361, doi: 10.1145/3297280.3297586.

Mor, B., Garhwal, S. and Kumar, A. (2020). A Systematic Review of Hidden Markov Models and Their Applications. *Archives of Computational Methods in Engineering*, doi: 10.1007/s11831-020-09422-4.

Munch, K. and Krogh, A. (2006). Automatic Generation of Gene Finders for Eukaryotic Species. *BMC Bioinformatics*, 7(263), doi: 10.1186/1471-2105-7-263.

Pachter, L., Alexandersson, M. and Cawley, S. (2002). Applications of Generalized Pair Hidden Markov Models to Alignment and Gene Finding Problems. *Journal of Computational Biology*, 9(2), pp. 389–399, doi: 10.1089/10665270252935520.

Podgórska, M., Śliwka, P., Topolewski, M. and Wszołek, M. (2002). *Łańcuchy Markowa w teorii i zastosowaniach*. Warszawa: Szkoła Główna Handlowa w Warszawie.

Rabin, M.O. (1963). Probabilistic Automata. *Information and Control*, 6(3), pp. 230–245, doi: 10.1016/S0019-9958(63)90290-0.

Rabiner, L.R. (1989). A Tutorial on Hidden Markov Models and Selected Applications in Speech Recognition. *Proceedings of the IEEE*, 77(2), pp. 257–286, doi: 10.1109/5.18626.

Smith, P.A. and Summers, P.M. (2005). How Well Do Markov Switching Models Describe Actual Business Cycles? The Case of Synchronization. *Journal of Applied Econometrics*, 20(2), pp. 253–274, doi: 10.1002/jae.845.

Vaseghi, S.V. (2000). *Advanced Digital Signal Processing and Noise Reduction*. 2nd ed. John Wiley & Sons, Ltd., doi: 10.1002/0470841621.

Viterbi, A. (1967). Error Bounds for Convolutional Codes and an Asymptotically Optimum Decoding Algorithm. *IEEE Transactions on Information Theory*, 13(2), pp. 260–269, doi: 10.1109/TIT.1967.1054010.

Yang, F., Balakrishnan, S. and Wainwright, M.J. (2017). Statistical and Computational Guarantees for the Baum-Welch Algorithm. *Journal of Machine Learning Research*, 18(125), pp. 1–53.

Yoon, B.-J. and Vaidyanathan, P.P. (2008). Structural Alignment of RNAs Using Profile-csHMMs and Its Application to RNA Homology Search: Overview and New Results. *IEEE Transactions on Automatic Control*, 53 (Special Issue), pp. 10–25, doi: 10.1109/TAC.2007.911322.

3 Different approaches to the regional convergence

3.1 Introduction

One of the directions of research in the field of economic convergence is the analysis at the regional level. The existing studies verify the existence of convergence of administrative units of a single country or a group of countries. The studies on regional convergence usually include top-level administrative units as regions, e.g. states in the USA, provinces in Canada, prefectures in Japan, or provinces in China. This approach allows finding some characteristics of economic growth paths of individual countries which cannot be observed at the national level. While both the methodology and the theoretical background of the study at the regional level are similar to those at the country level, there is one major empirical limitation that concerns the analysis at the regional level. Namely, in the conditional convergence model, the number of potential explanatory variables is limited because all the key economic growth factors that are defined at the national level and do not differ between regions must be excluded from the analysis: some of them (e.g. the level of democracy, economic freedom, or political stability) cannot be included in the conditional convergence model estimated on regional data because they exhibit zero variance on the cross-sectional level, while in some other cases (e.g. variables related to international trade), the appropriate data for individual regions cannot be collected.

In this chapter, we present the use of classical and unconventional methods to study the phenomenon of convergence at the regional level. The approaches discussed include the β convergence, stochastic convergence, and hidden Markov model (HMM) convergence. In the empirical part, we use the data on Polish voivodships,[1] US states, and Chinese provinces applying the same set of methods in order to obtain comparable results.

The key value added and novelty of this chapter refer to the wide picture of analysing the phenomenon of convergence. We examine various definitions of convergence using a variety of econometric techniques. We begin with the standard concept of β convergence which is tested in both absolute and conditional terms. Then, we switch to unconventional measures of convergence. We test stochastic convergence in two ways: without and with a trend. Finally, we apply HMMs to analyse the convergence process.

The analysis for Poland covers 16 voivodships observed in the 2000–2017 period. For the USA, the analysis includes 51 regions (50 states and District of Columbia) and the 2000–2019 period. The same period (2000–2019) is used for 31 Chinese provinces.

3.2 The review of the literature

There are many studies on regional convergence, including Poland, the USA, and China. As an example (the review of the literature itself is not the goal of the chapter), we focus here on the most important studies for Poland trying to show the gap existing in the literature and to justify the appropriateness of the approach undertaken in the current study.[2]

Tokarski and Gajewski (2003) examine β and σ convergence for the Polish regions in the 1995–2000 period. The β convergence is analysed in both absolute and conditional terms. In the conditional β convergence model, the regression equation includes the following control factors: investment rates, kilometres of roads, and urbanization rate for each voivodship, as well as some dummies. The data indicate that Poland recorded unconditional regional divergence as a result of very fast growth in mazowieckie, slaskie, and – to a lesser extent – pomorskie, dolnoslaskie, and swietokrzyskie voivodships. In conditional terms, however, the β convergence was evidenced. This study gives the idea of what kind of control factors can be introduced into the conditional β convergence model. Some of the variables applied by us correspond to those used in the cited study, but some others are different and reflect our own opinion as to the factors that best determine the GDP growth at the regional level.

One of the first articles about β and σ convergence at the regional level in Poland, published in economic journals, was the paper by Próchniak (2004). The cited author analysed absolute β and σ convergence for the Polish voivodships during the 1995–2000 period. The study concludes the lack of convergence – even in the narrower group of 15 voivodships, excluding the mazowieckie region which is supposed to tend to a different steady state.

Wójcik (2004) analyses convergence in the 1990–2001 period concluding that regional convergence was not the case in Poland, as the GDP per capita was very stable. Income polarization in that period was observed because relative differences between poor and rich regions were growing. The cited author also finds out that the situation in the first half of the 1990s was distinctively different from that in the second half of the decade. The latter finding means that the convergence process was not stable over time, suggesting the employment of new techniques in examining the catching-up process, like in our study.

Wolszczak-Derlacz (2009) verifies the impact of migration on regional convergence in Poland in the 1995–2006 period. The results demonstrate the lack of absolute and conditional convergence at the regional level.

The impact of inter- and intranational migration rates on the speed of divergence between Polish voivodships turned out to be statistically insignificant.

Markowska-Przybyła (2010), using methods of descriptive statistics and tests for the existence of β and σ convergence, finds out that there is an economic divergence at the regional level in Poland in the years 1999–2007, although when interpreting the results of estimated regression equations it is necessary to take into account weak statistics (especially for β convergence), a small number of observations, and a short period studied.

In another study, Markowska-Przybyła (2011) analyses the regional convergence in Poland according to classical and alternative approaches. According to the cited research, the Polish economy recorded regional divergence in the years 1999–2008, although the estimated function had weak statistical properties. σ convergence tests showed also the existence of divergence, but the estimated function had good statistical properties. The alternative methods of measuring convergence – Kendall's coefficient of concordance or the transition matrix analysis – indicate high stability of the GDP per capita distribution over time and no evidence of convergence. This study shows the necessity to use many definitions of convergence and many methods of its verification, like our research.

The study by Godziszewski, Kruszka, and Puziak (2013) is another one showing that disparities between Polish regions were increasing. The authors analyse income-level convergence (including the absolute β catching-up) between the Polish regions and within the EU27 group during the 1995–2007 period. There are some new approaches adopted in this study, e.g. population-weighted estimates of the β convergence regression. It turns out that population weighting does not significantly affect the results (especially in the EU27 group).

In the study by Matkowski and Próchniak (2013), the convergence hypothesis was verified for more than 200 EU27 regions (including Poland) at the NUTS2 level during the 1995–2009 period. EU regions, analysed together, confirmed the existence of some β and σ convergence.

Bal-Domańska (2013) analyses β (absolute and conditional) and σ convergence for 188 EU regions during 1999–2004 and 247 EU regions during 1999–2007 (at the NUTS2 level). Convergence studies using panel or cross-sectional models give ambiguous results because they are strongly dependent on the studied period and the objects (regions) covered by the model. The cited author states that convergence was only confirmed for some groups of regions. Since the findings are mixed, there is a necessity for further testing of the catching-up process, which is carried out by us in this research.

Borowiec (2015) analyses regional convergence in the EU28 countries in 2000–2011. The cited author uses various statistical methods, including descriptive statistics and correlation analysis. The results obtained confirm the occurrence of regional convergence in the EU. There is a negative correlation between the initial GDP per capita level and its growth rate in the EU member states. As a result, disparities in regional development decreased, especially between the least and the most developed regions. However, convergence did not take place in all less developed regions or transition regions.

Piętak (2015) analyses β and σ convergence in the selected EU countries at the regional level during the 2005–2011 period. The results indicate that Poland and the other CEE countries that accessed the EU in 2004 did not reveal regional income-level convergence. The catching-up process at the regional level took place in selected rich countries such as Austria, Belgium, and the Netherlands.

The lack of convergence in Poland was also confirmed in the study by Wędrowska and Wojciechowska (2015). The cited authors analysed Polish voivodships during the 2000–2012 period based on the absolute β convergence concept. They also calculated the coefficient of variation to assess changes in income differentiation over time.

According to the study by Borowiec (2017), who analysed β and σ convergence at the regional level in less developed EU countries, including those from Central-Eastern as well as Western Europe, β convergence did not occur in all less developed regions. Moreover, the cited study pointed out that β convergence was generally not accompanied by σ convergence.

Tylec (2017) examines the existence of β and σ convergence in the EU regions (including Western Europe and Central and Eastern Europe) during the 2000–2014 period. One of the findings is the regional GDP per capita divergence within the EU10 countries which are new EU member states.

Some studies focus on unconventional methods of analysing convergence and the application of Markov models to the analysis of the catching-up.

Wójcik (2008) examines GDP per capita convergence at the voivodship (NUTS2), sub-regional (NUTS3), and intra-voivodship levels in Poland during 1995–2005. The cited author estimates transition matrices derived from Markov processes and uses nonparametric Kernel estimators of the relative density function for relative GDP distribution per capita in subsequent years. The cited author finds out that voivodships, as well as sub-regions, were impoverished as a result of a faster-than-normal growth of the richest voivodships (mazowieckie) and sub-regions (large cities, mainly Warsaw and Poznan). The study also indicates that the club convergence can be seen at both NUTS2 and NUTS3 levels: relatively the poorest and – separately – the richest regions are becoming similar and converge at different income levels.

Łaźniewska and Górecki (2012) use the Markov analysis to evaluate GDP per capita convergence in Poland at the regional (NUTS3) level in the 1999–2008 period and on this basis they indicate, *inter alia*, which regions moved upwards, downwards, or remained unchanged within the considered classes in the GDP per capita ranking.

There are also studies in which the authors try to find the factors that affect regional income-level convergence or divergence. For example, Czudec and Kata (2016) analyse the EU structural funds and examine their role in the development of Polish regions.

Finally, it is worth mentioning the whole books which are devoted to the analysis of regional convergence. For the sake of conciseness, we are not going to present all the findings given in these works. The book by Kusideł (2013) demonstrates that regional GDP per capita in Poland is characterized by β divergence and σ divergence. However, the lack of convergence does not come from the fact that there is an increasing diversity between all voivodships but that the increasing diversity takes place between their groups (clusters). The book also shows interesting results for unconventional types of convergence, including γ convergence and stochastic convergence. Based on these findings, we are aware of the fact that the full picture of the catching-up process cannot be constrained to one type of convergence; hence, in the current study, a few concepts of convergence are being verified.

In another book fully devoted to regional and local convergence, Wójcik (2018) introduces an interesting concept of parallel convergence. Parallel convergence means the identical dynamics of economic convergence processes for the two phenomena in a given period. The cited author applies the concept of parallel convergence to various types of catching-up, among others β and σ types. The analysis is carried out at various levels of disaggregation (including NUTS2 and NUTS3 levels). The cited author also describes the variety of methods for the analysis of convergence – apart from the conventional types, also such concepts like γ, rho, and stochastic convergence.

Numerous studies on convergence for US states and Chinese provinces also exist. Restricting the attention to the latest US analysis, Miles (2020) analyses income convergence for US regions during the 1950–2018 period. The cited author models the differences in the logarithm of per capita income for the pairs of regions as an autoregressive series and conducts, among others, the ADF unit root test with and without trend on these differences. The results indicate predominantly no convergence and are in contrast to the β convergence tests. The method applied in the quoted study shows the need to extend the variety of tools for verifying the convergence hypothesis. Hence, the adoption of the concept of stochastic convergence in this chapter is fully justified.

Another study published recently for the US states was conducted by Kinfemichael and Morshed (2019). They verify the hypothesis of unconditional β convergence for US states at the sectoral level during the 1987–2015 period. The analysis is based on the linear regression model where the growth rate of GDP per worker is the dependent variable and the initial level of labour productivity is the independent variable. The cited authors do not include a variety of explanatory variables to account for different steady states. It is the justification for our approach which is also focused on unconditional convergence.

A number of studies consider the case of Chinese provinces. Sakamoto and Islam (2008) examine income-level convergence among Chinese provinces using Markov transition matrices. Their results demonstrate that the distribution of per capita income across Chinese regions was bi-modal during the 1952–2003 period. The cited study justifies our selection of various concepts of convergence. The adoption of the HMM approach in our study is a proper way of extending the research on GDP per capita convergence.

Another interesting study on convergence across Chinese regions was conducted by Tian et al. (2016). The cited study covers 31 provinces of China and the 1978–2013 period. It demonstrates that instead of one convergence at the national level, Chinese provinces confirm the club convergence hypothesis. Eight provinces[3] are converging into a high-income club, whereas the remaining ones into a low-income club. Moreover, income inequality within clubs decreases over time, while that between clubs reveals an increasing tendency. It is thus worth continuing the research on convergence across Chinese regions with the application of new economic concepts and new quantitative methods of analysis.

In summation, taking into account the increasing frequency of the application of alternative concepts of testing the convergence hypothesis, the approach adopted in the current research (stochastic convergence and the application of HMMs) seems to be justified. This seems particularly important given that the empirical evidence is mixed and partly depends on the economic types of convergence, the considered sample of countries, time period, and computational techniques. There is still much room for new research in this area. Studies on convergence require further testing using new theoretical concepts, methods, and approaches.

3.3 Methods of the analysis and data used

Three approaches adopted to test for the convergence at the regional level are based on the idea of β convergence (both absolute and conditional), the concept of stochastic convergence, and the application of HMMs. Such an analysis allows us to compare findings from the application of alternative approaches in testing convergence (stochastic convergence and HMM convergence) with the results derived from conventional methods (β convergence). In this section, we discuss the technical details of the procedures.

It needs to be noticed that a severe financial crisis took place in the middle of the analysed period. Such shocks often yield serious changes in the macroeconomic situation, including a change of convergence tendencies. In order to allow for the latter, we perform separate analyses for the pre- and post-crisis periods and the joint one.

3.3.1 The β convergence

The first of the two approaches used in the research is the β convergence analysis. The so-called Barro regression for panel data can be written as (Barro and Sala-i-Martin, 2003) follows:

$$\Delta \ln \text{GDP}_{it} = \beta_0 + \beta_1 \ln \text{GDP}_{i,\,t-1} + x'_{it}\beta + \alpha_i + \varepsilon_{it}, \tag{3.1}$$

where $\Delta\ln\text{GDP}_{it}$ is the change of $\ln\text{GDP}$ per capita for the ith region over the tth period, β_0 is the constant, $\ln\text{GDP}_{i,\,t-1}$ is the one-period lagged logarithm of the GDP per capita, x_{it} is a vector of the considered growth factors for the ith country over the tth period, α_i is the individual effect of the ith country, and ε_{it} is the error term. In the typical dynamic panel data analysis, equation (3.1) is transformed in a way that allows finding proper instruments in the generalized method of moments (GMM) scheme:

$$\ln\text{GDP}_{it} = \beta_0 + (\beta_1 + 1)\ln\text{GDP}_{i,\,t-1} + x'_{it}\beta + \alpha_i + \varepsilon_{it}. \tag{3.2}$$

Equation (3.2) enables estimation using instrumental variables or the GMM approach – technically the dynamic-fixed approach is also feasible; however, consistency of that estimator would require very long time series which are not available in this case. While choosing between the instrumental variables (IV) and GMM, one shall prefer the GMM for efficiency reasons and that is why Blundell and Bond (1998) system GMM is used. The vector x_{it} contains a set of considered variables, which are the selected GDP growth factors. It needs to be noticed that their selection is subject to the availability of the regional level data, which is to a certain extent limited.

The potential regressors are allowed to be endogenous, which is easily incorporable into the GMM framework. This choice is made based on economic theory and due to the undoubtful two-way relationship between the GDP growth and most of the macroeconomic indicators.

In the considered framework, β_1 determines the existence and the strength of regional convergence: with $\beta_1 < 0$, the lower developed regions grow faster and make up for the distance that separated them from the higher developed regions. $\beta_1 > 0$ would imply the existence of divergence – a situation that could be summarized as "the rich get richer". The latter is less frequent, yet possible, and seems likely especially on the regional level because of lower human capital migration barriers. Suppose that there exist a number of developed regions in a country. Unless particular measures are taken, this might attract the more energetic citizens to move to the higher developed regions. As a result, both the consumption and the production get polarized between regions, and they are usually the more dynamic humans who decide to migrate; thus, it is not only the quantity but also the quality of human capital that gets polarized which may enforce the divergence processes. While a similar process could take place in the cross-country framework, the migration barriers are much higher which prevents excessive movement of the human capital with its above-described consequences.

Two cases are analysed in this research. First, we consider an empty set of regressors in x'_{it}. The type of convergence which is thus investigated is called absolute (unconditional), and its existence implies that the convergence processes take place despite any changes in the GDP growth factors that may be included in x'_{it}. On the other hand, a non-empty set of regressors in x'_{it}

implies that the conclusions regarding convergence are conditional – the so-called conditional convergence considered in that case takes place if GDP per capita across regions levels up *ceteris paribus*, that is, conditional on no further differences in the GDP growth factors x'_{it}.

Taking into account the economic theory, the review of the literature, and data availability, two control growth factors are used in the case of Polish regions: the investment rate (% of GDP) [inv] and total expenditure of voivodships, poviats, and communes and cities with poviat rights (% of GDP) [gov]. The latter variable is a proxy for regional public spending. In order to control the effects of the global crisis, regression equations are estimated for the whole 2000–2017 period as well as for two shorter subperiods: 2000–2008 and 2009–2017. In the case of US states and Chinese provinces, the absolute convergence is verified and the regional convergence is analysed for the whole period as well as for the two shorter subperiods – like in the case of Poland.

The whole analysis uses regional GDP per capita data at constant prices (in PLN, USD, and CNY, respectively). All the statistics are taken from statistical offices in Poland, the USA, and China (supplemented by the authors' calculations when necessary).

The visualization of input data is given in Maps 3.1–3.9. The individual maps show the relative GDP per capita of a given region (compared with the richest one) in the initial year (2000), in 2008, and in the final year of the analysis (2017 or 2019). Black corresponds to a situation if a given region exceeds a certain relative development level compared with the richest region. Due to large differences in the polarization of regional development of individual countries, the cut-off point for the inclusion in the group marked by black (the relative highest-income group) was set at 80% in Poland, 50% in the USA, and 95% in China. The lighter colour denotes the lower relative development level of a given region.

The data presented in Maps 3.1–3.3 suggest the existence of regional divergence in Poland. In 2000, only three regions in Poland are marked by light grey, meaning that their GDP per capita is less than half of GDP per capita in the mazowieckie voivodship. In 2017, the number of voivodships which did not reach 50% of per capita income level observed in the mazowieckie voivodship increased to seven.

In the USA, the years 2000 and 2019 show a similar relative development level across US regions. The number of states which did not achieve 25% of per capita income level recorded in District of Columbia equalled seven in 2000 and eight in 2019, whereas the number of states with GDP per capita ranging from 30% to 50% of that observed in District of Columbia amounted to 22 in 2000 and 25 in 2019. The differences between these two years are not very high. However, in 2008, regional polarization in the USA was higher – 17 states recorded relative per capita income less than 25% of the richest region, while 10 states fell in the interval 30–50%. There is only the District of Columbia which was marked by black in Maps 3.4–3.6 because no other state exceeded half of the income per capita recorded in the capital region.

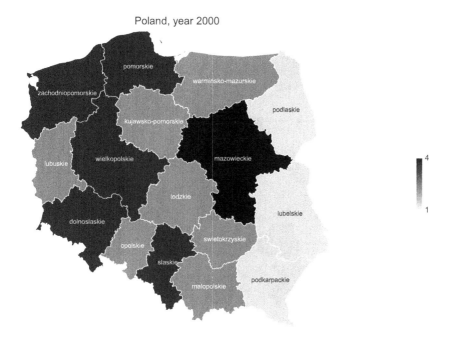

Map 3.1 Relative regional economic development in Poland, 2000.

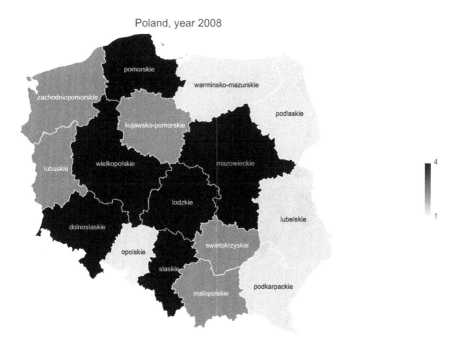

Map 3.2 Relative regional economic development in Poland, 2008.

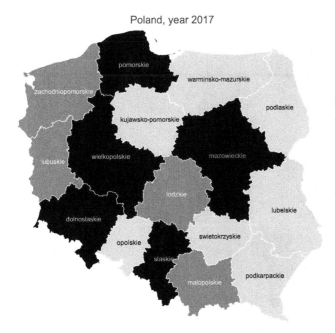

Map 3.3 Relative regional economic development in Poland, 2017.

Map 3.4 Relative regional economic development in the USA, 2000.

USA, year 2008

Map 3.5 Relative regional economic development in the USA, 2008.

USA, year 2019

Map 3.6 Relative regional economic development in the USA, 2019.

China, year 2000

Map 3.7 Relative regional economic development in China, 2000.

China, year 2008

Map 3.8 Relative regional economic development in China, 2008.

Map 3.9 Relative regional economic development in China, 2019.

The analysis of input data for Chinese regions suggests the existence of the catching-up. The analysis of Maps 3.7–3.9 indicates that the number of provinces marked by dark grey increased from 2000 to 2019. Indeed, in 2000, 15 provinces recorded per capita income less than 25% of Beijing; in 2019, this number fell to 5. The majority of provinces came closer to the richest region (Beijing) leading to the regional convergence.

3.3.2 Stochastic convergence

The stochastic convergence was defined in the literature in the early 1990s in the work by Bernard and Durlauf (1995). While the β convergence and the stochastic converge theoretically refer to the same idea of checking whether the process of interest is "getting similar" in different objects, there are probably more differences than similarities between these approaches from an econometric point of view. First of all, the convergence parameter in the case of β convergence is considered fixed and is estimable, while in Bernard and Durlauf's approach the existence of convergence is concluded based on stochastic properties of different objects or, actually, the properties of the stochastic process defined as differences between objects observed over time.

While concentrating on real GDP per capita convergence across regions, one can state the following. Let $\text{lnGDP}_{i,t}$ represent the logarithm of the

GDP per capita of region i in period (year) t. Then, regions i and j converge stochastically if

$$\lim_{k \to \infty} \left(\ln GDP_{i,t+k} - \ln GDP_{j,t+k} \mid I_t \right) = 0 \tag{3.3}$$

where I_t represents the set of information available at time t and $\ln GDP_{i,t}$ is the natural logarithm of the ith region's GDP per capita in year t. The econometric way to see and test for the above is to notice that for formula (3.3) to be fulfilled, a cointegrating vector $[1, -1]$ is required for the series $\ln GDP_{i,t}$ and $\ln GDP_{j,t}$. Thus, testing for convergence in the bivariate case of regions i and j requires computing the gap series:

$$dGDP_{ij,t} = \ln GDP_{i,t} - \ln GDP_{j,t} \tag{3.4}$$

and testing for the stationarity of the $dGDP_{ij,t}$ series. Usually, a variation of the augmented Dickey-Fuller (ADF) test would be used here (and we follow this classical approach), though Pesaran (2007) among others discusses also the Kwiatkowski-Phillips-Schmidt-Shin (KPSS)-type tests. Given that the conclusions are based on the results of a statistical test, those depend on the level of significance adopted in the research.

The natural extension to the group of $N > 2$ regions is to test for convergence replacing the series of gaps between two regions' output (3.4) with the series of a gap between $\ln GDP_{i,t}$ and its mean in a group of considered countries:

$$dGDP_{i,t} = \ln GDP_{i,t} - \overline{\ln GDP_t}. \tag{3.5}$$

Again, a popular approach is to test for stationarity of $dGDP_{i,t}$ with a variation of the ADF test. Nevertheless, we apply formula (3.4) in this research as we are interested in finding subgroups of regions which can be considered as converging and not only answering a general question such as "do regions of a given country converge?". The latter could technically be answered based on the fraction of pairs of regions that are found to be convergent if needed.

One might consider an alternative approach based on the use of $GDP_{i,t}$ (rather than $\ln GDP_{i,t}$) series while checking for the existence of the real GDP per capita convergence. However, we use the $\ln GDP_{i,t}$ for two reasons. First, it allows for at least partial unification of the conclusions with the ones attained in the β convergence analysis where the model was based on the $\ln GDP_{i,t}$ variable. Second, based on the elementary properties of the logarithmic function, the use of $\ln GDP_{i,t}$ series allows for the interpretation of the series of differences given by formula (3.4) as a relative (percentage) difference in the GDP per capita level.

Finally, it is an issue of what kind of stationarity should be tested or, to put it another way, what kind of testing ancillary equation should be applied in the ADF test used in the procedure. It can be observed that by applying the testing equation with constant we check only for stationarity of the differences computed in equation (3.4). The conclusion of $d\text{GDP}_{ij,t}$ being stationary implies that the logarithms of GDP per capita for the two regions of interest, in the long run, shall remain in the state of equilibrium and one can expect them to converge to the same level. However, if a trend is additionally included in the ADF equation, the rejection of the null hypothesis implies the presence of trend stationarity (and not necessarily the stationarity itself). As a result, the conclusion is not that the two regions are moving towards the same level: it would be if it were not for the trend in the difference. As a result, rejecting the null hypothesis in the trend-stationarity case implies the time series synchronization only: this may be interpreted as common trends in the GDP per capita ups and downs. We provide both results and demonstrate that the outcomes can be different.

3.3.3 HMM convergence

As an alternative to the econometric models, other quantitative methods are also used in convergence research. One of the most promising approaches is the exploration of the HMMs introduced by Bernardelli, Próchniak, and Witkowski (2018). The idea behind the HMM is to generalize the classical Markov model by adding a non-observable process, the states of which we want to determine based on the known, observable signals (see Cappé, Moulines and Ryden, 2005). The weak assumptions, compared to the econometric models, behind this method as well as effectiveness are the key reasons why this method is a popular tool in bioinformatics, cryptanalysis, and signal theory, but recently also in macroeconomics in synchronization of business cycle analysis, the phenomenon of convergence, and identification of turning points (Hamilton, 1994; Koskinen and Öller, 2004; Wójcik, 2008).

In convergence analyses, based on the article by Bernardelli, Próchniak, and Witkowski (2017), the Baum-Welch algorithm (Baum et al., 1970) is used for the identification of HMM parameters. This is a deterministic algorithm with the restriction that all initial probabilities must be given. In the case of this research, we assume that the probability distribution parameters associated with each state are defined as a Gaussian distribution and that the set of states consists of only two elements. The interpretation of the states is as follows: 0 is associated with periods of relatively good conditions, while 1 represents the situation that can be described as inferior. Nevertheless, the results strongly depend on the initial values and may be far from optimal. To increase the chance of finding an approximation of the solution, which is close enough to the globally optimal solution, a Monte Carlo simulation is used by performing the calculations repeatedly with the same data set and different initial values. In this study, 10,000 simulations were performed for each two-state HMM, and 25,000 simulations in the case of three-dimensional state space of HMM. A detailed description of this procedure and the selection of optimization criteria were presented in Chapter 2 and the article by Bernardelli (2013).

As an output of the Baum-Welch algorithm, the set of probabilities is given. Based on those probabilities, the unobserved path of states must be calculated. The economically recommended solution is not the maximization at each point, but rather the selection of the path of states which is optimal from the point of view of the whole considered period. To achieve this, the Viterbi algorithm is used (Viterbi, 1967), and the resulting path of states is called the Viterbi path.

Applying the concept of HMM and Viterbi path to the convergence analysis has evolved into a well-defined procedure (Bernardelli, Próchniak and Witkowski, 2017). In the previous chapter, the steps of the procedure adopted to the regional convergence problem have been described with the richest region chosen as the reference one. Let V be the set of all regions[4] of a given country except the richest one. In the considered case, the first step of the procedure includes the evaluation of the following formula:

$$\tilde{v}_t^{\text{region}} = v_t^{\text{reference region}} - v_t^{\text{region}}. \tag{3.6}$$

The analysed period is $t = 2000, 2001,..., T$, where $T = 2019$ for the USA and China, while $T = 2017$ in the case of Poland, region $\in V$.

In the second step, parameters of the HMM using the Baum-Welch algorithm are estimated and then the Viterbi paths are calculated. In this step, calculations for 15 models are performed in the case of Poland, 50 models for the USA, and 30 models for China.

In the third step, for each year the averages of the states of the Viterbi paths for all regions are calculated:

$$r_t = \frac{1}{n} \sum_{\text{region } \in V} VP_t^{\text{region}}, \tag{3.7}$$

where again $t = 2000, 2001,..., T$, and, in the considered case, $T = 2019$ for the USA and China, while $T = 2017$ in the case of Poland. In this context, the mean equal to 0 stands for the perfect similarity (convergence), while the year in which the average is equal to 1 is the period of a lack of similarity (divergence) between the richest region and other regions. The results of the estimation process are described in the subsequent sections for each of the considered cases of Poland, the USA, and China, respectively.

3.4 Empirical evidence

In this section, we present the empirical findings obtained in the analysis of convergence. The particular subsections are devoted to the analysis for Poland, the USA, and China. While there are some similarities in the convergence patterns across the exemplary countries from the different continents, of different size and various meaning for the world economy, many differences can be observed and discussed as well.

It should be mentioned that in the case of all the β convergence models discussed in this part of the text, we use a maximum of three lags of the regressors as instruments to avoid a proliferation of the instruments. Moreover, the macroeconomic regressors are treated as endogenous which minimizes the risk of the endogeneity of instruments. Another precaution taken to avoid inconsistency of the estimator is the classical Arellano-Bond test of autocorrelation which yields no ambiguous results (i.e. no autocorrelation of the error term is identified in any of the equations with the standard AR(2) autocorrelation test). These remarks refer to all the GDP growth Blundell-Bond regressions discussed here.

3.4.1 Polish voivodships

The results regarding the β convergence for Polish voivodships are presented in Tables 3.1 and 3.2. Table 3.1 includes the estimates of the regression equations with the initial GDP per capita only. Hence, the models presented in Table 3.1 allow us to verify the existence of the absolute β convergence.

The models shown in Table 3.2 refer to the conditional β convergence hypothesis. Regression equations include more explanatory variables – apart from initial GDP per capita, also investment rate and government expenditure (% of GDP).

Each table includes estimates of three models. The first one is estimated for the whole 2000–2017 period. The second model includes the period before the global crisis (until 2008, including this year). The third model covers the years after 2008, i.e. the period after the global crisis. The estimates are based on model (3.2); thus, it is essential to subtract 1 from the parameter on the initial lnGDP in order to obtain the β convergence parameter estimate.

The estimates in Table 3.1 demonstrate that Polish voivodships did not grow in line with the absolute β convergence hypothesis during the

Table 3.1 Absolute β convergence at the regional level in Poland

	(1)	(2)	(3)
	lnGDP	*lnGDP*	*lnGDP*
lnGDP(−1)	1.004	1.128[***]	1.015
	(0.84)	(8.02)	(1.48)
_cons	−0.00549	−1.231[***]	−0.124
	(−0.12)	(−7.82)	(−1.21)
N	272	128	144

Source: Own calculations.
t-statistics in parentheses; for the lagged ln GDP the convergence hypotheses tested, i.e. H0: $\beta = 1$.
[*]$p < 0.05$, [**]$p < 0.01$, [***]$p < 0.001$.

Table 3.2 Conditional β convergence at the regional level in Poland

	(1)	(2)	(3)
	lnGDP	*lnGDP*	*lnGDP*
lnGDP(−1)	1.004	1.142***	1.050***
	(0.87)	(6.47)	(3.51)
Inv	0.00119*	−0.00549**	0.00138*
	(2.28)	(−3.09)	(2.06)
gov	−0.00212**	0.00827***	0.00300*
	(−2.91)	(3.49)	(2.27)
_cons	−0.00214	−1.390***	−0.539***
	(−0.05)	(−6.52)	(−3.30)
N	272	128	144

Source: Own calculations.
t-statistics in parentheses; for the lagged ln GDP the convergence hypotheses tested, i.e.
H0: $\beta = 1$.
* $p < 0.05$, ** $p < 0.01$, *** $p < 0.001$.

2000–2017 period. The coefficient standing on the initial income level equals 1.004. Since its value is greater than 1, it means that in the untransformed convergence model the coefficient on initial income level would be positive. In such a case, Polish voivodships did not record a negative relationship between the initial income level and the future growth rate. However, since the obtained coefficient is not statistically significantly different from 1, divergence tendencies are not confirmed either. The results indicate that Polish regions have noted ambiguous results in terms of convergence/divergence since 2000. Nevertheless, income disparities have not been decreasing.

The lack of regional convergence is not a strange outcome. Empirical evidence shows that the EU countries converge at the national level but at the regional level they diverge (see also the review of the literature). Cross-country income differences diminish but within-country income differences rise. In the case of Poland, convergence tendencies were weakened, among others, by the behaviour of the mazowieckie voivodship with the capital in Warsaw. During the 2000–2017 period, the real GDP per capita of the mazowieckie voivodship almost doubled. Such a fast growth rate of the richest voivodship in Poland results from the atypical economic growth paths of Warsaw. Warsaw is the political, economic, and financial centre of Poland. It also hosts the headquarters of many companies that operate in the whole country. As a result, Warsaw was developing rapidly in the past two decades.

Regional divergence is often observed in other European countries. It is hard to expect that the north of Scotland will catch up with London; the same refers e.g. to the southern and northern regions of Italy. The agricultural regions of France are unlikely to catch up with Paris. Similar tendencies have been observed in Poland as confirmed by our results indicating the lack of convergence across Polish regions.

Models (2) and (3) presented in Table 3.1 allow us to analyse the stability of regional catching-up in Poland. It turns out that in both distinguished subperiods (till and after 2008) Polish voivodships were not converging. In both models, the coefficient on initial income is greater than 1. Moreover, in model (2), it is statistically significant indicating divergence tendencies. When comparing the absolute value of these coefficients (1.128 vs. 1.015), it turns out that the process of divergence was evident before the global crisis while after 2008 divergence tendencies were weaker and statistical models did not confirm either convergence or divergence (the coefficient 1.015 turned out to be statistically insignificantly different from 1). The likely reason for this outcome is the fact that the global crisis mostly affected the well-developed regions. Warsaw and the other big cities in Poland were negatively affected by the global crisis to a deeper extent than the less developed agricultural regions. For example, the global crisis reduced the profits of many companies – including international corporations whose headquarters are located in Polish large cities (Warsaw, Kraków, Wrocław, Gdańsk, Poznań, and Katowice) – resulting in a more palpable decrease in consumption, especially regarding the more expensive products than in the case of the less wealthy regions where spendings on luxurious goods have never been high. This is one of the reasons explaining the weakening of divergence tendencies after 2008: the "rich get richer" tendencies across regions resulting in increasing polarization were vastly reduced after the global financial crisis.

The models in Table 3.2 go further compared with the models presented in Table 3.1. They include the estimates of the conditional β convergence. Two additional explanatory variables are added to capture the impact of the differences in the steady states of the individual voivodships. It is necessary to emphasize some shortcomings of estimating the conditional convergence model at the regional level. Namely, the explanatory variables should be those that are responsible for different steady states to which individual economies are tending. In the case of cross-country regressions, many such determinants are available, including institutional variables. Institutions are treated as deep economic growth factors and they should be included in the set of explanatory variables to obtain the full picture of economic growth. However, at the regional level, such variables cannot be added. Institutions are the same for all Polish voivodships and they are not differentiated across them: even if there exist regional differences in this aspect, there are no publicly available data allowing for the cross-regional study of institutional factors; hence, such variables cannot be added to the regression model. As a result, in the case of regressions estimated on regional data, institutions can be considered primarily in the countries which are federations and whose regions have different legal systems (e.g. the USA or the UK). The institutional environment in California is partly different compared to that in North Dakota; hence, institutions are likely to explain a portion of economic growth differentiation between the states. Also in the country such as the United Kingdom of Great Britain and Ireland, we can include different institutions in England, Wales, Scotland, and Northern Ireland. However, in Poland, it is not possible. There also exist other variables that cannot be taken into account at the regional level but they affect economic growth at the national level, e.g. monetary policy variables or the variables related to international trade. That is why in the models presented in Table 3.2 the number of regressors is limited.

The estimates presented in Table 3.2 confirm in general the findings obtained for absolute convergence. First, throughout the whole 2000–2017 period, Polish voivodships did not reveal convergence tendencies. The coefficient on the initial income level equals 1.004. It is greater than 1, but it is also statistically insignificantly different from 1, pointing to the lack of convergence or divergence. The similarity of the outcomes for both unconditional and conditional convergence indicates that our results are stable and do not depend on the exact set of explanatory variables taken into account. Second, in both shorter subperiods (till and after 2008), convergence tendencies were not recorded either. In both subperiods, the coefficient on lagged GDP per capita is greater than 1 and statistically significantly different from 1, indicating divergence trends. At the same time, comparing the coefficients for the period before the global crisis (1.142) and after it (1.050), we may infer that divergence was faster in the period before 2008. After that year, divergence tendencies slowed down. This may to some extent indicate that the steps taken by the policymakers (or the market itself) prevented further divergence tendencies from before the global financial crisis – while observed on the *ceteris paribus* ground of conditional convergence was not observed in absolute terms.

The Dickey-Fuller unit root test *without trend* is used to check for the existence of stochastic convergence – that is to verify whether the difference in lnGDP per capita levels between the given pair of voivodships is stationary. Table 3.3 includes *p*-values for such a test. Assuming a 5% significance level, *p*-values less than 0.05 indicate the existence of regional stochastic convergence. Such cases are marked by grey cells.

The results in Table 3.3 indicate that regional convergence very rarely exists. In the vast majority of cases, the *p*-value is greater than 0.05, pointing to regional divergence. For example, the richest voivodship (mazowieckie) does not stochastically converge to any other voivodship. The same happens with the slaskie voivodship (the fourth richest Polish region in 2017). For these two voivodships, all the *p*-values are greater than 0.05. This indicates that these voivodships diverge from the remaining regions in terms of economic development. The same result (complete lack of convergence) has been observed in the case of four other voivodships: lubelskie, swietokrzyskie, kujawsko-pomorskie, and lubuskie. The lubelskie voivodship was the poorest region in Poland in 2017, and swietokrzyskie was also at the bottom. However, kujawsko-pomorskie and lubuskie both ranked in the middle in terms of GDP per capita. As we can see, full divergence was recorded by both the rich and poor Polish regions; there is no regularity in these terms. Hence, the voivodships as a whole did not converge – the pairwise convergence appears in Table 3.3 very seldom.

Table 3.3 Stochastic convergence of Polish voivodships: p-values for the stationarity test of stochastic convergence between the voivodships

	dolnoslaskie	kujawsko-pomorskie	lodzkie	lubelskie	lubuskie	malopolskie	mazowieckie	opolskie	podkarpackie	podlaskie	pomorskie	slaskie	swietokrzyskie	warminsko-mazurskie	wielkopolskie	zachodnio-pomorskie
dolnoslaskie		0.8429	0.0207	0.6532	0.6702	0.3637	0.5151	0.7537	0.0482	0.8859	0.0500[a]	0.0845	0.8558	0.8233	0.3585	0.6078
kujawsko-pomorskie			0.8591	0.7268	0.6244	0.7722	0.9544	0.1342	0.7240	0.4879	0.7997	0.9242	0.2465	0.1777	0.7740	0.0545
lodzkie				0.6339	0.6134	0.1762	0.2262	0.2863	0.7707	0.8460	0.2511	0.2986	0.9799	0.1213	0.3660	0.0265
lubelskie					0.5587	0.4340	0.4340	0.4044	0.4882	0.7681	0.3957	0.8181	0.7378	0.4400	0.4555	0.1791
lubuskie						0.3952	0.8762	0.4924	0.1849	0.6731	0.3361	0.6678	0.4616	0.5399	0.3559	0.2446
malopolskie							0.7432	0.6533	0.0030	0.7699	0.0060	0.5224	0.8262	0.8312	0.0275	0.4052
mazowieckie								0.7801	0.8553	0.9636	0.8022	0.1104	0.9575	0.8724	0.7843	0.4804
opolskie									0.2925	0.0112	0.4936	0.6213	0.1188	0.2064	0.6287	0.0304
podkarpackie										0.7772	0.0000	0.5913	0.8144	0.2000	0.0937	0.0141
podlaskie											0.8438	0.8736	0.4563	0.0001	0.7843	0.0001
pomorskie												0.4176	0.8039	0.5865	0.2204	0.1223
slaskie													0.9945	0.7380	0.5412	0.4507
swietokrzyskie														0.1655	0.7129	0.0907
warminsko-mazurskie															0.7249	0.1668
wielkopolskie																0.4086
zachodnio-pomorskie																

Source: Own calculations.
The grey cells indicate stochastic convergence.
[a] The exact value is 0.0500334.

The stochastic divergence at the regional level is consistent with the lack of β convergence (both absolute and conditional) described earlier. To some extent, such results could be expected by looking at the canonical β convergence analysis.

The existence of stochastic convergence confirmed on the basis of the unit root test with no constant implies instead the series of the GDP differences tending towards zero in infinite time horizon, while in the case of test *with trend*, this is attained after eliminating the trend factor from the series of differences, which reconciles more the confirmation of the existence of common trends in both series. It means that stochastic convergence is not a substitute for the β convergence analysis but it is more complementary. All in all, the estimates given in Table 3.3 are far from suggesting that in the infinite time horizon one could expect the level of development of the particular voivodships to level up.

Table 3.4 shows the results of the analysis using the trend-stationarity test. As it has been already pointed out, the unit root test is conducted to verify the hypothesis of stochastic convergence with a trend between each pair of voivodships. The p-values for this test are reported in Table 3.4. The values less than 0.05 indicate again the existence of stochastic convergence while those greater than 0.05 point to stochastic divergence. However, as stated above, the existence of a trend in the test equation results in confirming the existence of stochastic convergence also in the case when the lnGDP series actually do not converge to a common point but they would converge should a deterministic trend be eliminated which implies mostly the existence of a common trend in the behaviour of the series.

The results suggest that the Polish regions generally did not reveal stochastic convergence basing on the trend-stationarity test. The p-values lower than 0.05 do not frequently appear in the table. In the vast majority of pairs, stochastic divergence was recorded.

The grey cells indicate stochastic convergence.

There are four voivodships which reveal divergence against all the other voivodships. These are mazowieckie, slaskie, swietokrzyskie, and wielkopolskie. Except for swietokrzyskie, the remaining three ranked in top four in terms of GDP per capita in 2017. However, the inclusion of the swietokrzyskie voivodship means that there is no regularity here. This demonstrates that only in very few cases a common economic development trend of the different voivodships could be confirmed. On the one hand, this suggests their autonomy, which seems positive; on the other hand, it may imply a lack of sufficiently predominant national development policy.

When comparing the results given in Tables 3.3 and 3.4, it turns out that in the case of the stationarity test with a trend the number of converging voivodships is a little bit greater. This stationarity test is wider – if the difference between lnGDP per capita levels of the two regions is stationary around the trend, the stochastic convergence exists. As stated above, such a situation may be interpreted as the synchronization of business cycles between the voivodships. The grey cells presented in Table 3.4 imply that in a few cases there is some evidence of cyclical convergence between the

Table 3.4 Stochastic convergence of Polish voivodships: *p*-values for the trend-stationarity test of stochastic convergence between the voivodships

	dolnoslaskie	kujawsko-pomorskie	lodzkie	lubelskie	lubuskie	malopolskie	mazowieckie	opolskie	podkarpackie	podlaskie	pomorskie	slaskie	swietokrzyskie	warminsko-mazurskie	wielkopolskie	zachodniopomorskie
dolnoslaskie		0.3380	0.0867	0.0007	0.7356	0.3988	0.1019	0.4684	0.1358	0.0011	0.1091	0.1000	0.3999	0.1351	0.4672	0.3978
kujawsko-pomorskie	0.3380		0.5600	0.8839	0.0452	0.2260	0.2833	0.8152	0.2075	0.7549	0.1552	0.7428	0.7159	0.5923	0.5749	0.7895
lodzkie	0.0867	0.5600		0.8803	0.5973	0.0985	0.2281	0.7157	0.0216	0.6159	0.0001	0.6914	0.8182	0.7093	0.5913	0.8848
lubelskie	0.0007	0.8839	0.8803		0.8589	0.5962	0.5017	0.2522	0.8733	0.0061	0.3400	0.7416	0.9019	0.4346	0.7402	0.3270
lubuskie	0.7356	0.0452	0.5973	0.8589		0.6878	0.5701	0.8137	0.2744	0.7114	0.3949	0.6623	0.3928	0.7807	0.7336	0.9508
malopolskie	0.3988	0.2260	0.0985	0.5962	0.6878		0.5057	0.3380	0.0182	0.1452	0.0001	0.6736	0.6656	0.3775	0.0968	0.7976
mazowieckie	0.1019	0.2833	0.2281	0.5017	0.5701	0.5057		0.6808	0.1778	0.3078	0.3450	0.1009	0.3029	0.6714	0.7837	0.9793
opolskie	0.4684	0.8152	0.7157	0.2522	0.8137	0.3380	0.6808		0.4194	0.0078	0.5062	0.9005	0.9520	0.1608	0.2690	0.1154
podkarpackie	0.1358	0.2075	0.0216	0.8733	0.2744	0.0182	0.1778	0.4194		0.7786	0.0078	0.5394	0.4250	0.4857	0.3786	0.8100
podlaskie	0.0011	0.7549	0.6159	0.0061	0.7114	0.1452	0.3078	0.0078	0.7786		0.0000	0.3123	0.8182	0.0029	0.4636	0.0017
pomorskie	0.1091	0.1552	0.0001	0.3400	0.3949	0.0001	0.3450	0.5062	0.0078	0.0000		0.3123	0.4647	0.4105	0.4078	0.7159
slaskie	0.1000	0.7428	0.6914	0.7416	0.6623	0.6736	0.1009	0.9005	0.5394	0.3123	0.3123		0.7836	0.7543	0.7383	0.8487
swietokrzyskie	0.3999	0.7159	0.8182	0.9019	0.3928	0.6656	0.3029	0.9520	0.4250	0.8182	0.4647	0.7836		0.8670	0.7931	0.9006
warminsko-mazurskie	0.1351	0.5923	0.7093	0.4346	0.7807	0.3775	0.6714	0.1608	0.4857	0.0029	0.4105	0.7543	0.8670		0.3883	0.5764
wielkopolskie	0.4672	0.5749	0.5913	0.7402	0.7336	0.0968	0.7837	0.2690	0.3786	0.4636	0.4078	0.7383	0.7931	0.3883		0.6075
zachodnio-pomorskie	0.3978	0.7895	0.8848	0.3270	0.9508	0.7976	0.9793	0.1154	0.8100	0.0017	0.7159	0.8487	0.9006	0.5764	0.6075	

Source: Own calculation.

voivodships. No wonder that the convergence takes place between the neighbouring regions (e.g. warminsko-mazurskie with podlaskie and pomorskie, or malopolskie with podkarapckie), but sometimes also between the distant regions. In the latter case, there are deeper, hidden factors that drive convergence (e.g. factors at the national level). Moreover, it cannot be excluded that in some cases the evidence of convergence may be spurious.

Table 3.5 summarizes the results presented in Tables 3.3 and 3.4. It shows – for each voivodship – the number of regions towards which a given voivodship is converging or diverging for the two applied tests of stochastic convergence: without and with a trend. The data in Table 3.5 confirm a very weak stochastic convergence of Polish regions. The dominant tendency was stochastic divergence. These results support our earlier findings of the lack of existence of both absolute and conditional β convergence.

A comparison of the results from econometric models with the outcome of the approach based on HMM is one of the key goals of this research. Using the procedure described earlier, the states on Viterbi paths for the differences of GDP per capita for mazowieckie and every other voivodship were calculated. They are summarized in Table 3.6.

For each voivodship, the divergence to mazowieckie region is visible. The only difference is the time of switch between the states on the Viterbi path.

Table 3.5 Stochastic convergence of Polish voivodships: a summary

	Stochastic convergence without trend		Stochastic convergence with trend	
	The number of voivodships to/from which a given voivodship is:			
	Converging	Diverging	Converging	Diverging
dolnoslaskie	2	13	2	13
kujawsko-pomorskie	0	15	1	14
lodzkie	2	13	2	13
lubelskie	0	15	2	13
lubuskie	0	15	1	14
malopolskie	3	12	2	13
mazowieckie	0	15	0	15
opolskie	2	13	1	14
podkarpackie	4	11	3	12
podlaskie	3	12	5	10
pomorskie	2	13	4	11
slaskie	0	15	0	15
swietokrzyskie	0	15	0	15
warminsko-mazurskie	1	14	2	13
wielkopolskie	1	14	0	15
zachodnio-pomorskie	4	11	1	14

Source: Own calculations.

Table 3.6 HMM convergence of Polish voivodships: Viterbi paths

Year	dolnoslaskie	kujawsko-pomorskie	lodzkie	lubelskie	lubuskie	malopolskie	opolskie	podkarpackie	podlaskie	pomorskie	slaskie	swietokrzyskie	warminsko-mazurskie	wielkopolskie	zachodniopomorskie
2000	0	0	0	0	0	0	0	0	0	0	0	0	0	0	0
2001	0	0	0	0	0	0	0	0	0	0	0	0	0	0	0
2002	0	0	0	0	0	0	0	0	0	0	0	0	0	0	0
2003	0	0	0	0	0	0	0	0	0	0	0	0	0	0	0
2004	0	0	0	0	0	0	0	0	0	0	0	0	0	0	0
2005	0	1	0	1	0	0	1	0	0	0	0	1	1	0	0
2006	1	1	1	1	1	1	1	1	1	1	0	1	1	1	0
2007	1	1	1	1	1	1	1	1	1	1	0	1	1	1	1
2008	1	1	1	1	1	1	1	1	1	1	0	1	1	1	1
2009	1	1	1	1	1	1	1	1	1	1	1	1	1	1	1
2010	1	1	1	1	1	1	1	1	1	1	1	1	1	1	1
2011	1	1	1	1	1	1	1	1	1	1	1	1	1	1	1
2012	1	1	1	1	1	1	1	1	1	1	1	1	1	1	1
2013	1	1	1	1	1	1	1	1	1	1	1	1	1	1	1
2014	1	1	1	1	1	1	1	1	1	1	1	1	1	1	1
2015	1	1	1	1	1	1	1	1	1	1	1	1	1	1	1
2016	1	1	1	1	1	1	1	1	1	1	1	1	1	1	1
2017	1	1	1	1	1	1	1	1	1	1	1	1	1	1	1

Source: Own calculations.

The earliest signals of divergence are observed in 2005 for kujawsko-pomorskie, lubelskie, opolskie, swietokrzyskie, and warminsko-mazurskie. The latest change between the states is observed in 2009 for the slaskie region. Since divergence is proved for each voivodship, the obvious implication is the divergence of the whole group of voivodships to mazowieckie voivodship. The convergence function, which is calculated in the last step of the HMM convergence procedure, is given in Figure 3.1.

The results presented in Figure 3.1 support the lack of income-level convergence hypothesis as verified by econometric models. Exploring the HMM approach is an easy way to see how fast this divergence is. In economic terms, it means that mazowieckie voivodship is growing much faster than the other regions in Poland. Using a two-state HMM, the changes in the convergence function are found to be quite rapid. By allowing us to increase the number of states, we should get a smoother convergence function. Unfortunately, it comes with the cost. The more the states, the more numerically unstable computations are, and the more Monte Carlo simulations

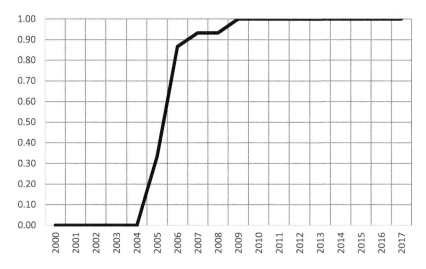

Figure 3.1 HMM convergence function of Polish voivodships to mazowieckie voivodship.

Table 3.7 Absolute β convergence at the regional level in the USA

	(1)	*(2)*	*(3)*
	lnGDP	*lnGDP*	*lnGDP*
lnGDP(−1)	0.95793***	0.98529	0.975173*
	(−5.01)	(−1.21)	(−1.77)
_cons	0.46479***	0.17172	0.27659*
	(−5.12)	1.31	(1.82)
N	969	408	561

Source: Own calculations.
t-statistics in parentheses; for the lagged ln GDP the convergence hypotheses tested, i.e. H0: $\beta = 1$.
* $p < 0.05$, ** $p < 0.01$, *** $p < 0.001$.

must be performed. Also, the length of the time series affects the feasibility of the solution.

3.4.2 US states

Table 3.7 shows the results of verification of the absolute β convergence hypothesis for 51 US regions (50 states plus the District of Columbia) during the 2000–2019 period: both for the entire period and separately for the pre- and post-crisis periods. The results confirm the existence of β convergence over the entire period. The estimated parameter on initial income level in the transformed convergence model is significantly less than 1 which implies a negative relationship between the initial level of income per capita and the rate of economic growth. A negative relationship between these variables was also observed in two shorter subperiods, although in the period till 2008 the estimated parameter turned out to be statistically insignificant which raises doubts regarding the homogeneous character of the regional convergence in both periods.

As we can see, the scheme of the β convergence strength and even existence for the US regions are completely different from the one regarding voivodships in Poland because in Poland absolute β convergence has not been confirmed either in the entire analysed period or in two separate subperiods. Despite the greater heterogeneity of US states due to, *inter alia*, differences in institutional systems (e.g. legal system, tax law), US regions behave according to the absolute β convergence hypothesis which can formally be confirmed for the entire 2000–2019 period and the years after 2008. One possible reason for this difference between the USA and Poland is the overall strength of the US economy and its currency and – apparently – the strength of the system of redistribution: despite the greater autonomy of the regions (states), the poorer benefit more from the centrally steered policy. On the other hand, it is likely that the more developed states suffered more from the effects of the global financial crisis which resulted in their lower rate of growth in the post-crisis era while the phenomenon could be far less palpable in the less developed states.

Tables 3.8–3.10 present the results of stochastic convergence analysis for the US regions. The structure of these tables is the same as in the case of Tables 3.3–3.4 for Poland. Similarly, Tables 3.8 and 3.9 provide the full documentation of the results, whereas Table 3.10 summarizes the outcomes.

The US states do not exhibit stochastic convergence in both models (without and with a trend). The stochastic convergence was confirmed only in the case of a few pairs of states. For example, Delaware was cyclically converging with 12 other states according to the model with a trend. Detailed analysis of the results shows that the convergence of Delaware occurred primarily with states in the Northern, Northeastern, and Eastern parts of the USA, including several states located nearby (e.g. Pennsylvania, West Virginia, New York, and Ohio). This means some synchronization of the business cycles in these states.

Table 3.11 and Figure 3.2 allow for the verification of the income convergence hypothesis based on HMMs. In this analysis, the reference region is the District of Columbia, which has been selected as the richest region in the USA. In the first part of the analysed period, most US regions increased their values of states on the Viterbi path from 0 to 1. As a result, the HMM convergence function plotted in Figure 3.2, showing the average values of

Table 3.8 Stochastic convergence of US states: p-values for the stationarity test of stochastic convergence between the states

	Alabama	Alaska	Arizona	Arkansas	California	Colorado	Connecticut	Delaware	District of Columbia	Florida	Georgia	Hawaii	Idaho	Illinois	Indiana	Iowa	Kansas
Alabama		0.3864	0.6046	0.4154	0.9976	0.6275	0.5378	0.5250	0.4212	0.7373	0.3358	0.9113	0.3811	0.8231	0.2619	0.6770	0.9102
Alaska	0.3864		0.5188	0.4281	0.9430	0.6205	0.3662	0.4095	0.0870	0.6153	0.5619	0.6028	0.4312	0.6440	0.3156	0.7092	0.8388
Arizona	0.6046	0.5188		0.6521	0.9946	0.8767	0.5080	0.4141	0.3912	0.0467	0.5698	0.8005	0.7964	0.8613	0.7704	0.6793	0.9117
Arkansas	0.4154	0.4281	0.6521		0.9988	0.5771	0.5673	0.5413	0.5539	0.7553	0.2613	0.8783	0.3653	0.7815	0.0548	0.6509	0.9125
California	0.9976	0.9430	0.9946	0.9988		0.5898	0.9969	0.9567	0.9954	0.9958	0.8657	0.9978	0.9180	0.9928	0.9670	0.9407	0.9328
Colorado	0.6275	0.6205	0.8767	0.5771	0.5898		0.8906	0.9414	0.6051	0.8738	0.8414	0.1125	0.4824	0.2547	0.1853	0.1192	0.2165
Connecticut	0.5378	0.3662	0.5080	0.5673	0.9969	0.8906		0.4907	0.0774	0.7063	0.6676	0.8981	0.6825	0.9138	0.6525	0.7911	0.9660
Delaware	0.5250	0.4095	0.4141	0.5413	0.9567	0.9414	0.4907		0.1501	0.5395	0.8396	0.7185	0.7920	0.8662	0.6952	0.6720	0.8653
District of Columbia	0.4212	0.0870	0.3912	0.5539	0.9954	0.6051	0.0774	0.1501		0.5353	0.3312	0.9445	0.4134	0.7755	0.4904	0.9353	0.9734
Florida	0.7373	0.6153	0.0467	0.7553	0.9958	0.8738	0.7063	0.5395	0.5353		0.4023	0.8066	0.8157	0.8817	0.7504	0.6928	0.8937
Georgia	0.3358	0.5619	0.5698	0.2613	0.8657	0.8414	0.6676	0.8396	0.3312	0.4023		0.1268	0.6951	0.5008	0.5089	0.1802	0.6066
Hawaii	0.9113	0.6028	0.8005	0.8783	0.9978	0.1125	0.8981	0.7185	0.9445	0.8066	0.1268		0.0117	0.2944	0.1716	0.4552	0.7217
Idaho	0.3811	0.4312	0.7964	0.3653	0.9180	0.4824	0.6825	0.7920	0.4134	0.8157	0.6951	0.0117		0.2229	0.1760	0.1363	0.4802
Illinois	0.8231	0.6440	0.8613	0.7815	0.9928	0.2547	0.9138	0.8662	0.7755	0.8817	0.5008	0.2944	0.2229		0.0012	0.1966	0.7551
Indiana	0.2619	0.3156	0.7704	0.0548	0.9670	0.1853	0.6525	0.6952	0.4904	0.7504	0.5089	0.1716	0.1760	0.0012		0.2258	0.6488
Iowa	0.6770	0.7092	0.6793	0.6509	0.9407	0.1192	0.7911	0.6720	0.9353	0.6928	0.1802	0.4552	0.1363	0.1966	0.2258		0.2567
Kansas	0.9102	0.8388	0.9117	0.9125	0.9328	0.2165	0.9660	0.8653	0.9734	0.8937	0.6066	0.7217	0.4802	0.7551	0.6488	0.2567	

Table 3.8 (Continued)

	Kentucky	Louisiana	Maine	Maryland	Massachusetts	Michigan	Minnesota	Mississippi	Missouri	Montana	Nebraska	Nevada	New Hampshire	New Jersey	New Mexico	New York	North Carolina
Alabama	0.2908	0.5532	0.4372	0.6033	0.9829	0.2580	0.9111	0.2672	0.1388	0.6595	0.7900	0.5517	0.9236	0.1975	0.0833	0.9549	0.1051
Alaska	0.3672	0.3904	0.5686	0.6810	0.9049	0.4396	0.5484	0.1281	0.2669	0.6350	0.7993	0.4913	0.7459	0.3819	0.6993	0.9644	0.3388
Arizona	0.7383	0.3614	0.5536	0.6352	0.9288	0.5966	0.8337	0.6617	0.5341	0.6821	0.7549	0.5056	0.8435	0.6206	0.4342	0.9096	0.6101
Arkansas	0.1098	0.6899	0.4479	0.5945	0.9828	0.1469	0.9741	0.5281	0.1401	0.6607	0.8091	0.5953	0.9612	0.2364	0.0889	0.9538	0.2190
California	0.9970	0.9837	0.9812	0.9590	0.8540	0.7776	0.9938	0.9984	0.9940	0.9868	0.8664	0.9763	0.9793	0.9977	0.9437	0.5161	0.9990
Colorado	0.6804	0.8078	0.5171	0.0066	0.1301	0.4600	0.2016	0.9036	0.9848	0.0398	0.0274	0.9488	0.0880	0.8943	0.2160	0.4625	0.9487
Connecticut	0.6205	0.1478	0.7383	0.7656	0.9855	0.5536	0.8371	0.1439	0.3566	0.7965	0.8429	0.5191	0.9119	0.5449	0.7364	0.9729	0.3082
Delaware	0.5996	0.2942	0.7352	0.6330	0.9199	0.6605	0.7734	0.4673	0.4932	0.6658	0.7457	0.3682	0.8516	0.5209	0.8747	0.9503	0.6212
District of Columbia	0.3857	0.1402	0.5476	0.9912	0.9955	0.2927	0.8840	0.0102	0.0073	0.9520	0.9800	0.1847	0.9474	0.1922	0.6704	0.9801	0.1041
Florida	0.7980	0.6005	0.7093	0.6438	0.9315	0.4707	0.8490	0.7168	0.6419	0.6955	0.7575	0.5167	0.8782	0.7179	0.6216	0.9287	0.6900
Georgia	0.5068	0.6224	0.3415	0.0417	0.5510	0.2079	0.3157	0.6601	0.7763	0.1648	0.1646	0.9537	0.3381	0.5460	0.2978	0.7331	0.6739
Hawaii	0.6600	0.8487	0.5810	0.1710	0.9232	0.1698	0.5216	0.8720	0.5711	0.4131	0.6176	0.6586	0.5424	0.7021	0.3134	0.8139	0.5119
Idaho	0.5503	0.7267	0.2087	0.0194	0.5358	0.5512	0.2762	0.7715	0.8999	0.0827	0.1939	0.9493	0.2327	0.6162	0.0047	0.6507	0.8157
Illinois	0.7030	0.8501	0.7445	0.0187	0.9102	0.2974	0.0711	0.8765	0.8347	0.0801	0.1825	0.8478	0.3148	0.8419	0.4457	0.9016	0.8500
Indiana	0.0526	0.6881	0.1890	0.0523	0.7463	0.3444	0.0876	0.6793	0.5477	0.1464	0.2926	0.8371	0.1556	0.3312	0.0107	0.7002	0.4411
Iowa	0.4625	0.8297	0.5308	0.2244	0.5814	0.1390	0.2994	0.6646	0.3918	0.3165	0.1365	0.5652	0.3600	0.5265	0.5112	0.5515	0.4217
Kansas	0.8826	0.9039	0.8375	0.2472	0.2499	0.5007	0.7119	0.9827	0.8792	0.5101	0.1551	0.8516	0.5794	0.9324	0.7015	0.2093	0.9106

Table 3.8 (Continued)

	North Dakota	Ohio	Oklahoma	Oregon	Pennsylvania	Rhode Island	South Carolina	South Dakota	Tennessee	Texas	Utah	Vermont	Virginia	Washington	West Virginia	Wisconsin	Wyoming
Alabama	0.7294	0.8576	0.7772	0.9932	0.9606	0.0561	0.4163	0.3308	0.8215	0.9423	0.9684	0.4188	0.0537	0.9957	0.6826	0.9363	0.4502
Alaska	0.8395	0.6092	0.8776	0.8655	0.8129	0.4568	0.5250	0.5890	0.6174	0.8865	0.8315	0.4578	0.3771	0.9558	0.5030	0.6813	0.1692
Arizona	0.7241	0.8919	0.7616	0.9750	0.8978	0.5028	0.7896	0.4786	0.8029	0.8996	0.9581	0.5840	0.6033	0.9936	0.7731	0.8664	0.4282
Arkansas	0.7269	0.8908	0.7886	0.9939	0.9686	0.0788	0.3363	0.3147	0.7897	0.9332	0.9552	0.3803	0.3470	0.9958	0.6792	0.9627	0.5414
California	0.5761	0.9557	0.6791	0.9159	0.9371	0.9973	0.9771	0.7188	0.9902	0.8810	0.9400	0.9755	0.9948	0.0896	0.9649	0.9902	0.9739
Colorado	0.4460	0.2819	0.0544	0.3341	0.0544	0.4309	0.8262	0.0432	0.1767	0.3202	0.1949	0.0790	0.5436	0.9611	0.5016	0.0576	0.5696
Connecticut	0.7611	0.8523	0.8633	0.9933	0.9672	0.4413	0.6911	0.4774	0.8384	0.9768	0.9897	0.6319	0.5001	0.9969	0.7911	0.9095	0.1675
Delaware	0.6908	0.8688	0.7658	0.9262	0.8811	0.4283	0.7477	0.4192	0.7846	0.9161	0.9095	0.5156	0.5683	0.9725	0.8144	0.8394	0.2557
District of Columbia	0.8732	0.7667	0.9623	0.9899	0.9913	0.4963	0.3991	0.8651	0.7436	0.9489	0.9501	0.9682	0.5141	0.9920	0.7059	0.9170	0.3380
Florida	0.7274	0.8898	0.7668	0.9736	0.9031	0.6522	0.7140	0.5024	0.8304	0.9127	0.9631	0.6239	0.7160	0.9913	0.8167	0.8874	0.5163
Georgia	0.5465	0.6482	0.3351	0.6936	0.5056	0.2412	0.3846	0.1400	0.3892	0.6638	0.6131	0.1303	0.3176	0.9640	0.6171	0.1969	0.4422
Hawaii	0.7006	0.3622	0.6019	0.9813	0.7898	0.8376	0.2798	0.2617	0.4529	0.6766	0.3771	0.4296	0.8069	0.9855	0.3872	0.5113	0.7233
Idaho	0.5457	0.5653	0.2542	0.6466	0.4508	0.1734	0.5472	0.0736	0.2553	0.5583	0.2941	0.0857	0.1774	0.9876	0.4550	0.1447	0.4092
Illinois	0.5958	0.3863	0.3388	0.9464	0.7430	0.6749	0.6047	0.0755	0.2527	0.8578	0.8571	0.0545	0.7384	0.9956	0.2941	0.0551	0.6609
Indiana	0.5957	0.3288	0.3827	0.8594	0.6458	0.0471	0.4315	0.0993	0.0018	0.6103	0.5196	0.0412	0.0874	0.9828	0.0399	0.0094	0.4908
Iowa	0.7360	0.1817	0.2575	0.5670	0.3843	0.7977	0.3114	0.0922	0.3296	0.2747	0.3667	0.4828	0.6780	0.8237	0.3006	0.3921	0.7919
Kansas	0.5965	0.6212	0.1648	0.6042	0.3460	0.9077	0.7152	0.1129	0.7469	0.1468	0.5271	0.6495	0.9114	0.9351	0.7017	0.7567	0.9225

Table 3.8 (Continued)

	Alabama	Alaska	Arizona	Arkansas	California	Colorado	Connecticut	Delaware	District of Columbia	Florida	Georgia	Hawaii	Idaho	Illinois	Indiana	Iowa	Kansas
Kentucky	0.2908	0.3672	0.7383	0.1098	0.9970	0.6804	0.6205	0.5996	0.3857	0.7980	0.5068	0.6600	0.5503	0.7030	0.0526	0.4625	0.8826
Louisiana	0.5532	0.3904	0.3614	0.6899	0.9837	0.8078	0.1478	0.2942	0.1402	0.6005	0.6224	0.8487	0.7267	0.8501	0.6881	0.8297	0.9039
Maine	0.4372	0.5686	0.5536	0.4479	0.9812	0.5171	0.7383	0.7352	0.5476	0.7093	0.3415	0.5810	0.2087	0.7445	0.1890	0.5308	0.8375
Maryland	0.6033	0.6810	0.6352	0.5945	0.9590	0.0066	0.7656	0.6330	0.9912	0.6438	0.0417	0.1710	0.0194	0.0187	0.0523	0.2244	0.2472
Massachusetts	0.9829	0.9049	0.9288	0.9828	0.8540	0.1301	0.9855	0.9199	0.9955	0.9315	0.5510	0.9232	0.5358	0.9102	0.7463	0.5814	0.2499
Michigan	0.2580	0.4396	0.5966	0.1469	0.7776	0.4600	0.5536	0.6605	0.2927	0.4707	0.2079	0.1698	0.5512	0.2974	0.3444	0.1390	0.5007
Minnesota	0.9111	0.5484	0.8337	0.9741	0.9938	0.2016	0.8371	0.7734	0.8840	0.8490	0.3157	0.5216	0.2762	0.0711	0.0876	0.2994	0.7119
Mississippi	0.2672	0.1281	0.6617	0.5281	0.9984	0.9036	0.1439	0.4673	0.0102	0.7168	0.6601	0.8720	0.7715	0.8765	0.6793	0.6646	0.9827
Missouri	0.1388	0.2669	0.5341	0.1401	0.9940	0.9848	0.3566	0.4932	0.0073	0.6419	0.7763	0.5711	0.8999	0.8347	0.5477	0.3918	0.8792
Montana	0.6595	0.6350	0.6821	0.6607	0.9868	0.0398	0.7965	0.6658	0.9520	0.6955	0.1648	0.4131	0.0827	0.0801	0.1464	0.3165	0.5101
Nebraska	0.7900	0.7993	0.7549	0.8091	0.8664	0.0274	0.8429	0.7457	0.9800	0.7575	0.1646	0.6176	0.1939	0.1825	0.2926	0.1365	0.1551
Nevada	0.5517	0.4913	0.5056	0.5953	0.9763	0.9488	0.5191	0.3682	0.1847	0.5167	0.9537	0.6586	0.9493	0.8478	0.8371	0.5652	0.8516
New Hampshire	0.9236	0.7459	0.8435	0.9612	0.9793	0.0880	0.9119	0.8516	0.9474	0.8782	0.3381	0.5424	0.2327	0.3148	0.1556	0.3600	0.5794
New Jersey	0.1975	0.3819	0.6206	0.2364	0.9977	0.8943	0.5449	0.5209	0.1922	0.7179	0.5460	0.7021	0.6162	0.8419	0.3312	0.5265	0.9324
New Mexico	0.0833	0.6993	0.4342	0.0889	0.9437	0.2160	0.7364	0.8747	0.6704	0.6216	0.2978	0.3134	0.0047	0.4457	0.0107	0.5112	0.7015
New York	0.9549	0.9644	0.9096	0.9538	0.5161	0.4625	0.9729	0.9503	0.9801	0.9287	0.7331	0.8139	0.6507	0.9016	0.7002	0.5515	0.2093
North Carolina	0.1051	0.3388	0.6101	0.2190	0.9990	0.9487	0.3082	0.6212	0.1041	0.6900	0.6739	0.5119	0.8157	0.8500	0.4411	0.4217	0.9106

Table 3.8 (Continued)

	Kentucky	Louisiana	Maine	Maryland	Massachusetts	Michigan	Minnesota	Mississippi	Missouri	Montana	Nebraska	Nevada	New Hampshire	New Jersey	New Mexico	New York	North Carolina
Kentucky		0.7098	0.3618	0.2111	0.9688	0.2784	0.7907	0.6154	0.3354	0.3705	0.5702	0.7487	0.8845	0.4198	0.0602	0.9386	0.4964
Louisiana	0.7098		0.7667	0.8683	0.9564	0.5450	0.8413	0.3730	0.4272	0.8345	0.8905	0.2681	0.9195	0.5483	0.7997	0.9755	0.4996
Maine	0.3618	0.7667		0.1440	0.9338	0.1814	0.6960	0.6780	0.2683	0.4694	0.5553	0.7400	0.8503	0.2016	0.1355	0.9380	0.2030
Maryland	0.2111	0.8683	0.1440		0.7795	0.0756	0.0674	0.6082	0.1093	0.0791	0.6518	0.5209	0.0521	0.3313	0.2991	0.7527	0.1700
Massachusetts	0.9688	0.9564	0.9338	0.7795		0.4752	0.9172	0.9889	0.9589	0.9396	0.1397	0.8827	0.9020	0.9744	0.8307	0.0474	0.9413
Michigan	0.2784	0.5450	0.1814	0.0756	0.4752		0.1791	0.5463	0.5488	0.1225	0.1534	0.9239	0.2197	0.3638	0.1547	0.5993	0.4854
Minnesota	0.7907	0.8413	0.6960	0.0674	0.9172	0.1791		0.8901	0.7843	0.2828	0.3698	0.8013	0.1394	0.7971	0.3850	0.8097	0.7329
Mississippi	0.6154	0.3730	0.6780	0.6082	0.9889	0.5463	0.8901		0.3409	0.6452	0.8086	0.6254	0.9296	0.6816	0.3994	0.9534	0.4401
Missouri	0.3354	0.4272	0.2683	0.1093	0.9589	0.5488	0.7843	0.3409		0.2652	0.4345	0.7429	0.8493	0.0974	0.2866	0.9402	0.3778
Montana	0.3705	0.8345	0.4694	0.0791	0.9396	0.1225	0.2828	0.6452	0.2652		0.7243	0.5623	0.3999	0.4440	0.4446	0.7930	0.2841
Nebraska	0.5702	0.8905	0.5553	0.6518	0.1397	0.1534	0.3698	0.8086	0.4345	0.7243		0.6642	0.3020	0.6302	0.5701	0.0955	0.4942
Nevada	0.7487	0.2681	0.7400	0.5209	0.8827	0.9239	0.8013	0.6254	0.7429	0.5623	0.6642		0.8180	0.7008	0.7446	0.8975	0.7766
New Hampshire	0.8845	0.9195	0.8503	0.0521	0.9020	0.2197	0.1394	0.9296	0.8493	0.3999	0.3020	0.8180		0.8958	0.6250	0.8650	0.8019
New Jersey	0.4198	0.5483	0.2016	0.3313	0.9744	0.3638	0.7971	0.6816	0.0974	0.4440	0.6302	0.7008	0.8958		0.0589	0.9438	0.0867
New Mexico	0.0602	0.7997	0.1355	0.2991	0.8307	0.1547	0.3850	0.3994	0.2866	0.4446	0.5701	0.7446	0.6250	0.0589		0.8677	0.0498
New York	0.9386	0.9755	0.9380	0.7527	0.0474	0.5993	0.8097	0.9534	0.9402	0.7930	0.0955	0.8975	0.8650	0.9438	0.8677		0.9187
North Carolina	0.4964	0.4996	0.2030	0.1700	0.9413	0.4854	0.7329	0.4401	0.3778	0.2841	0.4942	0.7766	0.8019	0.0867	0.0498	0.9187	

Table 3.8 (Continued)

	North Dakota	Ohio	Oklahoma	Oregon	Pennsylvania	Rhode Island	South Carolina	South Dakota	Tennessee	Texas	Utah	Vermont	Virginia	Washington	West Virginia	Wisconsin	Wyoming
Kentucky	0.6648	0.8721	0.6451	0.9818	0.9381	0.0447	0.5277	0.1635	0.7080	0.9046	0.9263	0.1002	0.1638	0.9959	0.5870	0.8835	0.4921
Louisiana	0.8261	0.8198	0.9035	0.9617	0.9181	0.7289	0.6320	0.6701	0.8000	0.9120	0.9328	0.7899	0.6866	0.9804	0.8211	0.8821	0.2015
Maine	0.6673	0.7068	0.6377	0.9436	0.8901	0.4472	0.1547	0.2351	0.5946	0.8681	0.8577	0.1815	0.3959	0.9837	0.6570	0.7698	0.5250
Maryland	0.7413	0.0538	0.6086	0.5836	0.3564	0.8828	0.0808	0.2663	0.1133	0.2036	0.1766	0.6874	0.6738	0.8239	0.0246	0.0935	0.8169
Massachusetts	0.5810	0.6534	0.1810	0.5563	0.5475	0.9919	0.7457	0.1656	0.8632	0.2093	0.5988	0.9681	0.9945	0.6537	0.8752	0.9472	0.9236
Michigan	0.4656	0.3022	0.2726	0.5972	0.3818	0.1533	0.1672	0.0749	0.1287	0.5149	0.4875	0.0857	0.2515	0.9358	0.3927	0.1291	0.4081
Minnesota	0.6384	0.2514	0.4820	0.9430	0.8555	0.7128	0.4728	0.1252	0.2363	0.6322	0.6007	0.1013	0.7819	0.9889	0.3610	0.0323	0.6794
Mississippi	0.7296	0.8774	0.8270	0.9955	0.9855	0.1258	0.7606	0.2796	0.8592	0.9472	0.9586	0.4154	0.0617	0.9985	0.8055	0.9012	0.2273
Missouri	0.6230	0.9217	0.5558	0.9735	0.9379	0.0281	0.7713	0.0777	0.8359	0.9058	0.8986	0.0244	0.0469	0.9974	0.8511	0.8024	0.2578
Montana	0.7366	0.1896	0.6439	0.8155	0.6690	0.8268	0.1631	0.1136	0.3219	0.5576	0.5009	0.1897	0.7020	0.9679	0.1524	0.3672	0.8257
Nebraska	0.6931	0.1224	0.1123	0.4772	0.1210	0.9299	0.1628	0.0788	0.3777	0.0546	0.3791	0.8265	0.8452	0.4992	0.2515	0.3582	0.9011
Nevada	0.6877	0.9123	0.6968	0.9491	0.8530	0.4339	0.8788	0.4064	0.8373	0.8793	0.9220	0.4936	0.5648	0.9852	0.8178	0.8186	0.2468
New Hampshire	0.6328	0.1674	0.4401	0.8388	0.5598	0.9902	0.5010	0.1504	0.4452	0.5312	0.5071	0.3081	0.9341	0.9592	0.4313	0.3673	0.7723
New Jersey	0.6773	0.8523	0.6778	0.9856	0.9667	0.1152	0.5915	0.1967	0.8156	0.9419	0.9427	0.2210	0.1367	0.9977	0.7616	0.8642	0.3997
New Mexico	0.6660	0.4050	0.6143	0.8431	0.7531	0.4738	0.1266	0.2772	0.3088	0.7892	0.6504	0.3174	0.1580	0.9420	0.3932	0.4419	0.5628
New York	0.5234	0.6823	0.1043	0.3635	0.2027	0.9916	0.8082	0.1900	0.8265	0.2737	0.6595	0.8804	0.9854	0.2262	0.8837	0.8838	0.9023
North Carolina	0.6536	0.8869	0.5556	0.9964	0.9001	0.0807	0.7025	0.1678	0.7858	0.9108	0.9732	0.1740	0.0752	0.9978	0.7494	0.7985	0.2865

Table 3.8 (Continued)

	Alabama	Alaska	Arizona	Arkansas	California	Colorado	Connecticut	Delaware	District of Columbia	Florida	Georgia	Hawaii	Idaho	Illinois	Indiana	Iowa	Kansas
North Dakota	0.7294	0.8395	0.7241	0.7269	0.5761	0.4460	0.7611	0.6908	0.8732	0.7274	0.5465	0.7006	0.5457	0.5958	0.5957	0.7360	0.5965
Ohio	0.8576	0.6092	0.8919	0.8908	0.9557	0.2819	0.8523	0.8688	0.7667	0.8898	0.6482	0.3622	0.5653	0.3863	0.3288	0.1817	0.6212
Oklahoma	0.7772	0.8776	0.7616	0.7886	0.6791	0.0544	0.8633	0.7658	0.9623	0.7668	0.3351	0.6019	0.2542	0.3388	0.3827	0.2575	0.1648
Oregon	0.9932	0.8655	0.9750	0.9939	0.9159	0.3341	0.9933	0.9262	0.9899	0.9736	0.6936	0.9813	0.6466	0.9464	0.8594	0.5670	0.6042
Pennsylvania	0.9606	0.8129	0.8978	0.9686	0.9371	0.0544	0.9672	0.8811	0.9913	0.9031	0.5056	0.7898	0.4508	0.7430	0.6458	0.3843	0.3460
Rhode Island	0.0561	0.4568	0.5028	0.0788	0.9973	0.4309	0.4413	0.4283	0.4963	0.6522	0.2412	0.8376	0.1734	0.6749	0.0471	0.7977	0.9077
South Carolina	0.4163	0.5250	0.7896	0.3363	0.9771	0.8262	0.6911	0.7477	0.3991	0.7140	0.3846	0.2798	0.5472	0.6047	0.4315	0.3114	0.7152
South Dakota	0.3308	0.5890	0.4786	0.3147	0.7188	0.0432	0.4774	0.4192	0.8651	0.5024	0.1400	0.2617	0.0736	0.0755	0.0993	0.0922	0.1129
Tennessee	0.8215	0.6174	0.8029	0.7897	0.9902	0.1767	0.8384	0.7846	0.7436	0.8304	0.3892	0.4529	0.2553	0.2527	0.0018	0.3296	0.7469
Texas	0.9423	0.8865	0.8996	0.9332	0.8810	0.3202	0.9768	0.9161	0.9489	0.9127	0.6638	0.6766	0.5583	0.8578	0.6103	0.2747	0.1468
Utah	0.9684	0.8315	0.9581	0.9552	0.9400	0.1949	0.9897	0.9095	0.9501	0.9631	0.6131	0.3771	0.2941	0.8571	0.5196	0.3667	0.5271
Vermont	0.4188	0.4578	0.5840	0.3803	0.9755	0.0790	0.6319	0.5156	0.9682	0.6239	0.1303	0.4296	0.0857	0.0545	0.0412	0.4828	0.6495
Virginia	0.0537	0.3771	0.6033	0.3470	0.9948	0.5436	0.5001	0.5683	0.5141	0.7160	0.3176	0.8069	0.1774	0.7384	0.0874	0.6780	0.9114
Washington	0.9957	0.9558	0.9936	0.9958	0.0896	0.9611	0.9969	0.9725	0.9920	0.9913	0.9640	0.9855	0.4550	0.9956	0.9828	0.8237	0.9351
West Virginia	0.6826	0.5030	0.7731	0.6792	0.9649	0.5016	0.7911	0.8144	0.7059	0.8167	0.6171	0.3872	0.5113	0.2941	0.0399	0.3006	0.7017
Wisconsin	0.9363	0.6813	0.8664	0.9627	0.9902	0.0576	0.9095	0.8394	0.9170	0.8874	0.1969	0.5113	0.1447	0.0551	0.0094	0.3921	0.7567
Wyoming	0.4502	0.1692	0.4282	0.5414	0.9739	0.5696	0.1675	0.2557	0.3380	0.5163	0.4422	0.7233	0.4092	0.6609	0.4908	0.7919	0.9225

Table 3.8 (Continued)

	Kentucky	Louisiana	Maine	Maryland	Massachusetts	Michigan	Minnesota	Mississippi	Missouri	Montana	Nebraska	Nevada	New Hampshire	New Jersey	New Mexico	New York	North Carolina
North Dakota	0.6648	0.8261	0.6673	0.7413	0.5810	0.4656	0.6384	0.7296	0.6230	0.7366	0.6931	0.6877	0.6328	0.6773	0.6660	0.5234	0.6536
Ohio	0.8721	0.8198	0.7068	0.0538	0.6534	0.3022	0.2514	0.8774	0.9217	0.1896	0.1224	0.9123	0.1674	0.8523	0.4050	0.6823	0.8869
Oklahoma	0.6451	0.9035	0.6377	0.6086	0.1810	0.2726	0.4820	0.8270	0.5558	0.6439	0.1123	0.6968	0.4401	0.6778	0.6143	0.1043	0.5556
Oregon	0.9818	0.9617	0.9436	0.5836	0.5563	0.5972	0.9430	0.9955	0.9735	0.8155	0.4772	0.9491	0.8388	0.9856	0.8431	0.3635	0.9964
Pennsylvania	0.9381	0.9181	0.8901	0.3564	0.5475	0.3818	0.8555	0.9855	0.9379	0.6690	0.1210	0.8530	0.5598	0.9667	0.7531	0.2027	0.9001
Rhode Island	0.0447	0.7289	0.4472	0.8828	0.9919	0.1533	0.7128	0.1258	0.0281	0.8268	0.9299	0.4339	0.9902	0.1152	0.4738	0.9916	0.0807
South Carolina	0.5277	0.6320	0.1547	0.0808	0.7457	0.1672	0.4728	0.7606	0.7713	0.1631	0.1628	0.8788	0.5010	0.5915	0.1266	0.8082	0.7025
South Dakota	0.1635	0.6701	0.2351	0.2663	0.1656	0.0749	0.1252	0.2796	0.0777	0.1136	0.0788	0.4064	0.1504	0.1967	0.2772	0.1900	0.1678
Tennessee	0.7080	0.8000	0.5946	0.1133	0.8632	0.1287	0.2363	0.8592	0.8359	0.3219	0.3777	0.8373	0.4452	0.8156	0.3088	0.8265	0.7858
Texas	0.9046	0.9120	0.8681	0.2036	0.2093	0.5149	0.6322	0.9472	0.9058	0.5576	0.0546	0.8793	0.5312	0.9419	0.7892	0.2737	0.9108
Utah	0.9263	0.9328	0.8577	0.1766	0.5988	0.4875	0.6007	0.9586	0.8986	0.5009	0.3791	0.9220	0.5071	0.9427	0.6504	0.6595	0.9732
Vermont	0.1002	0.7899	0.1815	0.6874	0.9681	0.0857	0.1013	0.4154	0.0244	0.1897	0.8265	0.4936	0.3081	0.2210	0.3174	0.8804	0.1740
Virginia	0.1638	0.6866	0.3959	0.6738	0.9945	0.2515	0.7819	0.0617	0.0469	0.7020	0.8452	0.5648	0.9341	0.1367	0.1580	0.9854	0.0752
Washington	0.9959	0.9804	0.9837	0.8239	0.6537	0.9358	0.9889	0.9985	0.9974	0.9679	0.4992	0.9852	0.9592	0.9977	0.9420	0.2262	0.9978
West Virginia	0.5870	0.8211	0.6570	0.0246	0.8752	0.3927	0.3610	0.8055	0.8511	0.1524	0.2515	0.8178	0.4313	0.7616	0.3932	0.8837	0.7494
Wisconsin	0.8835	0.8821	0.7698	0.0935	0.9472	0.1291	0.0323	0.9012	0.8024	0.3672	0.3582	0.8186	0.3673	0.8642	0.4419	0.8838	0.7985
Wyoming	0.4921	0.2015	0.5250	0.8169	0.9236	0.4081	0.6794	0.2273	0.2578	0.8257	0.9011	0.2468	0.7723	0.3997	0.5628	0.9023	0.2865

Table 3.8 (Continued)

	North Dakota	Ohio	Oklahoma	Oregon	Pennsylvania	Rhode Island	South Carolina	South Dakota	Tennessee	Texas	Utah	Vermont	Virginia	Washington	West Virginia	Wisconsin	Wyoming
North Dakota		0.5385	0.6937	0.5936	0.5945	0.7835	0.5858	0.8136	0.6168	0.5436	0.6066	0.7756	0.7404	0.4224	0.5964	0.6385	0.8757
Ohio	0.5385		0.2811	0.7996	0.5010	0.6134	0.7995	0.0712	0.0477	0.5913	0.6071	0.1194	0.6918	0.9803	0.5467	0.0770	0.6527
Oklahoma	0.6937	0.2811		0.3967	0.2084	0.8820	0.4151	0.2193	0.4797	0.0559	0.3770	0.7696	0.8114	0.2349	0.3966	0.5129	0.9567
Oregon	0.5936	0.7996	0.3967		0.6079	0.9876	0.8827	0.3534	0.9520	0.5234	0.4823	0.8900	0.9793	0.6263	0.8751	0.9322	0.9379
Pennsylvania	0.5945	0.5010	0.2084	0.6079		0.9595	0.6517	0.1330	0.7624	0.0102	0.4791	0.8173	0.9653	0.8964	0.7405	0.8237	0.8844
Rhode Island	0.7835	0.6134	0.8820	0.9876	0.9595		0.2670	0.4787	0.5768	0.9496	0.9554	0.6119	0.1779	0.9906	0.4587	0.9274	0.5338
South Carolina	0.5858	0.7995	0.4151	0.8827	0.6517	0.2670		0.1089	0.4141	0.7641	0.7742	0.1420	0.3570	0.9911	0.6220	0.3704	0.4874
South Dakota	0.8136	0.0712	0.2193	0.3534	0.1330	0.4787	0.1089		0.1312	0.0935	0.2323	0.2620	0.3603	0.4772	0.0324	0.1679	0.7824
Tennessee	0.6168	0.0477	0.4797	0.9520	0.7624	0.5768	0.4141	0.1312		0.7813	0.7113	0.1316	0.6086	0.9819	0.5316	0.1417	0.6421
Texas	0.5436	0.5913	0.0559	0.5234	0.0102	0.9496	0.7641	0.0935	0.7813		0.6770	0.5187	0.9254	0.8901	0.7714	0.7669	0.8884
Utah	0.6066	0.6071	0.3770	0.4823	0.4791	0.9554	0.7742	0.2323	0.7113	0.6770		0.5064	0.9482	0.9489	0.7231	0.7430	0.8864
Vermont	0.7756	0.1194	0.7696	0.8900	0.8173	0.6119	0.1420	0.2620	0.1316	0.5187	0.5064		0.4521	0.9202	0.0176	0.2328	0.7185
Virginia	0.7404	0.6918	0.8114	0.9793	0.9653	0.1779	0.3570	0.3603	0.6086	0.9254	0.9482	0.4521		0.9940	0.6341	0.9036	0.4950
Washington	0.4224	0.9803	0.2349	0.6263	0.8964	0.9906	0.9911	0.4772	0.9819	0.8901	0.9489	0.9202	0.9940		0.9896	0.9868	0.9619
West Virginia	0.5964	0.5467	0.3966	0.8751	0.7405	0.4587	0.6220	0.0324	0.5316	0.7714	0.7231	0.0176	0.6341	0.9896		0.3747	0.6160
Wisconsin	0.6385	0.0770	0.5129	0.9322	0.8237	0.9274	0.3704	0.1679	0.1417	0.7669	0.7430	0.2328	0.9036	0.9868	0.3747		0.7407
Wyoming	0.8757	0.6527	0.9567	0.9379	0.8844	0.5338	0.4874	0.7824	0.6421	0.8884	0.8864	0.7185	0.4950	0.9619	0.6160	0.7407	

Source: Own calculations.
The grey cells indicate stochastic convergence.

Table 3.9 Stochastic convergence of US states: p-values for the trend-stationarity test of stochastic convergence between the states

	Alabama	Alaska	Arizona	Arkansas	California	Colorado	Connecticut	Delaware	District of Columbia	Florida	Georgia	Hawaii	Idaho	Illinois	Indiana	Iowa	Kansas
Alabama		0.7952	0.8663	0.7278	0.8979	0.8655	0.7310	0.2429	0.7782	0.9783	0.9872	0.4574	0.6060	0.5481	0.2309	0.6025	0.4761
Alaska	0.7952		0.9113	0.8053	0.9303	0.9475	0.7942	0.8668	0.2091	0.9533	0.9629	0.8022	0.8537	0.8887	0.7026	0.6910	0.7281
Arizona	0.8663	0.9113		0.9107	0.1035	0.4771	0.8775	0.5702	0.9594	0.1915	0.7545	0.8230	0.0117	0.7472	0.5432	0.9531	0.8087
Arkansas	0.7278	0.8053	0.9107		0.9626	0.9250	0.7759	0.1035	0.7841	0.9845	0.9951	0.8068	0.8213	0.4361	0.0623	0.4527	0.5935
California	0.8979	0.9303	0.1035	0.9626		0.7694	0.9137	0.4732	0.8602	0.0010	0.8569	0.9631	0.4316	0.9601	0.7613	0.9891	0.9715
Colorado	0.8655	0.9475	0.4771	0.9250	0.7694		0.9087	0.3812	0.7525	0.2507	0.7739	0.9225	0.8158	0.9700	0.6602	0.9871	0.9850
Connecticut	0.7310	0.7942	0.8775	0.7759	0.9137	0.9087		0.6828	0.5991	0.9674	0.9725	0.5666	0.5808	0.8325	0.6428	0.8155	0.4192
Delaware	0.2429	0.8668	0.5702	0.1035	0.4732	0.3812	0.6828		0.6266	0.6994	0.7695	0.3578	0.2482	0.0512	0.0052	0.4845	0.1665
District of Columbia	0.7782	0.2091	0.9594	0.7841	0.8602	0.7525	0.5991	0.6266		0.9873	0.9645	0.6645	0.6486	0.5532	0.5751	0.3247	0.2545
Florida	0.9783	0.9533	0.1915	0.9845	0.0010	0.2507	0.9674	0.6994	0.9873		0.4066	0.9549	0.0007	0.8426	0.5951	0.9895	0.8252
Georgia	0.9872	0.9629	0.7545	0.9951	0.8569	0.7739	0.9725	0.7695	0.9645	0.4066		0.9914	0.9045	0.9931	0.9240	0.9962	0.9770
Hawaii	0.4574	0.8022	0.8230	0.8068	0.9631	0.9225	0.5666	0.3578	0.6645	0.9549	0.9914		0.6414	0.7750	0.4957	0.8276	0.6215
Idaho	0.6060	0.8537	0.0117	0.8213	0.4316	0.8158	0.5808	0.2482	0.6486	0.0007	0.9045	0.6414		0.6928	0.5687	0.9528	0.7959
Illinois	0.5481	0.8887	0.7472	0.4361	0.9601	0.9700	0.8325	0.0512	0.5532	0.8426	0.9931	0.7750	0.6928		0.0001	0.9589	0.7129
Indiana	0.2309	0.7026	0.5432	0.0623	0.7613	0.6602	0.6428	0.0052	0.5751	0.5951	0.9240	0.4957	0.5687	0.0001		0.8067	0.4534
Iowa	0.6025	0.6910	0.9531	0.4527	0.9891	0.9871	0.8155	0.4845	0.3247	0.9895	0.9962	0.8276	0.9528	0.9589	0.8067		0.7146
Kansas	0.4761	0.7281	0.8087	0.5935	0.9715	0.9850	0.4192	0.1665	0.2545	0.8252	0.9770	0.6215	0.7959	0.7129	0.4534	0.7146	

Table 3.9 (Continued)

	Kentucky	Louisiana	Maine	Maryland	Massachusetts	Michigan	Minnesota	Mississippi	Missouri	Montana	Nebraska	Nevada	New Hampshire	New Jersey	New Mexico	New York	North Carolina
Alabama	0.6109	0.4592	0.8816	0.4998	0.5691	0.8638	0.6458	0.5821	0.5500	0.6804	0.6700	0.9769	0.7133	0.5676	0.3562	0.4821	0.4790
Alaska	0.7918	0.5882	0.9435	0.7557	0.8274	0.8983	0.7970	0.4722	0.7911	0.6093	0.6568	0.9238	0.8865	0.8454	0.9695	0.8958	0.8284
Arizona	0.8770	0.7422	0.6689	0.9141	0.8031	0.6073	0.8281	0.9334	0.7759	0.9767	0.9632	0.2580	0.7777	0.8104	0.2410	0.6641	0.6491
Arkansas	0.5225	0.7007	0.9175	0.6320	0.6243	0.8694	0.2569	0.8128	0.6135	0.8059	0.7583	0.9722	0.6823	0.5982	0.4200	0.4338	0.7592
California	0.9585	0.7146	0.5376	0.9048	0.9514	0.7706	0.9664	0.9820	0.9560	0.9842	0.9853	0.5599	0.9164	0.9178	0.3119	0.8205	0.9758
Colorado	0.9222	0.7125	0.3292	0.8948	0.9757	0.6017	0.9604	0.9770	0.9727	0.9848	0.9916	0.7118	0.8776	0.8675	0.4253	0.8550	0.9312
Connecticut	0.7896	0.1829	0.9253	0.6993	0.8007	0.8836	0.7964	0.2475	0.7463	0.6973	0.7724	0.9422	0.8466	0.8086	0.8546	0.7473	0.6208
Delaware	0.0071	0.7000	0.2201	0.1819	0.0301	0.2502	0.0111	0.3076	0.0075	0.4503	0.0968	0.7321	0.0224	0.0512	0.6367	0.0183	0.2338
District of Columbia	0.6904	0.1781	0.9739	0.7492	0.2140	0.8424	0.5876	0.1213	0.2768	0.2099	0.4379	0.9650	0.6945	0.7559	0.9602	0.4436	0.6603
Florida	0.9466	0.8997	0.8416	0.9836	0.8587	0.5000	0.9015	0.9593	0.8689	0.9917	0.9815	0.1849	0.8905	0.9133	0.4796	0.7644	0.8091
Georgia	0.9867	0.8825	0.9037	0.9888	0.9864	0.3596	0.9957	0.9828	0.9821	0.9930	0.9953	0.8410	0.9878	0.9698	0.8033	0.9497	0.9815
Hawaii	0.8290	0.3759	0.8017	0.5464	0.8170	0.9124	0.8648	0.7883	0.8059	0.8529	0.8583	0.9674	0.8399	0.7257	0.1358	0.6545	0.4962
Idaho	0.8418	0.4371	0.1622	0.6437	0.7853	0.8624	0.9178	0.9082	0.8781	0.9044	0.9076	0.4509	0.6920	0.5060	0.0157	0.6560	0.3125
Illinois	0.0455	0.6367	0.4513	0.4308	0.6836	0.8477	0.2178	0.8353	0.2322	0.9170	0.8885	0.9054	0.3270	0.1064	0.4616	0.3331	0.6363
Indiana	0.0076	0.5276	0.0282	0.1512	0.1121	0.9142	0.0120	0.7502	0.0519	0.6692	0.3639	0.8327	0.0033	0.0131	0.0138	0.0666	0.1898
Iowa	0.6255	0.4610	0.9720	0.3119	0.9180	0.9719	0.8762	0.4312	0.7973	0.3139	0.3011	0.9854	0.9162	0.7491	0.9883	0.8200	0.7764
Kansas	0.5572	0.4000	0.5064	0.2050	0.5278	0.9237	0.7134	0.5311	0.4336	0.5754	0.6567	0.8802	0.6387	0.2481	0.3924	0.3470	0.5375

Table 3.9 (Continued)

	North Dakota	Ohio	Oklahoma	Oregon	Pennsylvania	Rhode Island	South Carolina	South Dakota	Tennessee	Texas	Utah	Vermont	Virginia	Washington	West Virginia	Wisconsin	Wyoming
Alabama	0.9555	0.8072	0.6049	0.7602	0.7073	0.2890	0.9515	0.8905	0.8281	0.5315	0.7539	0.8209	0.2084	0.4480	0.6903	0.8222	0.8130
Alaska	0.8118	0.8884	0.7280	0.8897	0.8136	0.8052	0.9352	0.3070	0.9008	0.8573	0.9218	0.6283	0.7909	0.8907	0.8226	0.8943	0.3944
Arizona	0.9781	0.6931	0.9222	0.0843	0.8324	0.9207	0.7393	0.9695	0.6842	0.7029	0.2728	0.9476	0.8980	0.0372	0.8081	0.8351	0.9363
Arkansas	0.9564	0.7948	0.6069	0.8879	0.6360	0.4160	0.9853	0.8845	0.7742	0.3892	0.8376	0.7899	0.6902	0.6192	0.7735	0.7926	0.8444
California	0.9847	0.8950	0.9749	0.7998	0.9554	0.9378	0.5997	0.9684	0.8904	0.9374	0.7184	0.9454	0.8621	0.3958	0.9288	0.8958	0.8696
Colorado	0.9894	0.8402	0.9879	0.7777	0.9887	0.9116	0.2842	0.9757	0.7757	0.9748	0.8090	0.9351	0.8178	0.3619	0.9691	0.8592	0.8500
Connecticut	0.9453	0.8670	0.7873	0.7829	0.8426	0.7450	0.9350	0.7380	0.8792	0.7613	0.8099	0.8321	0.6310	0.5536	0.7475	0.8878	0.6879
Delaware	0.9299	0.0497	0.2403	0.4404	0.0013	0.3128	0.2666	0.4650	0.0615	0.0226	0.5206	0.1703	0.3492	0.1862	0.0221	0.0408	0.8319
District of Columbia	0.8658	0.7434	0.5327	0.7561	0.2719	0.6499	0.9355	0.2777	0.7917	0.4224	0.7914	0.7298	0.7782	0.3887	0.4028	0.8041	0.6972
Florida	0.9776	0.6691	0.9613	0.0501	0.8817	0.9920	0.6231	0.9855	0.7725	0.8038	0.4099	0.9811	0.9748	0.0125	0.8846	0.9130	0.9594
Georgia	0.9882	0.9773	0.9844	0.9466	0.9859	0.9898	0.8658	0.9878	0.9813	0.9747	0.9494	0.9893	0.9780	0.6838	0.9742	0.9927	0.9321
Hawaii	0.9621	0.8932	0.7413	0.8302	0.8388	0.5701	0.9721	0.8884	0.9019	0.6877	0.6193	0.8523	0.4170	0.6000	0.7959	0.8792	0.7691
Idaho	0.9784	0.8821	0.8788	0.0048	0.8500	0.7212	0.5647	0.9395	0.7313	0.7668	0.0137	0.8392	0.4839	0.4999	0.8736	0.6298	0.7527
Illinois	0.9791	0.7967	0.8465	0.8872	0.2637	0.5934	0.9395	0.8925	0.4841	0.3337	0.9049	0.7123	0.4858	0.6556	0.6231	0.2079	0.8058
Indiana	0.9711	0.5606	0.3334	0.5644	0.1263	0.2038	0.6004	0.7568	0.0138	0.0665	0.3898	0.4674	0.1573	0.4725	0.1571	0.0000	0.7659
Iowa	0.9332	0.9763	0.2569	0.9722	0.8994	0.0224	0.9870	0.4032	0.9433	0.8310	0.9617	0.3604	0.4464	0.9676	0.7819	0.9699	0.6617
Kansas	0.9670	0.9055	0.5905	0.9185	0.6708	0.4115	0.9737	0.7616	0.8058	0.4358	0.8320	0.5065	0.2229	0.9283	0.4550	0.7468	0.5900

Table 3.9 (Continued)

	Alabama	Alaska	Arizona	Arkansas	California	Colorado	Connecticut	Delaware	District of Columbia	Florida	Georgia	Hawaii	Idaho	Illinois	Indiana	Iowa	Kansas
Kentucky	0.6109	0.7918	0.8770	0.5225	0.9585	0.9222	0.7896	0.0071	0.6904	0.9466	0.9867	0.8290	0.8418	0.0455	0.0076	0.6255	0.5572
Louisiana	0.4592	0.5882	0.7422	0.7007	0.7146	0.7125	0.1829	0.7000	0.1781	0.8997	0.8825	0.3759	0.4371	0.6367	0.5276	0.4610	0.4000
Maine	0.8816	0.9435	0.6689	0.9175	0.5376	0.3292	0.9253	0.2201	0.9739	0.8416	0.9037	0.8017	0.1622	0.4513	0.0282	0.9720	0.5064
Maryland	0.4998	0.7557	0.9141	0.6320	0.9048	0.8948	0.6993	0.1819	0.7492	0.9836	0.9888	0.5464	0.6437	0.4308	0.1512	0.3119	0.2050
Massachusetts	0.5691	0.8274	0.8031	0.6243	0.9514	0.9757	0.8007	0.0301	0.2140	0.8587	0.9864	0.8170	0.7853	0.6836	0.1121	0.9180	0.5278
Michigan	0.8638	0.8983	0.6073	0.8694	0.7706	0.6017	0.8836	0.2502	0.8424	0.5000	0.3596	0.9124	0.8624	0.8477	0.9142	0.9719	0.9237
Minnesota	0.6458	0.7970	0.8281	0.2569	0.9664	0.9604	0.7964	0.0111	0.5876	0.9015	0.9957	0.8648	0.9178	0.2178	0.0120	0.8762	0.7134
Mississippi	0.5821	0.4722	0.9334	0.8128	0.9820	0.9770	0.2475	0.3076	0.1213	0.9593	0.9828	0.7883	0.9082	0.8353	0.7502	0.4312	0.5311
Missouri	0.5500	0.7911	0.7759	0.6135	0.9560	0.9727	0.7463	0.0075	0.2768	0.8689	0.9821	0.8059	0.8781	0.2322	0.0519	0.7973	0.4336
Montana	0.6804	0.6093	0.9767	0.8059	0.9842	0.9848	0.6973	0.4503	0.2099	0.9917	0.9930	0.8529	0.9044	0.9170	0.6692	0.3139	0.5754
Nebraska	0.6700	0.6568	0.9632	0.7583	0.9853	0.9916	0.7724	0.0968	0.4379	0.9815	0.9953	0.8583	0.9076	0.8885	0.3639	0.3011	0.6567
Nevada	0.9769	0.9238	0.2580	0.9722	0.5599	0.7118	0.9422	0.7321	0.9650	0.1849	0.8410	0.9674	0.4509	0.9054	0.8327	0.9854	0.8802
New Hampshire	0.7133	0.8865	0.7777	0.6823	0.9164	0.8776	0.8466	0.0224	0.6945	0.8905	0.9878	0.8399	0.6920	0.3270	0.0033	0.9162	0.6387
New Jersey	0.5676	0.8454	0.8104	0.5982	0.9178	0.8675	0.8086	0.0512	0.7559	0.9133	0.9698	0.7257	0.5060	0.1064	0.0131	0.7491	0.2481
New Mexico	0.3562	0.9695	0.2410	0.4200	0.3119	0.4253	0.8546	0.6367	0.9602	0.4796	0.8033	0.1358	0.0157	0.4616	0.0138	0.9883	0.3924
New York	0.4821	0.8958	0.6641	0.4338	0.8205	0.8550	0.7473	0.0183	0.4436	0.7644	0.9497	0.6545	0.6560	0.3331	0.0666	0.8200	0.3470
North Carolina	0.4790	0.8284	0.6491	0.7592	0.9758	0.9312	0.6208	0.2338	0.6603	0.8091	0.9815	0.4962	0.3125	0.6363	0.1898	0.7764	0.5375

Table 3.9 (Continued)

	Kentucky	Louisiana	Maine	Maryland	Massachusetts	Michigan	Minnesota	Mississippi	Missouri	Montana	Nebraska	Nevada	New Hampshire	New Jersey	New Mexico	New York	North Carolina
Kentucky		0.6858	0.7092	0.4557	0.3417	0.8977	0.1245	0.8528	0.3447	0.8128	0.4730	0.9500	0.3331	0.5401	0.2506	0.1611	0.8230
Louisiana	0.6858		0.8240	0.6368	0.5426	0.7694	0.6594	0.2953	0.5922	0.3493	0.6403	0.8139	0.7317	0.6387	0.7292	0.5688	0.5466
Maine	0.7092	0.8240		0.9906	0.3335	0.5945	0.6290	0.9479	0.3909	0.9658	0.9787	0.8092	0.6444	0.5234	0.2319	0.3105	0.5013
Maryland	0.4557	0.6368	0.9906		0.1625	0.8454	0.4874	0.2315	0.1899	0.2807	0.2610	0.9634	0.6164	0.4132	0.7090	0.2653	0.5434
Massachusetts	0.3417	0.5426	0.3335	0.1625		0.9001	0.6940	0.7966	0.0964	0.8870	0.8744	0.9083	0.5756	0.2805	0.4424	0.0645	0.6951
Michigan	0.8977	0.7694	0.5945	0.8454	0.9001		0.9120	0.9275	0.8659	0.9534	0.9439	0.8005	0.7911	0.8242	0.5287	0.7179	0.8631
Minnesota	0.1245	0.6594	0.6290	0.4874	0.6940	0.9120		0.8783	0.6733	0.8441	0.7726	0.9428	0.1460	0.4240	0.2800	0.2823	0.7593
Mississippi	0.8528	0.2953	0.9479	0.2315	0.7966	0.9275	0.8783		0.9053	0.0985	0.5691	0.9338	0.8806	0.9569	0.7277	0.5911	0.8886
Missouri	0.3447	0.5922	0.3909	0.1899	0.0964	0.8659	0.6733	0.9053		0.7385	0.4460	0.8932	0.2961	0.2596	0.2721	0.1065	0.7022
Montana	0.8128	0.3493	0.9658	0.2807	0.8870	0.9534	0.8441	0.0985	0.7385		0.6067	0.9796	0.9150	0.8348	0.9413	0.6973	0.8569
Nebraska	0.4730	0.6403	0.9787	0.2610	0.8744	0.9439	0.7726	0.5691	0.4460	0.6067		0.9693	0.9289	0.6542	0.9381	0.4362	0.9106
Nevada	0.9500	0.8139	0.8092	0.9634	0.9083	0.8005	0.9428	0.9338	0.8932	0.9796	0.9693		0.8959	0.8836	0.5624	0.8295	0.9004
New Hampshire	0.3331	0.7317	0.6444	0.6164	0.5756	0.7911	0.1460	0.8806	0.2961	0.9150	0.9289	0.8959		0.4637	0.4985	0.3105	0.7047
New Jersey	0.5401	0.6387	0.5234	0.4132	0.2805	0.8242	0.4240	0.9569	0.2596	0.8348	0.6542	0.8836	0.4637		0.0949	0.2348	0.3267
New Mexico	0.2506	0.7292	0.2319	0.7090	0.4424	0.5287	0.2800	0.7277	0.2721	0.9413	0.9381	0.5624	0.4985	0.0949		0.5497	0.0627
New York	0.1611	0.5688	0.3105	0.2653	0.0645	0.7179	0.2823	0.5911	0.1065	0.6973	0.4362	0.8295	0.3105	0.2348	0.5497		0.4742
North Carolina	0.8230	0.5466	0.5013	0.5434	0.6951	0.8631	0.7593	0.8886	0.7022	0.8569	0.9106	0.9004	0.7047	0.3267	0.0627	0.4742	

Table 3.9 (Continued)

	North Dakota	Ohio	Oklahoma	Oregon	Pennsylvania	Rhode Island	South Carolina	South Dakota	Tennessee	Texas	Utah	Vermont	Virginia	Washington	West Virginia	Wisconsin	Wyoming
Kentucky	0.9672	0.8067	0.5572	0.8791	0.3654	0.4941	0.9742	0.8499	0.7099	0.1596	0.8080	0.7153	0.4954	0.6169	0.5449	0.3032	0.8315
Louisiana	0.9364	0.7340	0.7103	0.5302	0.6372	0.7661	0.7979	0.4976	0.7405	0.5635	0.5446	0.7395	0.5081	0.3799	0.5876	0.7465	0.5776
Maine	0.9786	0.5246	0.9185	0.2961	0.6163	0.9901	0.5423	0.9795	0.5510	0.4938	0.4971	0.9956	0.9173	0.0221	0.5993	0.6373	0.9085
Maryland	0.9316	0.7908	0.4769	0.7671	0.4621	0.3628	0.9634	0.7592	0.7844	0.3046	0.7806	0.7493	0.2774	0.4414	0.4027	0.8173	0.8207
Massachusetts	0.9743	0.8673	0.6998	0.8939	0.5024	0.5333	0.9599	0.8196	0.7740	0.4458	0.8317	0.5256	0.1879	0.7571	0.0487	0.7437	0.7669
Michigan	0.9849	0.6956	0.8824	0.8464	0.8787	0.8585	0.5246	0.9527	0.5878	0.8378	0.8368	0.8922	0.8215	0.8303	0.8540	0.7817	0.8642
Minnesota	0.9695	0.9346	0.6172	0.9127	0.6727	0.3856	0.9829	0.8646	0.2797	0.2865	0.7977	0.7014	0.5977	0.7942	0.7089	0.1239	0.8108
Mississippi	0.9584	0.9240	0.6038	0.9559	0.8893	0.3829	0.9842	0.4493	0.9303	0.6425	0.8372	0.5956	0.1568	0.8573	0.7326	0.9038	0.6557
Missouri	0.9743	0.8380	0.6469	0.8608	0.2559	0.4340	0.9469	0.8365	0.8164	0.2112	0.6875	0.5618	0.3053	0.7208	0.3370	0.4264	0.7830
Montana	0.9391	0.9495	0.3495	0.9540	0.8644	0.2098	0.9919	0.4097	0.9204	0.7038	0.9685	0.2712	0.4350	0.8920	0.7883	0.9703	0.7215
Nebraska	0.9260	0.9612	0.2198	0.9696	0.7514	0.2187	0.9959	0.3946	0.9000	0.4423	0.9596	0.0176	0.7692	0.9088	0.6658	0.9726	0.7949
Nevada	0.9748	0.8801	0.9425	0.6613	0.9089	0.9695	0.8145	0.9724	0.8943	0.8836	0.7679	0.9702	0.9417	0.4440	0.9037	0.9248	0.9262
New Hampshire	0.9708	0.5622	0.7439	0.8328	0.2482	0.8221	0.9130	0.9024	0.3288	0.3854	0.8094	0.8373	0.7066	0.5195	0.6033	0.1830	0.8390
New Jersey	0.9714	0.7016	0.7192	0.6761	0.4327	0.6629	0.9477	0.9007	0.7243	0.1889	0.5342	0.8220	0.4686	0.2409	0.4926	0.4820	0.8476
New Mexico	0.9797	0.5114	0.9266	0.0706	0.5363	0.9793	0.3852	0.9779	0.4905	0.6124	0.2405	0.9533	0.5782	0.0723	0.6031	0.4147	0.9003
New York	0.9717	0.4649	0.5386	0.6523	0.0451	0.5068	0.6197	0.6814	0.3945	0.2293	0.7579	0.3604	0.3350	0.5750	0.0260	0.2781	0.7349
North Carolina	0.9707	0.8630	0.9081	0.8328	0.7614	0.6716	0.9499	0.8926	0.8452	0.5377	0.2336	0.8483	0.4199	0.3010	0.7980	0.7696	0.8066

Table 3.9 (Continued)

	Alabama	Alaska	Arizona	Arkansas	California	Colorado	Connecticut	Delaware	District of Columbia	Florida	Georgia	Hawaii	Idaho	Illinois	Indiana	Iowa	Kansas
North Dakota	0.9555	0.8118	0.9781	0.9564	0.9847	0.9894	0.9453	0.9299	0.8658	0.9776	0.9882	0.9621	0.9784	0.9791	0.9711	0.9332	0.9670
Ohio	0.8072	0.8884	0.6931	0.7948	0.8950	0.8402	0.8670	0.0497	0.7434	0.6691	0.9773	0.8932	0.8821	0.7967	0.5606	0.9763	0.9055
Oklahoma	0.6049	0.7280	0.9222	0.6069	0.9749	0.9879	0.7873	0.2403	0.5327	0.9613	0.9844	0.7413	0.8788	0.8465	0.3334	0.2569	0.5905
Oregon	0.7602	0.8897	0.0843	0.8879	0.7998	0.7777	0.7829	0.4404	0.7561	0.0501	0.9466	0.8302	0.0048	0.8872	0.5644	0.9722	0.9185
Pennsylvania	0.7073	0.8136	0.8324	0.6360	0.9554	0.9887	0.8426	0.0013	0.2719	0.8817	0.9859	0.8388	0.8500	0.2637	0.1263	0.8994	0.6708
Rhode Island	0.2890	0.8052	0.9207	0.4160	0.9378	0.9116	0.7450	0.3128	0.6499	0.9920	0.9898	0.5701	0.7212	0.5934	0.2038	0.0224	0.4115
South Carolina	0.9515	0.9352	0.7393	0.9853	0.5997	0.2842	0.9350	0.2666	0.9355	0.6231	0.8658	0.9721	0.5647	0.9395	0.6004	0.9870	0.9737
South Dakota	0.8905	0.3070	0.9695	0.8845	0.9684	0.9757	0.7380	0.4650	0.2777	0.9855	0.9878	0.8884	0.9395	0.8925	0.7568	0.4032	0.7616
Tennessee	0.8281	0.9008	0.6842	0.7742	0.8904	0.7757	0.8792	0.0615	0.7917	0.7725	0.9813	0.9019	0.7313	0.4841	0.0138	0.9433	0.8058
Texas	0.5315	0.8573	0.7029	0.3892	0.9374	0.9748	0.7613	0.0226	0.4224	0.8038	0.9747	0.6877	0.7668	0.3337	0.0665	0.8310	0.4358
Utah	0.7539	0.9218	0.2728	0.8376	0.7184	0.8090	0.8099	0.5206	0.7914	0.4099	0.9494	0.6193	0.0137	0.9049	0.3898	0.9617	0.8320
Vermont	0.8209	0.6283	0.9476	0.7899	0.9454	0.9351	0.8321	0.1703	0.7298	0.9811	0.9893	0.8523	0.8392	0.7123	0.4674	0.3604	0.5065
Virginia	0.2084	0.7909	0.8980	0.6902	0.8621	0.8178	0.6310	0.3492	0.7782	0.9748	0.9780	0.4170	0.4839	0.4858	0.1573	0.4464	0.2229
Washington	0.4480	0.8907	0.0372	0.6192	0.3958	0.3619	0.5536	0.1862	0.3887	0.0125	0.6838	0.6000	0.4999	0.6556	0.4725	0.9676	0.9283
West Virginia	0.6903	0.8226	0.8081	0.7735	0.9288	0.9691	0.7475	0.0221	0.4028	0.8846	0.9742	0.7959	0.8736	0.6231	0.1571	0.7819	0.4550
Wisconsin	0.8222	0.8943	0.8351	0.7926	0.8958	0.8592	0.8878	0.0408	0.8041	0.9130	0.9927	0.8792	0.6298	0.2079	0.0000	0.9699	0.7468
Wyoming	0.8130	0.3944	0.9363	0.8444	0.8696	0.8500	0.6879	0.8319	0.6972	0.9594	0.9321	0.7691	0.7527	0.8058	0.7659	0.6617	0.5900

Table 3.9 (Continued)

	Kentucky	Louisiana	Maine	Maryland	Massachusetts	Michigan	Minnesota	Mississippi	Missouri	Montana	Nebraska	Nevada	New Hampshire	New Jersey	New Mexico	New York	North Carolina
North Dakota	0.9672	0.9364	0.9786	0.9316	0.9743	0.9849	0.9695	0.9584	0.9743	0.9391	0.9260	0.9748	0.9708	0.9714	0.9797	0.9717	0.9707
Ohio	0.8067	0.7340	0.5246	0.7908	0.8673	0.6956	0.9346	0.9240	0.8380	0.9495	0.9612	0.8801	0.5622	0.7016	0.5114	0.4649	0.8630
Oklahoma	0.5572	0.7103	0.9185	0.4769	0.6998	0.8824	0.6172	0.6038	0.6469	0.3495	0.2198	0.9425	0.7439	0.7192	0.9266	0.5386	0.9081
Oregon	0.8791	0.5302	0.2961	0.7671	0.8939	0.8464	0.9127	0.9559	0.8608	0.9540	0.9696	0.6613	0.8328	0.6761	0.0706	0.6523	0.8328
Pennsylvania	0.3654	0.6372	0.6163	0.4621	0.5024	0.8787	0.6727	0.8893	0.2559	0.8644	0.7514	0.9089	0.2482	0.4327	0.5363	0.0451	0.7614
Rhode Island	0.4941	0.7661	0.9901	0.3628	0.5333	0.8585	0.3856	0.3829	0.4340	0.2098	0.2187	0.9695	0.8221	0.6629	0.9793	0.5068	0.6716
South Carolina	0.9742	0.7979	0.5423	0.9634	0.9599	0.5246	0.9829	0.9842	0.9469	0.9919	0.9959	0.8145	0.9130	0.9477	0.3852	0.6197	0.9499
South Dakota	0.8499	0.4976	0.9795	0.7592	0.8196	0.9527	0.8646	0.4493	0.8365	0.4097	0.3946	0.9724	0.9024	0.9007	0.9779	0.6814	0.8926
Tennessee	0.7099	0.7405	0.5510	0.7844	0.7740	0.5878	0.2797	0.9303	0.8164	0.9204	0.9000	0.8943	0.3288	0.7243	0.4905	0.3945	0.8452
Texas	0.1596	0.5635	0.4938	0.3046	0.4458	0.8378	0.2865	0.6425	0.2112	0.7038	0.4423	0.8836	0.3854	0.1889	0.6124	0.2293	0.5377
Utah	0.8080	0.5446	0.4971	0.7806	0.8317	0.8368	0.7977	0.8372	0.6875	0.9685	0.9596	0.7679	0.8094	0.5342	0.2405	0.7579	0.2336
Vermont	0.7153	0.7395	0.9956	0.7493	0.5256	0.8922	0.7014	0.5956	0.5618	0.2712	0.0176	0.9702	0.8373	0.8220	0.9533	0.3604	0.8483
Virginia	0.4954	0.5081	0.9173	0.2774	0.1879	0.8215	0.5977	0.1568	0.3053	0.4350	0.7692	0.9417	0.7066	0.4686	0.5782	0.3350	0.4199
Washington	0.6169	0.3799	0.0221	0.4414	0.7571	0.8303	0.7942	0.8573	0.7208	0.8920	0.9088	0.4440	0.5195	0.2409	0.0723	0.5750	0.3010
West Virginia	0.5449	0.5876	0.5993	0.4027	0.0487	0.8540	0.7089	0.7326	0.3370	0.7883	0.6658	0.9037	0.6033	0.4926	0.6031	0.0260	0.7980
Wisconsin	0.3032	0.7465	0.6373	0.8173	0.7437	0.7817	0.1239	0.9038	0.4264	0.9703	0.9726	0.9248	0.1830	0.4820	0.4147	0.2781	0.7696
Wyoming	0.8315	0.5776	0.9085	0.8207	0.7669	0.8642	0.8108	0.6557	0.7830	0.7215	0.7949	0.9262	0.8390	0.8476	0.9003	0.7349	0.8066

Table 3.9 (Continued)

	North Dakota	Ohio	Oklahoma	Oregon	Pennsylvania	Rhode Island	South Carolina	South Dakota	Tennessee	Texas	Utah	Vermont	Virginia	Washington	West Virginia	Wisconsin	Wyoming
North Dakota		0.9830	0.9551	0.9781	0.9716	0.9248	0.9853	0.8230	0.9788	0.9682	0.9756	0.9213	0.9530	0.9886	0.9719	0.9774	0.8619
Ohio	0.9830		0.8929	0.8862	0.8579	0.7891	0.7398	0.9566	0.1080	0.6499	0.8528	0.8710	0.7662	0.7659	0.8550	0.5558	0.8505
Oklahoma	0.9551	0.8929		0.9406	0.6327	0.4030	0.9655	0.4460	0.9022	0.4280	0.9334	0.4618	0.6217	0.8917	0.7599	0.8614	0.7942
Oregon	0.9781	0.8862	0.9406		0.8886	0.8511	0.7890	0.9525	0.8957	0.8446	0.1180	0.9261	0.6246	0.2203	0.8627	0.8309	0.8197
Pennsylvania	0.9716	0.8579	0.6327	0.8886		0.5414	0.9749	0.8530	0.6440	0.0520	0.8221	0.6560	0.5804	0.7659	0.3095	0.5402	0.8005
Rhode Island	0.9248	0.7891	0.4030	0.8511	0.5414		0.9613	0.5481	0.8187	0.4200	0.8811	0.3749	0.6076	0.6264	0.6285	0.8791	0.8180
South Carolina	0.9853	0.7398	0.9655	0.7890	0.9749	0.9613		0.9876	0.5746	0.8315	0.8229	0.9762	0.9333	0.1268	0.9285	0.9537	0.9144
South Dakota	0.8230	0.9566	0.4460	0.9525	0.8530	0.5481	0.9876		0.9521	0.7276	0.9468	0.2883	0.7344	0.9300	0.8940	0.9468	0.7323
Tennessee	0.9788	0.1080	0.9022	0.8957	0.6440	0.8187	0.5746	0.9521		0.5519	0.7714	0.9148	0.7565	0.5138	0.8411	0.1205	0.8618
Texas	0.9682	0.6499	0.4280	0.8446	0.0520	0.4200	0.8315	0.7276	0.5519		0.9143	0.4225	0.3987	0.8401	0.4056	0.3333	0.7095
Utah	0.9756	0.8528	0.9334	0.1180	0.8221	0.8811	0.8229	0.9468	0.7714	0.9143		0.8728	0.6849	0.1020	0.8396	0.8492	0.8318
Vermont	0.9213	0.8710	0.4618	0.9261	0.6560	0.3749	0.9762	0.2883	0.9148	0.4225	0.8728		0.7353	0.7068	0.4868	0.9270	0.8224
Virginia	0.9530	0.7662	0.6217	0.6246	0.5804	0.6076	0.9333	0.7344	0.7565	0.3987	0.6849	0.7353		0.2916	0.4334	0.8101	0.8279
Washington	0.9886	0.7659	0.8917	0.2203	0.7659	0.6264	0.1268	0.9300	0.5138	0.8401	0.1020	0.7068	0.2916		0.7371	0.3932	0.6357
West Virginia	0.9719	0.8550	0.7599	0.8627	0.3095	0.6285	0.9285	0.8940	0.8411	0.4056	0.8396	0.4868	0.4334	0.7371		0.7120	0.7881
Wisconsin	0.9774	0.5558	0.8614	0.8309	0.5402	0.8791	0.9537	0.9468	0.1205	0.3333	0.8492	0.9270	0.8101	0.3932	0.7120		0.8666
Wyoming	0.8619	0.8505	0.7942	0.8197	0.8005	0.8180	0.9144	0.7323	0.8618	0.7095	0.8318	0.8224	0.8279	0.6357	0.7881	0.8666	

Source: Own calculation.
The grey cells indicate stochastic convergence.

Table 3.10 Stochastic convergence of US states: a summary

State	Stochastic convergence without trend		Stochastic convergence with trend	
	The number of US states to/from which a given state is:			
	Converging	*Diverging*	*Converging*	*Diverging*
Alabama	0	50	0	50
Alaska	0	50	0	50
Arizona	1	49	2	48
Arkansas	0	50	0	50
California	0	50	1	49
Colorado	4	46	0	50
Connecticut	0	50	0	50
Delaware	0	50	12	38
District of Columbia	2	48	0	50
Florida	1	49	3	47
Georgia	1	49	0	50
Hawaii	1	49	0	50
Idaho	3	47	5	45
Illinois	2	48	2	48
Indiana	7	43	10	40
Iowa	0	50	1	49
Kansas	0	50	0	50
Kentucky	1	49	3	47
Louisiana	0	50	0	50
Maine	0	50	2	48
Maryland	5	45	0	50
Massachusetts	1	49	2	48
Michigan	0	50	0	50
Minnesota	1	49	2	48
Mississippi	1	49	0	50
Missouri	4	46	1	49
Montana	1	49	0	50
Nebraska	1	49	1	49
Nevada	0	50	0	50
New Hampshire	0	50	2	48
New Jersey	0	50	1	49
New Mexico	3	47	2	48
New York	1	49	3	47
North Carolina	1	49	0	50
North Dakota	0	50	0	50
Ohio	1	49	1	49
Oklahoma	0	50	0	50
Oregon	0	50	1	49
Pennsylvania	1	49	2	48
Rhode Island	3	47	1	49
South Carolina	0	50	0	50
South Dakota	2	48	0	50
Tennessee	2	48	1	49
Texas	1	49	1	49
Utah	0	50	1	49
Vermont	3	47	1	49
Virginia	1	49	0	50
Washington	0	50	3	47
West Virginia	4	46	3	47
Wisconsin	2	48	2	48
Wyoming	0	50	0	50

Source: Own calculations.

Table 3.11 HMM convergence of US states: Viterbi paths

Year	Alabama	Alaska	Arizona	Arkansas	California	Colorado	Connecticut	Delaware	Florida	Georgia	Hawaii	Idaho	Illinois	Indiana	Iowa	Kansas	Kentucky	Louisiana	Maine	Maryland	Massachusetts	Michigan	Minnesota	Mississippi	Missouri	Montana	Nebraska	Nevada	New Hampshire	New Jersey	New Mexico	New York	North Carolina	North Dakota	Ohio	Oklahoma	Oregon	Pennsylvania	Rhode Island	South Carolina	South Dakota	Tennessee	Texas	Utah	Vermont	Virginia	Washington	West Virginia	Wisconsin	Wyoming
2000	0	0	0	0	0	0	0	0	0	0	0	0	1	1	1	0	0	0	0	0	0	0	1	0	0	1	0	0	0	1	0	0	0	1	1	0	0	0	1	0	1	0	0	0	1	0	0	1	1	0
2001	0	0	0	0	0	0	0	0	0	0	0	0	1	1	1	0	0	0	0	0	0	0	1	0	0	1	0	0	0	1	0	0	0	1	1	0	0	0	1	0	1	0	0	0	1	0	0	1	1	0
2002	0	0	0	0	0	0	0	0	0	0	0	0	1	1	1	0	0	0	0	0	0	0	1	0	0	1	0	0	0	1	0	0	0	1	1	0	0	0	1	0	1	0	0	0	1	0	0	1	0	0
2003	0	1	0	0	1	0	0	1	0	0	1	1	1	1	1	0	0	0	0	0	0	0	1	0	0	1	0	0	0	1	0	0	0	1	1	0	0	0	1	0	1	0	0	1	1	0	1	1	0	1
2004	0	1	1	0	1	1	1	1	1	1	1	1	1	1	1	1	0	1	1	1	1	1	1	0	0	1	0	0	1	1	1	1	1	1	1	1	1	1	1	1	1	0	1	1	1	1	1	1	1	1
2005	0	1	1	1	1	1	1	1	1	1	1	1	1	1	1	1	0	1	1	1	1	1	1	0	0	1	0	0	1	1	1	1	1	1	1	1	1	1	1	1	1	0	1	1	1	1	1	1	1	1
2006	0	1	1	0	1	1	1	1	1	1	1	1	1	1	1	1	0	1	1	1	1	1	1	0	0	1	0	0	1	1	1	1	1	1	1	1	1	1	1	1	1	0	1	1	1	1	1	1	1	1
2007	0	1	1	1	0	1	1	1	1	1	1	1	1	1	1	1	0	1	1	1	1	1	1	0	0	1	0	0	1	1	1	1	1	1	1	1	1	1	1	1	1	0	1	1	1	1	1	1	1	1
2008	0	1	1	0	1	1	1	1	1	1	1	1	1	1	1	1	0	1	1	1	1	1	1	0	0	1	0	0	1	0	1	1	1	1	1	1	1	1	1	1	1	0	1	1	1	1	1	1	1	1
2009	0	1	1	1	1	1	1	1	1	1	1	1	1	1	1	1	0	1	1	1	1	1	1	0	0	0	0	1	1	0	1	1	1	1	1	1	1	1	1	1	1	0	1	1	1	1	1	1	1	1
2010	0	1	1	0	1	1	1	1	1	1	1	1	1	1	1	1	0	1	1	1	1	1	1	1	1	0	1	1	1	0	1	1	1	1	1	1	1	0	0	1	1	0	0	1	1	1	1	0	1	1
2011	0	1	1	1	0	1	1	1	1	1	1	1	1	1	1	1	0	1	0	1	1	1	1	1	1	0	1	1	1	0	1	1	1	0	1	0	0	0	0	1	0	0	0	1	0	1	1	0	1	1
2012	0	1	1	0	1	1	1	1	1	1	1	1	1	0	1	1	0	1	0	0	0	1	0	1	1	0	1	1	1	0	1	1	1	0	1	0	0	0	0	1	0	0	0	1	0	1	0	0	1	1
2013	1	1	1	1	1	1	1	1	1	1	1	1	1	0	0	0	1	1	0	0	0	1	0	1	1	0	1	1	0	0	1	1	1	0	0	0	0	0	0	1	0	1	0	1	0	1	0	0	1	1
2014	1	1	1	1	0	1	1	1	1	1	1	1	0	0	0	0	1	1	0	0	0	1	0	1	1	0	1	1	0	0	1	1	1	0	0	0	0	0	0	0	0	1	0	1	0	1	0	0	1	1
2015	1	1	1	1	1	1	1	1	1	1	1	1	0	0	0	0	1	1	0	0	0	1	0	1	1	0	1	1	0	0	1	1	1	0	0	0	0	0	0	0	0	1	0	1	0	1	0	0	0	1
2016	1	1	1	0	0	1	1	1	1	1	1	1	0	0	0	0	1	1	0	0	0	1	0	1	1	0	1	1	0	0	1	1	1	0	0	0	0	0	0	0	0	1	0	1	0	1	0	0	0	1
2017	1	1	1	1	1	1	1	1	1	1	1	1	0	0	0	0	1	1	0	0	0	1	0	1	1	0	1	1	0	0	1	1	1	0	0	0	0	0	0	0	0	1	0	1	0	1	0	0	0	1
2018	1	1	1	0	0	1	1	1	1	1	1	1	0	0	0	0	1	1	0	0	0	1	0	1	1	0	1	1	0	0	1	1	1	0	0	0	0	0	0	0	0	1	0	1	0	1	0	0	0	1
2019	1	1	1	1	1	1	1	1	1	1	1	1	0	0	0	0	1	1	0	0	0	1	0	1	1	0	1	1	0	0	1	1	1	0	0	0	0	0	0	0	0	1	0	1	0	1	0	0	0	1

Source: Own calculations.

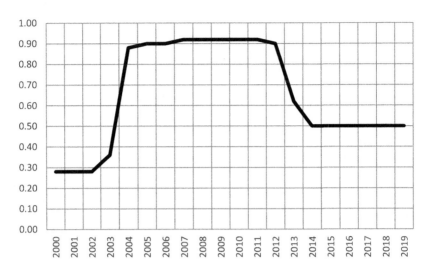

Figure 3.2 HMM convergence function of US states to District of Columbia.

states on the Viterbi path, increased from 0.3 to 0.9. This indicates a tendency towards HMM divergence. On the other hand, in the second part of the analysed period, many US regions changed their states on the Viterbi path downwards from 1 to 0. As a result, the HMM convergence function plotted in Figure 3.2 became downward sloping, which corresponds to HMM convergence. As can be seen, the results obtained are partly in line with the β convergence outcomes because β convergence was confirmed in the second part of the analysed period, i.e. after 2008, whereas in the first part of the period the results for β convergence were ambiguous.

As we can see, the results for HMM convergence partly follow those for β convergence (obviously, some differences appear as well). From the two of considered subperiods, β convergence took place only in that one which begins in 2008. The HMM approach also indicates some convergence tendencies in the final years of the analysis, whereas in the initial years divergence trends were primarily recorded. Instead, the stochastic convergence gives slightly different results. The paths of stochastic divergence were mostly evidenced which do not match with β convergence outcomes. It is caused by the fact that stochastic convergence is verified across all the pairs of countries, whereas HMM convergence is verified against only the richest region.

3.4.3 Chinese provinces

Table 3.12 contains the estimates of the income-level β convergence for the 31 Chinese provinces during 2000–2019 in the same layout as presented in Sections 3.4.1 and 3.4.2. The conclusions obtained in this part of the analysis

Table 3.12 Absolute β convergence at the regional level in China

	(1)	*(2)*	*(3)*
	lnGDP	*lnGDP*	*lnGDP*
lnGDP(−1)	0.945718***	1.050104***	0.884639***
	(−23.15)	(10.83)	(−18.18)
_cons	0.62616***	−0.34471***	1.255929***
	(27.01)	(−8.03)	(19.23)
N	589	248	341

Source: Own calculations. *t*-statistics in parentheses; for the lagged ln GDP the convergence hypotheses tested, i.e. H0: $\beta = 1$.
$^{*} p < 0.05$, $^{**} p < 0.01$, $^{***} p < 0.001$.

are probably the most interesting outcome of the regional convergence analysis. The model constructed based on the entire period suggests that Chinese regions were on an economic growth path consistent with the unconditional β convergence hypothesis. The estimated parameter standing on the initial level of per capita income in the transformed convergence model equals 0.95 and is statistically significantly lower than 1 which suggests a negative relationship between the initial income level and the rate of economic growth among Chinese regions during 2000–2019. Thus, in light of these results, the neoclassical model of economic growth correctly describes the economic growth paths of Chinese provinces.

However, a detailed analysis of the results for China indicates that economic growth paths were completely different in the pre- and post-crisis periods. Namely, before 2008, the results confirmed the existence of a statistically significant income-level divergence, as the estimated parameter on the initial per capita income level for the model calculated for the period until 2008 is greater than 1 and statistically significant. In turn, after the outbreak of the global crisis; that is after 2008, the previous growth trends reversed. In 2009–2019, the provinces of China demonstrated absolute β convergence which was statistically significant.

Such a strong difference in the conclusions between the two considered periods has a couple of implications. At first, it emphasizes the importance of proper care that needs to be taken of the structural break. While in the cases of the USA and Poland there clearly existed the differences between the modelled convergence process before and after the global financial crisis, in the Chinese case failing to take it into consideration would lead to the conclusions that would shade its picture, suggesting its permanence over time while the overall convergence parameter is merely an "average" of the divergence before and convergence after the global crisis. In reality, the "rich were getting richer" in the pre-crisis era faced a spectacular end at the global crisis time. In 2008, the provinces of Shanghai and Beijing were topping the list of the richest Chinese provinces. One year earlier, Beijing was one of the fastest developing provinces with spectacular annual GDP per capita growth. However, in 2008 both of them faced the disappointing approximately 2% increases in the GDP per capita which was by far the worst result of all the Chinese regions that year. This is very much in line with the American path and suggests the overall tendency of the economic leaders suffering the most during the sever crises. No wonder the financial sector, mostly developed in the above-mentioned cities, was trailing in the economy due to the crisis. As a result, this enabled the lower developed provinces to catch up – sadly, not as a result of their true progress but mostly because of the cooling down of the leaders. Still, the results suggest the process' continuation in subsequent years as well.

Interestingly, considering the three analysed countries, the process of post-crises regional convergence seems to be the weakest in the case of Poland which is known for having suffered relatively little due to the global financial crisis but also the weakest economy of the three analysed in this chapter. It suggests that the immediate strengthening of the regional convergence processes after the crises to a large extent is the result of the leaders' cooldown and followers' holding on to their positions; thus, the stronger the leaders, the more observable the levelling-up of the economic development level after a large crises may be.

Tables 3.13–3.15 present the results of the analysis of stochastic convergence at the regional level for China. Their structure is the same as in the case of the tables describing the stochastic convergence of Polish voivodships and US states. With few exceptions, China's provinces did not reveal stochastic convergence. There are very few pairs of provinces for which the stochastic convergence in the model with or without a trend was confirmed. Apparently, the current state and heterogeneity of the Chinese region still do not imply that the real GDP seems to be converging to the same level in the future.

Table 3.16 and Figure 3.3 present the results of verifying the HMM convergence hypothesis for Chinese regions. In the entire analysed period of 2000–2019, the mean outcomes show an increasing divergence of Chinese provinces against Beijing, i.e. the richest province in 2019. The HMM convergence function presented in Figure 3.3 demonstrates a significant change in states on the Viterbi path between 2006 and 2007, i.e. just before the outbreak of the global crisis. During this two-year period, the change in the values of states from 0 to 1 on the Viterbi path occurred in most provinces of China. Comparing the results of HMM convergence for Chinese provinces, US states, and Polish voivodships, a high similarity between the regions of China and Poland can be noticed. In both countries, the HMMs showed the income-level divergence of individual regions against the richest region of a given country (Beijing and mazowieckie voivodship, respectively).

The similarity between China and Poland in terms of HMM convergence results primarily, in our opinion, from the fact that both these countries

Table 3.13 Stochastic convergence of Chinese provinces: *p*-values for the stationarity test of stochastic convergence between the provinces

	Anhui	Beijing	Chongqing	Fujian	Gansu	Guangdong	Guangxi	Guizhou	Hainan	Hebei	Heilongjiang	Henan	Hubei	Hunan	Inner Mongolia	Jiangsu
Anhui		0.9590	0.3035	0.6265	0.9953	0.9904	0.9974	0.8652	0.9833	0.9979	0.9972	0.9746	0.3040	0.9665	0.9423	0.9624
Beijing	0.9590		0.8743	0.9716	0.7973	0.6272	0.7751	0.9743	0.8378	0.8893	0.9566	0.7844	0.9502	0.7938	0.5617	0.7201
Chongqing	0.3035	0.8743		0.2551	0.9482	0.9647	0.9820	0.9941	0.6928	0.9969	0.9966	0.9082	0.1817	0.9701	0.9858	0.9508
Fujian	0.6265	0.9716	0.2551		0.9945	0.9957	0.9529	0.8927	0.9975	0.9985	0.9981	0.8362	0.4986	0.4829	0.7960	0.5852
Gansu	0.9953	0.7973	0.9482	0.9945		0.6740	0.5500	0.9963	0.8464	0.9712	0.9889	0.8035	0.9944	0.7783	0.2043	0.6130
Guangdong	0.9904	0.6272	0.9647	0.9957	0.6740		0.8159	0.9955	0.8574	0.9772	0.9831	0.9436	0.9909	0.8989	0.5377	0.8808
Guangxi	0.9974	0.7751	0.9820	0.9529	0.5500	0.8159		0.9975	0.3064	0.9824	0.9901	0.7893	0.9978	0.8079	0.5458	0.7380
Guizhou	0.8652	0.9743	0.9941	0.8927	0.9963	0.9955	0.9975		0.9908	0.9988	0.9988	0.9918	0.9552	0.9976	0.9949	0.9955
Hainan	0.9833	0.8378	0.6928	0.9975	0.8464	0.8574	0.3064	0.9908		0.9940	0.9972	0.3232	0.9838	0.0873	0.4120	0.0338
Hebei	0.9979	0.8893	0.9969	0.9985	0.9712	0.9772	0.9824	0.9988	0.9940		0.9568	0.9981	0.9983	0.9962	0.2516	0.9976
Heilongjiang	0.9972	0.9566	0.9966	0.9981	0.9889	0.9831	0.9901	0.9988	0.9972	0.9568		0.9954	0.9976	0.9959	0.3405	0.9947
Henan	0.9746	0.7844	0.9082	0.8362	0.8035	0.9436	0.7893	0.9918	0.3232	0.9981	0.9954		0.9699	0.6871	0.7433	0.3082
Hubei	0.3040	0.9502	0.1817	0.4986	0.9944	0.9909	0.9978	0.9552	0.9838	0.9983	0.9976	0.9699		0.9845	0.9319	0.9598
Hunan	0.9665	0.7938	0.9701	0.4829	0.7783	0.8989	0.8079	0.9976	0.0873	0.9962	0.9959	0.6871	0.9845		0.8342	0.5976
Inner Mongolia	0.9423	0.5617	0.9858	0.7960	0.2043	0.5377	0.5458	0.9949	0.4120	0.2516	0.3405	0.7433	0.9319	0.8342		0.8140
Jiangsu	0.9624	0.7201	0.9508	0.5852	0.6130	0.8808	0.7380	0.9955	0.0338	0.9976	0.9947	0.3082	0.9598	0.5976	0.8140	

Table 3.13 (Continued)

	Jiangxi	Jilin	Liaoning	Ningxia	Qinghai	Shaanxi	Shandong	Shanghai	Shanxi	Sichuan	Tianjin	Tibet	Xinjiang	Yunnan	Zhejiang
Anhui	0.9411	0.9957	0.9966	0.9873	0.9977	0.4924	0.9927	0.9477	0.9881	0.8695	0.9960	0.9071	0.9780	0.2414	0.9929
Beijing	0.8474	0.8494	0.8726	0.7203	0.7471	0.7489	0.6847	0.5502	0.5236	0.9340	0.8933	0.9089	0.5381	0.9785	0.4698
Chongqing	0.8895	0.9983	0.9907	0.9984	0.9945	0.7482	0.9965	0.8058	0.9885	0.3381	0.9981	0.8141	0.8152	0.2283	0.9733
Fujian	0.2997	0.9932	0.9955	0.8696	0.9938	0.2082	0.9838	0.9693	0.9667	0.5578	0.9951	0.4916	0.9781	0.2930	0.9923
Gansu	0.9586	0.8657	0.9105	0.3445	0.0214	0.6929	0.2015	0.7608	0.2311	0.9961	0.9511	0.9321	0.5308	0.9962	0.4568
Guangdong	0.9607	0.8974	0.8988	0.7544	0.7487	0.8537	0.7253	0.3593	0.4359	0.9878	0.9588	0.9933	0.0955	0.9899	0.1021
Guangxi	0.9875	0.9820	0.9451	0.1131	0.8798	0.8402	0.9087	0.6944	0.7933	0.9893	0.9892	0.8985	0.5301	0.8846	0.8389
Guizhou	0.9934	0.9991	0.9980	0.9990	0.9988	0.9946	0.9988	0.9551	0.9964	0.9722	0.9989	0.9671	0.9783	0.7009	0.9945
Hainan	0.3858	0.9696	0.9764	0.1688	0.7687	0.1712	0.7895	0.8573	0.6952	0.9810	0.9848	0.5899	0.7608	0.9902	0.7171
Hebei	0.9979	0.7653	0.4671	0.9673	0.9511	0.9881	0.4902	0.6805	0.4376	0.9986	0.8017	0.9970	0.8306	0.9978	0.9643
Heilongjiang	0.9963	0.6056	0.3779	0.9867	0.9833	0.9909	0.8920	0.8616	0.8755	0.9980	0.0992	0.9964	0.9817	0.9981	0.9756
Henan	0.8463	0.9861	0.9796	0.6782	0.9796	0.7123	0.9923	0.6476	0.9378	0.9343	0.9949	0.8090	0.5433	0.7131	0.9382
Hubei	0.9386	0.9972	0.9963	0.9935	0.9983	0.2581	0.9944	0.9273	0.9848	0.8288	0.9969	0.8868	0.9569	0.3803	0.9907
Hunan	0.5288	0.9966	0.9829	0.9608	0.9879	0.6928	0.9883	0.7062	0.9451	0.4976	0.9969	0.8102	0.5936	0.4220	0.9197
Inner Mongolia	0.8924	0.3756	0.2879	0.6409	0.3125	0.9778	0.4448	0.3737	0.5775	0.8474	0.7293	0.8424	0.3045	0.7576	0.6285
Jiangsu	0.7652	0.9920	0.9735	0.7453	0.9565	0.7990	0.9970	0.5268	0.9481	0.8199	0.9967	0.7879	0.3852	0.4434	0.9464

Table 3.13 (Continued)

	Anhui	Beijing	Chongqing	Fujian	Gansu	Guangdong	Guangxi	Guizhou	Hainan	Hebei	Heilongjiang	Henan	Hubei	Hunan	Inner Mongolia	Jiangsu
Jiangxi	0.9411	0.8474	0.8895	0.2997	0.9586	0.9607	0.9875	0.9934	0.3858	0.9979	0.9963	0.8463	0.9386	0.5288	0.8924	0.7652
Jilin	0.9957	0.8494	0.9983	0.9932	0.8657	0.8974	0.9820	0.9991	0.9696	0.7653	0.6056	0.9861	0.9972	0.9966	0.3756	0.9920
Liaoning	0.9966	0.8726	0.9907	0.9955	0.9105	0.8988	0.9451	0.9980	0.9764	0.4671	0.3779	0.9796	0.9963	0.9829	0.2879	0.9735
Ningxia	0.9873	0.7203	0.9984	0.8696	0.3445	0.7544	0.1131	0.9990	0.1688	0.9673	0.9867	0.6782	0.9935	0.9608	0.6409	0.7453
Qinghai	0.9977	0.7471	0.9945	0.9938	0.0214	0.7487	0.8798	0.9988	0.7687	0.9511	0.9833	0.9796	0.9983	0.9879	0.3125	0.9565
Shaanxi	0.4924	0.7489	0.7482	0.2082	0.6929	0.8537	0.8402	0.9946	0.1712	0.9881	0.9909	0.7123	0.2581	0.6928	0.9778	0.7990
Shandong	0.9927	0.6847	0.9965	0.9838	0.2015	0.7253	0.9087	0.9988	0.7895	0.4902	0.8920	0.9923	0.9944	0.9883	0.4448	0.9970
Shanghai	0.9477	0.5502	0.8058	0.9693	0.7608	0.3593	0.6944	0.9551	0.8573	0.6805	0.8616	0.6476	0.9273	0.7062	0.3737	0.5268
Shanxi	0.9881	0.5236	0.9885	0.9667	0.2311	0.4359	0.7933	0.9964	0.6952	0.4376	0.8755	0.9378	0.9848	0.9451	0.5775	0.9481
Sichuan	0.8695	0.9340	0.3381	0.5578	0.9961	0.9878	0.9893	0.9722	0.9810	0.9986	0.9980	0.9343	0.8288	0.4976	0.8474	0.8199
Tianjin	0.9960	0.8933	0.9981	0.9951	0.9511	0.9588	0.9892	0.9989	0.9848	0.8017	0.0992	0.9949	0.9969	0.9969	0.7293	0.9967
Tibet	0.9071	0.9089	0.8141	0.4916	0.9321	0.9933	0.8985	0.9671	0.5899	0.9970	0.9964	0.8090	0.8868	0.8102	0.8424	0.7879
Xinjiang	0.9780	0.5381	0.8152	0.9781	0.5308	0.0955	0.5301	0.9783	0.7608	0.8306	0.9817	0.5433	0.9569	0.5936	0.3045	0.3852
Yunnan	0.2414	0.9785	0.2283	0.2930	0.9962	0.9899	0.8846	0.7009	0.9902	0.9978	0.9981	0.7131	0.3803	0.4220	0.7576	0.4434
Zhejiang	0.9929	0.4698	0.9733	0.9923	0.4568	0.1021	0.8389	0.9945	0.7171	0.9643	0.9756	0.9382	0.9907	0.9197	0.6285	0.9464

Table 3.13 (Continued)

	Jiangxi	Jilin	Liaoning	Ningxia	Qinghai	Shaanxi	Shandong	Shanghai	Shanxi	Sichuan	Tianjin	Tibet	Xinjiang	Yunnan	Zhejiang
Jiangxi		0.9954	0.9875	0.9693	0.9974	0.5149	0.9937	0.7524	0.9796	0.2038	0.9966	0.7766	0.7256	0.2933	0.9734
Jilin	0.9954		0.2179	0.9923	0.9066	0.9959	0.9129	0.7384	0.7832	0.9963	0.9316	0.9861	0.7619	0.9859	0.9004
Liaoning	0.9875	0.2179		0.9303	0.8859	0.9829	0.6226	0.7810	0.7021	0.9956	0.0946	0.9866	0.9283	0.9963	0.8873
Ningxia	0.9693	0.9923	0.9303		0.7688	0.9758	0.9345	0.6216	0.8863	0.9642	0.9950	0.8708	0.4198	0.7716	0.7994
Qinghai	0.9974	0.9066	0.8859	0.7688		0.9691	0.4103	0.6342	0.5437	0.9982	0.9755	0.9779	0.3669	0.9891	0.7441
Shaanxi	0.5149	0.9959	0.9829	0.9758	0.9691		0.9896	0.6544	0.9790	0.0898	0.9964	0.7246	0.5380	0.2002	0.9012
Shandong	0.9937	0.9129	0.6226	0.9345	0.4103	0.9896		0.5046	0.4164	0.9923	0.9929	0.9821	0.3243	0.9629	0.7698
Shanghai	0.7524	0.7384	0.7810	0.6216	0.6342	0.6544	0.5046		0.3488	0.9135	0.7254	0.7989	0.7931	0.9894	0.1641
Shanxi	0.9796	0.7832	0.7021	0.8863	0.5437	0.9790	0.4164	0.3488		0.9847	0.9235	0.9578	0.1307	0.9510	0.5292
Sichuan	0.2038	0.9963	0.9956	0.9642	0.9982	0.0898	0.9923	0.9135	0.9847		0.9965	0.7952	0.9588	0.4581	0.9870
Tianjin	0.9966	0.9316	0.0946	0.9950	0.9755	0.9964	0.9929	0.7254	0.9235	0.9965		0.9943	0.8551	0.9915	0.9666
Tibet	0.7766	0.9861	0.9866	0.8708	0.9779	0.7246	0.9821	0.7989	0.9578	0.7952	0.9943		0.7659	0.9967	0.9944
Xinjiang	0.7256	0.7619	0.9283	0.4198	0.3669	0.5380	0.3243	0.7931	0.1307	0.9588	0.8551	0.7659		0.0286	0.0108
Yunnan	0.2933	0.9859	0.9963	0.7716	0.9891	0.2002	0.9629	0.9894	0.9510	0.4581	0.9915	0.9967	0.0286		0.9783
Zhejiang	0.9734	0.9004	0.8873	0.7994	0.7441	0.9012	0.7698	0.1641	0.5292	0.9870	0.9666	0.9944	0.0108	0.9783	

Source: Own calculations.

The grey cells indicate stochastic convergence.

Table 3.14 Stochastic convergence of Chinese provinces: *p*-values for the trend-stationarity test of stochastic convergence between the provinces

	Anhui	Beijing	Chongqing	Fujian	Gansu	Guangdong	Guangxi	Guizhou	Hainan	Hebei	Heilongjiang	Henan	Hubei	Hunan	Inner Mongolia	Jiangsu
Anhui		0.7240	0.8329	0.8019	0.9719	0.6485	0.9952	0.3109	0.7113	0.9440	0.9657	0.8917	0.6623	0.9185	0.9968	0.8888
Beijing	0.7240		0.9700	0.4577	0.9781	0.9889	0.9901	0.5087	0.8762	0.9943	0.9908	0.9611	0.7853	0.9827	1.0000	0.9870
Chongqing	0.8329	0.9700		0.9937	0.6575	0.7390	0.7852	0.5171	0.5415	0.6997	0.8928	0.7433	0.8400	0.0014	0.9955	0.5406
Fujian	0.8019	0.4577	0.9937		0.9907	0.5403	0.9970	0.6356	0.9937	0.9836	0.9887	0.9581	0.9969	0.9946	1.0000	0.9812
Gansu	0.9719	0.9781	0.6575	0.9907		0.8155	0.7689	0.7893	0.9331	0.2477	0.7404	0.7984	0.9383	0.5904	0.9961	0.4739
Guangdong	0.6485	0.9889	0.7390	0.5403	0.8155		0.9661	0.1127	0.5492	0.9894	0.9840	0.6005	0.4357	0.9224	0.9970	0.9473
Guangxi	0.9952	0.9901	0.7852	0.9970	0.7689	0.9661		0.8631	0.9925	0.5029	0.4532	0.9749	0.9926	0.8365	0.9921	0.9356
Guizhou	0.3109	0.5087	0.5171	0.6356	0.7893	0.1127	0.8631		0.1521	0.6206	0.9254	0.5170	0.3648	0.1531	0.9904	0.3235
Hainan	0.7113	0.8762	0.5415	0.9937	0.9331	0.5492	0.9925	0.1521		0.8907	0.9745	0.8318	0.4158	0.5356	0.9957	0.7286
Hebei	0.9440	0.9943	0.6997	0.9836	0.2477	0.9894	0.5029	0.6206	0.8907		0.9321	0.9682	0.8793	0.8980	0.9947	0.9509
Heilongjiang	0.9657	0.9908	0.8928	0.9887	0.7404	0.9840	0.4532	0.9254	0.9745	0.9321		0.9749	0.9533	0.9473	0.9472	0.9672
Henan	0.8917	0.9611	0.7433	0.9581	0.7984	0.6005	0.9749	0.5170	0.8318	0.9682	0.9749		0.7838	0.9533	1.0000	0.7208
Hubei	0.6623	0.7853	0.8400	0.9969	0.9383	0.4357	0.9926	0.3648	0.4158	0.8793	0.9533	0.7838		0.7102	0.9967	0.7282
Hunan	0.9185	0.9827	0.0014	0.9946	0.5904	0.9224	0.8365	0.1531	0.5356	0.8980	0.9473	0.9118	0.7102		0.9963	0.8296
Inner Mongolia	0.9968	1.0000	0.9955	1.0000	0.9961	0.9970	0.9921	0.9904	0.9957	0.9947	0.9472	1.0000	0.9967	0.9963		0.9966
Jiangsu	0.8888	0.9870	0.5406	0.9812	0.4739	0.9473	0.9356	0.3235	0.7286	0.9509	0.9672	0.7208	0.7282	0.8296	0.9966	

Table 3.14 (Continued)

	Jiangxi	Jilin	Liaoning	Ningxia	Qinghai	Shaanxi	Shandong	Shanghai	Shanxi	Sichuan	Tianjin	Tibet	Xinjiang	Yunnan	Zhejiang
Anhui	0.9393	0.9942	0.9853	0.9868	0.9837	0.9917	0.9736	0.9089	0.7530	0.5451	0.9826	0.6382	0.6895	0.9879	0.4575
Beijing	0.9750	0.9963	0.9884	0.9941	0.9928	0.9929	0.9964	0.5176	0.9859	0.7709	0.9959	0.8635	0.7031	0.3056	0.9921
Chongqing	0.5263	0.9947	0.9338	0.9626	0.7757	0.9304	0.9141	0.9828	0.4905	0.7688	0.9751	0.9635	0.6116	0.9950	0.4648
Fujian	0.9917	0.9968	0.9917	0.9966	0.9945	0.9970	0.9924	0.7819	0.8415	0.9923	0.9927	0.1738	0.7768	0.9036	0.2724
Gansu	0.7809	0.9907	0.9004	0.7268	0.3269	0.7836	0.8152	0.9927	0.2464	0.9619	0.9557	0.9806	0.9299	0.9969	0.5601
Guangdong	0.7267	0.9957	0.9777	0.9845	0.9796	0.9681	0.9962	1.0000	0.8919	0.3432	0.9945	0.9811	0.4162	0.8310	0.4754
Guangxi	0.9877	0.9825	0.8081	0.3967	0.3757	0.5121	0.7797	0.9961	0.5501	0.9920	0.9176	0.9945	0.9634	1.0000	0.9252
Guizhou	0.4124	0.9951	0.9581	0.8756	0.7393	0.8985	0.8842	0.7630	0.3388	0.4996	0.9720	0.1312	0.4535	0.9607	0.0645
Hainan	0.7082	0.9964	0.9742	0.9852	0.9676	0.9818	0.9734	0.9705	0.6164	0.6918	0.9873	0.8605	0.6432	0.9955	0.1613
Hebei	0.8594	0.9950	0.8038	0.6376	0.3743	0.3290	0.9690	0.9968	0.4429	0.9007	0.9922	0.9946	0.9129	0.9908	0.9771
Heilongjiang	0.9413	0.9949	0.5029	0.7039	0.5378	0.6308	0.7968	0.9953	0.8717	0.9692	0.9853	0.9934	0.9684	0.9929	0.9734
Henan	0.7826	0.9951	0.9739	0.9726	0.9829	0.9687	0.9929	0.9956	0.5034	0.7524	0.9899	0.9783	0.7436	0.9865	0.2945
Hubei	0.7975	0.9950	0.9783	0.9854	0.9661	0.9892	0.9617	0.9366	0.5851	0.3991	0.9802	0.7204	0.6125	0.9962	0.1953
Hunan	0.6313	0.9960	0.9519	0.9889	0.9296	0.9416	0.9655	0.9925	0.7047	0.6913	0.9861	0.9920	0.7012	0.9953	0.8065
Inner Mongolia	0.9970	0.7404	0.8284	0.9918	0.9960	0.9922	0.9821	1.0000	0.9919	0.9966	0.6934	0.9970	0.9964	1.0000	0.9970
Jiangsu	0.4371	0.9951	0.9623	0.9562	0.9316	0.9030	0.9925	0.9970	0.5659	0.6908	0.9901	0.9927	0.6734	0.9903	0.4780

Table 3.14 (Continued)

	Anhui	Beijing	Chongqing	Fujian	Gansu	Guangdong	Guangxi	Guizhou	Hainan	Hebei	Heilongjiang	Henan	Hubei	Hunan	Inner Mongolia	Jiangsu
Jiangxi	0.9393	0.9750	0.5263	0.9917	0.7809	0.7267	0.9877	0.4124	0.7082	0.8594	0.9413	0.7826	0.7975	0.6313	0.9970	0.4371
Jilin	0.9942	0.9963	0.9947	0.9968	0.9907	0.9957	0.9825	0.9951	0.9964	0.9950	0.9949	0.9951	0.9950	0.9960	0.7404	0.9951
Liaoning	0.9853	0.9884	0.9338	0.9917	0.9004	0.9777	0.8081	0.9581	0.9742	0.8038	0.5029	0.9739	0.9783	0.9519	0.8284	0.9623
Ningxia	0.9868	0.9941	0.9626	0.9966	0.7268	0.9845	0.3967	0.8756	0.9852	0.6376	0.7039	0.9726	0.9854	0.9889	0.9918	0.9562
Qinghai	0.9837	0.9928	0.7757	0.9945	0.3269	0.9796	0.3757	0.7393	0.9676	0.3743	0.5378	0.9829	0.9661	0.9296	0.9960	0.9316
Shaanxi	0.9917	0.9929	0.9304	0.9970	0.7836	0.9681	0.5121	0.8985	0.9818	0.3290	0.6308	0.9687	0.9892	0.9416	0.9922	0.9030
Shandong	0.9736	0.9964	0.9141	0.9924	0.8152	0.9962	0.7797	0.8842	0.9734	0.9690	0.7968	0.9929	0.9617	0.9655	0.9821	0.9925
Shanghai	0.9089	0.5176	0.9828	0.7819	0.9927	1.0000	0.9961	0.7630	0.9705	0.9968	0.9953	0.9956	0.9366	0.9925	1.0000	0.9970
Shanxi	0.7530	0.9859	0.4905	0.8415	0.2464	0.8919	0.5501	0.3388	0.6164	0.4429	0.8717	0.5034	0.5851	0.7047	0.9919	0.5659
Sichuan	0.5451	0.7709	0.7688	0.9923	0.9619	0.3432	0.9920	0.4996	0.6918	0.9007	0.9692	0.7524	0.3991	0.6913	0.9966	0.6908
Tianjin	0.9826	0.9959	0.9751	0.9927	0.9557	0.9945	0.9176	0.9720	0.9873	0.9922	0.9853	0.9899	0.9802	0.9861	0.6934	0.9901
Tibet	0.6382	0.8635	0.9635	0.1738	0.9806	0.9811	0.9945	0.1312	0.8605	0.9946	0.9934	0.9783	0.7204	0.9920	0.9970	0.9927
Xinjiang	0.6895	0.7031	0.6116	0.7768	0.9299	0.4162	0.9634	0.4535	0.6432	0.9129	0.9684	0.7436	0.6125	0.7012	0.9964	0.6734
Yunnan	0.9879	0.3056	0.9950	0.9036	0.9969	0.8310	1.0000	0.9607	0.9955	0.9908	0.9929	0.9865	0.9962	0.9953	1.0000	0.9903
Zhejiang	0.4575	0.9921	0.4648	0.2724	0.5601	0.4754	0.9252	0.0645	0.1613	0.9771	0.9734	0.2945	0.1953	0.8065	0.9970	0.4780

Table 3.14 (Continued)

	Jiangxi	Jilin	Liaoning	Ningxia	Qinghai	Shaanxi	Shandong	Shanghai	Shanxi	Sichuan	Tianjin	Tibet	Xinjiang	Yunnan	Zhejiang
Jiangxi		0.9945	0.9593	0.9817	0.9741	0.9780	0.9640	0.9922	0.5071	0.7379	0.9821	0.9777	0.5621	0.9963	0.3444
Jilin	0.9945		0.2593	0.9909	0.9860	0.9834	0.9857	0.9968	0.9739	0.9958	0.2993	0.9967	0.9928	0.9969	0.9940
Liaoning	0.9593	0.2593		0.7710	0.8368	0.8387	0.7526	0.9926	0.8848	0.9811	0.3971	0.9919	0.9868	0.9955	0.9696
Ningxia	0.9817	0.9909	0.7710		0.5612	0.2941	0.8255	0.9958	0.6840	0.9900	0.9580	0.9950	0.9603	0.9967	0.9650
Qinghai	0.9741	0.9860	0.8368	0.5612		0.3084	0.7754	0.9963	0.5930	0.9785	0.9484	0.9953	0.9795	0.9970	0.9551
Shaanxi	0.9780	0.9834	0.8387	0.2941	0.3084		0.7394	0.9951	0.3895	0.9959	0.9217	0.9939	0.9729	1.0000	0.9072
Shandong	0.9640	0.9857	0.7526	0.8255	0.7754	0.7394		1.0000	0.7260	0.9724	0.9775	0.9964	0.9727	0.9946	0.9927
Shanghai	0.9922	0.9968	0.9926	0.9958	0.9963	0.9951	1.0000		0.9894	0.9426	0.9967	0.9606	0.9426	0.4379	0.9927
Shanxi	0.5071	0.9739	0.8848	0.6840	0.5930	0.3895	0.7260	0.9894		0.5071	0.9752	0.9714	0.7486	0.9281	0.8758
Sichuan	0.7379	0.9958	0.9811	0.9900	0.9785	0.9959	0.9724	0.9426	0.5071		0.9847	0.7313	0.5497	0.9970	0.0923
Tianjin	0.9821	0.2993	0.3971	0.9580	0.9484	0.9217	0.9775	0.9967	0.9752	0.9847		0.9958	0.9841	0.9940	0.9933
Tibet	0.9777	0.9967	0.9919	0.9950	0.9953	0.9939	0.9964	0.9606	0.9714	0.7313	0.9958		0.6679	0.0455	0.9776
Xinjiang	0.5621	0.9928	0.9868	0.9603	0.9795	0.9729	0.9727	0.9426	0.7486	0.5497	0.9841	0.6679		0.9661	0.1865
Yunnan	0.9963	0.9969	0.9955	0.9967	0.9970	1.0000	0.9946	0.4379	0.9281	0.9970	0.9940	0.0455	0.9661		0.7267
Zhejiang	0.3444	0.9940	0.9696	0.9650	0.9551	0.9072	0.9927	0.9927	0.8758	0.0923	0.9933	0.9776	0.1865	0.7267	

Source: Own calculations.
The grey cells indicate stochastic convergence.

Table 3.15 Stochastic convergence of Chinese provinces: a summary

Province	Stochastic convergence without trend		Stochastic convergence with trend	
	The number of Chinese provinces to/from which a given province is:			
	Converging	Diverging	Converging	Diverging
Anhui	0	30	0	30
Beijing	0	30	0	30
Chongqing	0	30	1	29
Fujian	0	30	0	30
Gansu	1	29	0	30
Guangdong	0	30	0	30
Guangxi	0	30	0	30
Guizhou	0	30	0	30
Hainan	1	29	0	30
Hebei	0	30	0	30
Heilongjiang	0	30	0	30
Henan	0	30	0	30
Hubei	0	30	0	30
Hunan	0	30	1	29
Inner Mongolia	0	30	0	30
Jiangsu	1	29	0	30
Jiangxi	0	30	0	30
Jilin	0	30	0	30
Liaoning	0	30	0	30
Ningxia	0	30	0	30
Qinghai	1	29	0	30
Shaanxi	0	30	0	30
Shandong	0	30	0	30
Shanghai	0	30	0	30
Shanxi	0	30	0	30
Sichuan	0	30	0	30
Tianjin	0	30	0	30
Tibet	1	29	1	29
Xinjiang	1	29	0	30
Yunnan	1	29	1	29
Zhejiang	1	29	0	30

Source: Own calculations.

are monocentric, whereas the USA is the polycentric country. In the USA, there are many important regions and important large cities which constitute the core of the American economy. It is at least New York, Chicago, and California which are treated as well prospering regions, being headquarters of numerous nationwide and international companies. From the point of view of an average citizen, it needn't be Washington, DC to settle to get the most profitable job – even better economic conditions to live are offered by New York or California. The opposite situation exists in Poland and – partly – China. In Poland, the highest salaries prevail in the capital

Table 3.16 HMM convergence of Chinese provinces: Viterbi paths

Year	Anhui	Chongqing	Fujian	Gansu	Guangdong	Guangxi	Guizhou	Hainan	Hebei	Heilongjiang	Henan	Hubei	Hunan	Inner Mongolia	Jiangsu	Jiangxi	Jilin	Liaoning	Ningxia	Qinghai	Shaanxi	Shandong	Shanghai	Shanxi	Sichuan	Tianjin	Tibet	Xinjiang	Yunnan	Zhejiang
2000	○	○	○	○	○	○	○	○	○	○	○	○	○	—	○	○	—	—	○	○	○	—	○	○	○	○	○	○	○	○
2001	○	○	○	○	○	○	○	○	○	○	○	○	○	—	○	○	—	—	○	○	○	—	○	○	○	○	○	○	○	○
2002	○	○	○	○	○	○	○	○	○	○	○	○	○	—	○	○	—	—	○	○	○	—	○	○	○	○	○	○	○	○
2003	○	○	○	○	○	○	○	○	○	○	○	○	○	—	○	○	—	—	○	○	○	—	○	○	○	○	○	○	○	○
2004	○	○	○	○	○	○	○	○	○	○	○	○	○	○	○	○	—	—	○	○	○	—	○	○	○	○	○	○	○	○
2005	—	○	○	○	○	○	○	○	○	○	○	○	○	○	○	○	—	—	○	○	○	—	○	○	○	○	○	○	○	○
2006	—	—	—	○	○	○	○	○	○	○	○	○	○	○	○	○	○	○	○	○	○	○	○	○	○	○	○	○	○	○
2007	—	—	—	—	—	—	—	—	—	—	—	—	—	○	○	—	○	○	—	—	—	○	—	—	—	○	—	—	—	—
2008	—	—	—	—	—	—	—	—	—	—	—	—	—	○	—	—	○	○	—	—	—	○	—	—	—	○	—	—	—	—
2009	—	—	—	—	—	—	—	—	—	—	—	—	—	○	—	—	○	○	—	—	—	○	—	—	—	○	—	—	—	—
2010	—	—	—	—	—	—	—	—	—	—	—	—	—	○	—	—	○	○	—	—	—	○	—	—	—	○	—	—	—	—
2011	—	—	—	—	—	—	—	—	—	—	—	—	—	○	—	—	○	○	—	—	—	○	—	—	—	○	—	—	—	—
2012	—	—	—	—	—	—	—	—	—	—	—	—	—	○	—	—	○	○	—	—	—	○	—	—	—	○	—	—	—	—
2013	—	—	—	—	—	—	—	—	—	—	—	—	—	○	—	—	○	○	—	—	—	○	—	—	—	○	—	—	—	—
2014	—	—	—	—	—	—	—	—	—	—	—	—	—	○	—	—	—	○	—	—	—	○	—	—	—	○	—	—	—	○
2015	—	—	○	—	—	—	—	—	—	—	—	—	—	○	—	—	—	○	—	—	—	○	—	—	—	○	—	—	—	○
2016	—	○	○	—	—	—	—	—	—	—	—	—	—	○	○	—	—	—	—	—	—	—	—	—	—	—	—	—	—	○
2017	—	○	○	—	—	—	—	—	—	—	—	—	—	—	○	—	—	—	—	—	—	—	—	—	—	—	—	—	—	○
2018	—	○	○	—	—	—	—	—	—	—	—	—	—	—	○	—	—	—	—	—	—	—	—	—	—	—	—	—	—	○
2019	—	○	○	—	—	—	—	—	—	—	—	—	—	—	○	—	—	—	—	—	—	—	—	—	—	—	—	—	—	○

Source: Own calculations.

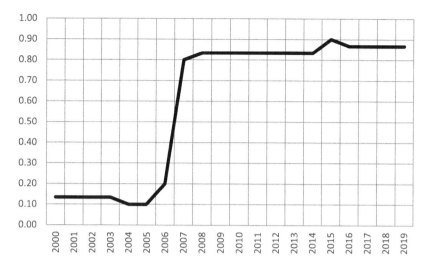

Figure 3.3 HMM convergence function of Chinese provinces to the province of Beijing.

of Warsaw. Warsaw attracts many young people from the whole country because it offers the best living conditions from the economic point of view, strengthening the divergence tendencies at the regional level. China is not so monocentric like Poland because there is, among others, Shanghai which is also the city of a similar rank as Beijing; however, the degree of polycentrism in China is relatively low (many eastern parts are underdeveloped), and thus, divergence tendencies on the basis of HMM were identified.

3.5 Regional convergence: main conclusions from the analysis

This study examines economic convergence in Poland, the USA, and China at the regional level. The analysis covers 16 voivodships in Poland, 51 US regions (50 states and District of Columbia), and 31 Chinese provinces. Various definitions of convergence are incorporated using a variety of estimation techniques. We begin with the standard concept of absolute and conditional β convergence (conditional convergence is examined only in the case of Poland). Then, a few unconventional measures of convergence are tested: stochastic convergence and the convergence based on HMMs. The analysis covers the 2000–2019 period (for Poland, 2000–2017).

In the majority of cases, the results indicate the lack of regional convergence. However, the exact outcomes differ across the individual methods applied. The most frequent confirmation of the existence of catching-up took place for β type of convergence. On the other side, the stochastic analysis indicated predominantly regional income-level divergence.

Divergence against the richest region was also the most frequent conclusion from HMMs. Hence, the outcomes obtained for stochastic and HMM convergence give an interesting supplementary picture of the catching-up process.

Comparing the results of β convergence for Poland, China, and the USA, we see the lack of stability of this process over time. The outcomes for the entire period are not the same as those for individual subperiods. This applies to Polish voivodships, US states, and Chinese provinces. Such findings imply the need to analyse the stability of the results over time and to verify macroeconomic phenomena also in shorter subperiods and the relevance of taking structural breaks into consideration. Models estimated on long time series produce aggregated results which might be misleading with the key example of Chinese provinces. On their basis, it is difficult to characterize in detail economic growth paths in shorter time intervals, as the conclusions drawn on the basis of models estimated for much longer periods may not be reliable for shorter subperiods. This is especially true if there was a strong structural break during the studied period, usually caused by some kind of an external shock (e.g. a global crisis or, in future research, the coronavirus pandemic that emerged in 2020). The approach presented in this book (also in the next chapter), where we estimate β convergence models also for shorter subperiods, taking into account the structural break due to the global crisis, seems to be entirely justified.

Different convergence models may produce different results in terms of the characteristics of the convergence phenomenon. The various approaches presented in this book should be regarded as complementary, not substitutable for each other. For example, the regional data for China show that the existence of β income-level convergence does not necessarily imply that there is stochastic or HMM convergence. This is a consequence of the existence of different definitions of the phenomenon of convergence, which do not necessarily mean the same. It is worth emphasizing here that the results of β convergence are average outcomes for the entire studied sample, i.e. in our case all regions of a given country. On the other hand, the stochastic convergence study analyses individual regions separately in the form of pairwise comparisons. In turn, in HMM convergence, individual regions are compared to one selected (richest) region. Therefore, the results of verification of individual types of convergence do not have to be the same and in order to get a complete picture of the catching-up process, convergence should be tested using different methods. Naturally, this is due to the fact that while the general concept of convergence is clear, the detailed definitions in finite time horizon may lead to contradictory conclusions.

The outcomes are important for policymakers. The results of stochastic and HMM convergence show the individual paths according to which the individual regions are developing. Using the results of the β convergence hypothesis and the factors affecting the process of economic growth and real income-level convergence, the study gives hints about which regions should be the main focus of policymakers to decrease the country's income differences and what to do to achieve this goal.

Regional convergence studies should be continued. They give a slightly different picture of the catching-up process compared to the analyses at the national level. National growth paths need not translate in the same way to the growth paths of individual regions. One of the directions of future research is also the application of these tools to examine convergence at the most disaggregated regional level (e.g. NUTS3 or poviats in Poland).

Notes

1 NUTS2 regions.
2 The review of the literature does not include country-level studies on convergence. Such studies are numerous (see, e.g., Rapacki and Próchniak, 2019 and Matkowski, Próchniak and Rapacki, 2016 for the EU countries; or Rapacki and Próchniak, 2007 for a wider group of transition economies).
3 Seven east-coastal provinces (Shanghai, Tianjin, Jiangsu, Zhejiang, Guangdong, Shandong, and Fujian) and Inner Mongolia.
4 Regions are administrative units: voivodships in Poland, states in the USA, and provinces in China. The richest region being the point of reference is the mazowieckie voivodship in Poland, District of Columbia in the USA, and Beijing in China. As we can see, the richest regions are the ones with a capital city.

References

Bal-Domańska, B. (2013). Procesy konwergencji wydajności pracy w regionach Unii Europejskiej. *Wiadomości Statystyczne*, 2, pp. 1–14.

Barro, R. and Sala-i-Martin, X. (2003). *Economic Growth*. Cambridge – London: The MIT Press.

Baum, L.E., Petrie, T., Soules, G. and Weiss, N. (1970). A Maximization Technique Occurring in the Statistical Analysis of Probabilistic Functions of Markov Chains. *Annals of Mathematical Statistics*, 41(1), pp. 164–171, doi: 10.1214/aoms/1177697196.

Bernard, A.B., and Durlauf, S.N. (1995). Convergence in International Output. *Journal of Applied Econometrics*, 10(2), pp. 97–108.

Bernardelli, M. (2013). Nieklasyczne modele Markowa w analizie cykli koniunktury gospodarczej w Polsce. *Roczniki Kolegium Analiz Ekonomicznych SGH*, 30, pp. 59–74.

Bernardelli, M., Próchniak, M. and Witkowski, B. (2017). Cycle and Income-Level Convergence in the EU Countries: An Identification of Turning Points Based on the Hidden Markov Models. *Roczniki Kolegium Analiz Ekonomicznych SGH*, 47, pp. 27–42.

Bernardelli, M., Próchniak, M. and Witkowski, B. (2018). Przydatność ukrytych modeli Markowa do oceny podobieństwa krajów w zakresie synchronizacji wahań cyklicznych i wyrównywania się poziomów dochodu. *Roczniki Kolegium Analiz Ekonomicznych SGH*, 53, 77–96.

Blundell, R. and Bond, S. (1998). Initial Conditions and Moment Restrictions in Dynamic Panel Data Models. *Journal of Econometrics*, 87(1), pp. 115–143, doi: 10.1016/s0304-4076(98)00009-8.

Borowiec, J. (2015). Konwergencja regionalna w Unii Europejskiej. *Prace Naukowe Uniwersytetu Ekonomicznego we Wrocławiu*, 380, pp. 15–25.

Borowiec, J. (2017). Konwergencja regionalna w regionach słabiej rozwiniętych Unii Europejskiej w latach 2001–2014. *Prace Naukowe Uniwersytetu Ekonomicznego we Wrocławiu*, 466, pp. 50–62.

Cappé, O., Moulines, E. and Ryden, T. (2005). *Inference in Hidden Markov Models*. New York: Springer-Verlag.

Czudec, A. and Kata, R. (2016). Processes of Regional Convergence in Poland in the Context of the Use of European Union Funds. *Lex Localis – Journal of Local Self-Government*, 14(4), pp. 715–737, doi: 10.4335/14.4.715-737(2016).

Godziszewski, B., Kruszka, M. and Puziak, M. (2013). Income Distribution and Regional Convergence in Poland and the European Union. *Olsztyn Economic Journal*, 8/1, pp. 45–60.

Hamilton, J.D. (1994). *Time Series Analysis*. Princeton, NJ: Princeton University Press.

Kinfemichael, B. and Morshed, A.K.M.M. (2019). Convergence of Labor Productivity Across the US States. *Economic Modelling*, 76, pp. 270–280, doi: 10.1016/j.econmod.2018.08.008.

Koskinen, L. and Öller, L.E. (2004). A Classifying Procedure for Signaling Turning Points. *Journal of Forecasting*, 23(3), pp. 197–214, doi: 10.1002/for.905.

Kusideł, E. (2013). *Konwergencja gospodarcza w Polsce i jej znaczenie w osiąganiu celów polityki spójności*. Łódź: Wydawnictwo Uniwersytetu Łódzkiego.

Łaźniewska, E. and Górecki, T. (2012). Analiza konwergencji podregionów za pomocą łańcuchów Markowa. *Wiadomości Statystyczne*, 5, pp. 1–9.

Markowska-Przybyła, U. (2010). Konwergencja regionalna w Polsce w latach 1999–2007. *Gospodarka Narodowa*, 11–12, pp. 85–110.

Markowska-Przybyła, U. (2011). Integracja a konwergencja realna. Konwergencja regionalna w Polsce według klasycznych i alternatywnych metod badań. *Ekonomia*, 16, pp. 77–97.

Matkowski, Z. and Próchniak, M. (2013). Real Income Convergence. In: M.A. Weresa, ed., *Poland. Competitiveness Report 2013. National and Regional Dimensions*. Warsaw: World Economy Research Institute, SGH Warsaw School of Economics, pp. 44–64.

Matkowski, Z., Próchniak, M. and Rapacki, R. (2016). Real Income Convergence between Central Eastern and Western Europe: Past, Present, and Prospects. *Ekonomista*, 6, pp. 853–892.

Miles, W. (2020). Regional Convergence – And Divergence – In the US. *Research in Economics*, 74(2), pp. 131–139, doi: 10.1016/j.rie.2020.02.005.

Pesaran, M.H. (2007). A Pair-wise Approach to Testing for Output and Growth Convergence. *Journal of Econometrics*, 138(1), pp. 312–355, doi: 10.1016/j.jeconom.2006.05.024.

Piętak, Ł. (2015). Convergence Across Polish Regions, 2005–2011. *Comparative Economic Research*, 18(2), pp. 99–118, doi: 10.1515/cer-2015-0014.

Próchniak, M. (2004). Analiza zbieżności wzrostu gospodarczego województw w latach 1995–2000. *Gospodarka Narodowa*, 3, pp. 27–44.

Rapacki, R. and Próchniak, M. (2007). Konwergencja beta i sigma w krajach postsocjalistycznych w latach 1990–2005. *Bank i Kredyt*, 8–9, pp. 42–60.

Rapacki, R. and Próchniak, M. (2019). EU Membership and Economic Growth: Empirical Evidence for the CEE Countries. *European Journal of Comparative Economics*, 16(1), pp. 3–40, doi: 10.25428/1824–2979/201901-3-40.

Sakamoto, H. and Islam, N. (2008). Convergence Across Chinese Provinces: An Analysis Using Markov Transition Matrix. *China Economic Review*, 19(1), pp. 66–79, doi: 10.1016/j.chieco.2006.07.002.

Tian, X., Zhang, X., Zhou, Y. and Yu, X. (2016). Regional Income Inequality in China Revisited: A Perspective from Club Convergence. *Economic Modelling*, 56, pp. 50–58, doi: 10.1016/j.econmod.2016.02.028.

Tokarski, T. and Gajewski, P. (2003). *Real Convergence in Poland. A Regional Approach*. Paper presented at the NBP Conference "Potential Output and Barriers to Growth", Zalesie Górne (Poland). Available at: https://www.nbp.pl/konferencje/zalesie/pdf/tokarski_gajewski.pdf [Accessed 15 Sep. 2019].

Tylec, T. (2017). Konwergencja gospodarcza na poziomie regionalnym w wybranych grupach państw Unii Europejskiej w latach 2000–2014. *Studia Ekonomiczne. Zeszyty Naukowe Uniwersytetu Ekonomicznego w Katowicach*, 319, pp. 259–267.

Viterbi, A. (1967). Error Bounds for Convolutional Codes and an Asymptotically Optimum Decoding Algorithm. *IEEE Transactions on Information Theory*, 13, pp. 260–269.

Wędrowska, E. and Wojciechowska, K. (2015). Konwergencja gospodarcza w województwach Polski w latach 2000–2012. *Roczniki Kolegium Analiz Ekonomicznych*, 36, pp. 403–412.

Wolszczak-Derlacz, J. (2009). The Impact of Internal and International Migration on Regional Convergence in Poland. In: M. Duszczyk, M. Lesińska, eds., *Współczesne migracje: dylematy Europy i Polski*. Warszawa: Ośrodek Badań nad Migracjami Uniwersytetu Warszawskiego, pp. 92–117.

Wójcik, P. (2004). Konwergencja regionów Polski w latach 1990–2001. *Gospodarka Narodowa*, 11–12, pp. 69–86.

Wójcik, P. (2008). Dywergencja czy konwergencja: dynamika rozwoju polskich regionów. *Studia Regionalne i Lokalne*, 9, pp. 41–60.

Wójcik, P. (2018). *Metody pomiaru realnej konwergencji gospodarczej w ujęciu regionalnym i lokalnym. Konwergencja równoległa*. Warszawa: Wydawnictwa Uniwersytetu Warszawskiego.

4 Conventional convergence in the worldwide perspective

4.1 Introduction

This chapter presents the convergence analysis in the various groups of countries from the whole world. We consider ten groups of countries, while some of the countries belong to more than one of them. The distinction is made based on the geographical, political, or historical criteria. We consider the following groups:

- European Union (EU28),
- Europe,
- North Africa and the Middle East,
- sub-Saharan Africa,
- South America,
- Caribbean,
- South-East Asia,
- Australia and Oceania,
- post-socialist countries,
- OECD countries.

The EU28 group includes 28 European Union countries (as of 2019, that is with the UK[1]). The exact list of countries included in the remaining groups is presented in Table 4.1.

For each group, the convergence analysis is carried out using the same methodology based on the examination of β convergence both in absolute and conditional terms. The calculations are made for the whole period (1995–2019) as well as for two shorter subperiods – before the global crisis (i.e. till 2008) and after it (from 2009 onwards). Such an analysis makes it possible to carry out a comparative analysis in four dimensions:

- between groups of countries,
- before and after the global crisis,
- absolute versus conditional convergence.

Table 4.1 Countries included in the individual groups

Europe	North Africa and the Middle East	Sub-Saharan Africa	South America	Caribbean	South-East Asia	Australia and Oceania	Post-socialist countries	OECD countries
Albania	Algeria	Angola	Argentina	Antigua and Barbuda	Bangladesh	Australia	Albania	Australia
Austria	Bahrain	Benin	Bolivia	Aruba	Bhutan	Fiji	Armenia	Austria
Belarus	Egypt	Botswana	Brazil	Barbados	Brunei Darussalam	Kiribati	Azerbaijan	Belgium
Bosnia and Herzegovina	Israel	Burkina Faso	Chile	Belize	Cambodia	Micronesia	Belarus	Canada
Bulgaria	Jordan	Burundi	Colombia	Costa Rica	China	New Zealand	Bosnia and Herzegovina	Chile
Croatia	Kuwait	Cabo Verde	Ecuador	Dominica	Hong Kong	Papua New Guinea	Bulgaria	Czech Rep.
Cyprus	Lebanon	Cameroon	Guyana	Dominican Rep.	India	Samoa	Croatia	Denmark
Czech Rep.	Libya	Central African Rep.	Paraguay	El Salvador	Indonesia	Solomon Islands	Czech Rep.	Estonia
Denmark	Morocco	Chad	Peru	Grenada	Iran	Tonga	Estonia	Finland
Estonia	Oman	Comoros	Suriname	Guatemala	Japan	Tuvalu	Georgia	France
Finland	Qatar	Côte d'Ivoire	Uruguay	Haiti	Korea	Vanuatu	Hungary	Germany
France	Saudi Arabia	Dem. Rep. of the Congo	Venezuela	Honduras	Lao P.D.R.		Kazakhstan	Greece
Germany	Tunisia	Djibouti		Jamaica	Malaysia		Kyrgyz Rep.	Hungary
Greece	United Arab Emirates	Equatorial Guinea		Mexico	Maldives		Latvia	Iceland
Hungary	Yemen	Eritrea		Nicaragua	Mongolia		Lithuania	Ireland
Iceland		Eswatini		Panama	Myanmar		Moldova	Israel
Ireland		Ethiopia		Puerto Rico	Nepal		Montenegro	Italy
Italy		Gabon		St. Kitts and Nevis	Pakistan			Japan
Latvia		Ghana		St. Lucia	Philippines			Korea
Lithuania		Guinea		St. Vincent and the Grenadines	Singapore			Latvia
Luxembourg		Guinea-Bissau		The Bahamas	Sri Lanka			Lithuania
Malta		Kenya		Trinidad and Tobago	Taiwan			Luxembourg
Moldova		Lesotho			Thailand			Mexico
Montenegro		Madagascar			Vietnam			Netherlands
Netherlands		Malawi						New Zealand
North Macedonia								Norway
								Poland

(Continued)

Europe	North Africa and the Middle East	Sub-Saharan Africa	South America	Caribbean	South-East Asia	Australia and Oceania	Post-socialist countries	OECD countries
Norway		Mali						Portugal
Poland		Mauritania						Slovak Rep.
Portugal		Mauritius						Slovenia
Romania		Mozambique						Spain
Russia		Namibia						Sweden
Serbia		Niger						Switzerland
Slovak Rep.		Nigeria						Turkey
Slovenia		Rep. of Congo						UK
Spain		Rwanda						USA
Sweden		São Tomé and Príncipe						
Switzerland		Senegal						
Turkey		Seychelles						
Ukraine		Sierra Leone						
UK		South Africa						
		Sudan						
		Tanzania						
		The Gambia						
		Togo						
		Uganda						
		Zambia						
		Zimbabwe						

Source: Own elaboration.

The calculations in this chapter are performed using the same dataset and the same groups of countries as in the next chapter where the HMM-based approach is tested. Hence, the results of conventional convergence can be directly compared with the results of HMM convergence. The comparison between classical concepts (β convergence) and alternative approaches (HMM) is a key value added to this analysis.

4.2 Methodology of testing β convergence

The analysis of the β convergence is based on panel data for the different groups of countries and the estimation technique is mostly the same as in Chapter 3. While in the early 1990s most research was based on the sets of cross-sectional (cross-country) data which resulted in a low number of observations in the considered samples, however, with the increasing popularity of panel data studies, most researchers would use an adapted form of the so-called Barro regression:

$$\Delta \ln\text{GDP}_{it} = \beta_0 + \beta_1 \ln\text{GDP}_{i,\,t-1} + x'_{it}\gamma + \alpha_i + \varepsilon_{it}, \qquad (4.1)$$

where $\Delta \ln\text{GDP}_{it}$ is the change of log GDP per capita (at constant PPP prices) for the ith country over the tth period, β_0 is the constant, $\ln\text{GDP}_{i,\,t-1}$ is the one period lagged log GDP per capita, x_{it} is a vector of the considered growth factors for the ith country over the tth period (γ is the associated coefficient), α_i is the individual effect of the ith country, and ε_{it} is the error term.

The core difference as compared to the cross-sectional studies is the lag of the GDP – while in the cross-sectional studies the lagged value of the gross domestic product from an initial t_0 period would be included, in the case of panel data studies, this would mean that the length of the delay would be increasing over time. Thus in most studies, it is the $\ln\text{GDP}_{i,\,t-1}$ which replaces the $\ln\text{GDP}_{i,\,t_0}$ from the cross-sectional case. An important difference between these studies is the length of a single period t – while it would be reasonable to cover as much time as possible by a single period because of the long-term nature of the growth phenomena and the incurred possibility to eliminate short-term incidental changes of the GDP, that implicitly means lowering the number of the available observations over time. In consequence, if the considered time series that constitute a panel are short themselves, such an analysis becomes infeasible and it is essential to consider observations whose lengths would be as low as a single year. This is what we assume in this research: while the analysed series are quite lengthy (1995–2019), eliminating incomplete observations and dividing the series into pre- and post-crisis observations require the use of one year per observation modelling strategy.

The β convergence exists if β_1 in equation (4.1) is statistically significantly negative. In such a case, it is possible to calculate the β-coefficient which reflects the rate of convergence as

$$\beta = -\frac{1}{T}\ln(1+\beta_1 T), \tag{4.2}$$

where T is the length of a single period in equation (4.1), so simply

$$\beta = -\ln(1+\beta_1) \tag{4.3}$$

in the considered case.

Huge literature exists that regards the methods of estimation of equation (4.1). It is most popular to use the instrumental variables type of approach; usually the Blundell and Bond (1998; BB hereafter, frequently referred to as a system GMM or just sys-GMM) being the first choice which replaced the formerly popular Arellano and Bond (1991) estimator. In this chapter, as it took place also in Chapter 3, we use the BB approach (although some refer more to Arellano and Bover than Blundell and Bond given that Arellano and Bover's contribution to the delivery of this estimator was much more crucial than the Blundell and Bond's, yet most applied scholars would use the Blundell and Bond's article referring to its construction), although it needs to be noticed that it does have certain drawbacks. Just like all the GMM estimators, this one also is developed typically for large samples, which is not exactly the case in cross-country studies. However, alternative possibilities are usually less attractive: the simple *fixed effects* estimator is only asymptotically unbiased and requires a large time dimension and the interesting Kiviet's estimator is only valid if the regressors are all assumed to be strictly exogenous. In consequence, they cannot be used in short macroeconomic data.

Equation (4.1) can be written as

$$\ln GDP_{it} = \beta_0 + (\beta_1 + 1)\ln GDP_{i,\,t-1} + x'_{it}\gamma + \alpha_i + \varepsilon_{it} \tag{4.4}$$

which is a typical dynamic panel data regression with $(\beta_1 + 1)$ being a parameter on a lagged dependent variable. As described in Chapter 3, $\beta_1 < 0$ implies the existence of the β convergence as the less developed countries grow faster and make up for the distance that separated them from the more developed countries, while $\beta_1 > 0$ would imply the existence of the real GDP divergence which is the typical "the rich get richer" situation.

In the first part of the research, we estimate a series of models based on samples from different parts of the world, thus verifying the existence and rate of convergence in different groups of countries. For each country group, we consider separately three periods: the entire period of the analysis (1995–2019), the pre-crisis (1995–2008) period, and the post-crisis (2009–2019) period. The latter is aimed at reflecting possible instability of the convergence processes over time and the probable existence of a structural break at the period of the global financial crisis which could be observed in some cases of the regional convergence discussed in Chapter 3 and indeed can be observed in the case of many country groups. Additionally, we distinguish between the absolute and the conditional convergence. The former takes place if the convergence parameter is significantly negative without considering any growth factors – i.e. when x_{it} contains no variables in Equation (4.4). The latter is conditional upon values of the considered growth factors in x_{it}.

The analysis of the conditional convergence was not performed in most cases of the regional data considered in Chapter 3. The reason for that was either unavailability or cross-sectional constancy of the considered growth factors that enforced restricting attention mostly to the absolute convergence. The analysis is possible using the country-level data. However, it must be noticed that the conclusion regarding the existence of the conditional convergence is not always robust to the selection of regressors in x_{it}. On the contrary, in particular, in the case of the GMM class of estimators, there exists a high risk of getting different results depending on the construction of x_{it}. In consequence, different attempts have been made over time in order to attain robustness of the conditional β convergence inference. Probably Leamer (1978) was the first author who proposed a more complex and objective approach called extreme bound analysis (EBA). In brief, his proposal consisted of the estimation of all the possible models with every possible subset of the initially considered regressors. Afterwards, a regressor was found to have a robust effect on the dependent variable if it was found statistically significant in a given fraction of the estimated models (say, 95% or even 100% of them). Such a construction of the algorithm made it difficult for virtually any variable to be found robustly significant and had a number of other deficits. To begin with, in this algorithm, it actually plays no role what the statistics of significance is for a variable in a given regression and it only matters whether it falls within or outside a critical range which makes the results strongly dependent on the preassumed level of significance.

In this research, we use a different approach that has gained recently a lot of popularity, namely, the Bayesian Model Averaging (BMA). It was first popularized in the growth and convergence studies in the milestone paper by Sala-i-Martin, Doppelhofer, and Miller (2004, SDM hereafter) who used the simplest version of the BMA algorithm called Bayesian Averaging of Classical Estimates (BACE), which is a BMA procedure applied to the model estimated with the basic OLS.

In SDM's research, the cited authors considered more than 60 growth factors which they planned to include in a convergence model. Since for each of them, the decision was binomial (whether to include the regressor in the equation or not), there was a total of over 2^{60} models that could be estimated and used to draw conclusions regarding the modelled relation. This meant over 2^{60} possible estimates of the parameter of convergence based on the different models, many of them being contradictory. Clearly, the conclusion regarding the estimate of the convergence or any other parameter and the significance of the influence of a given growth factor depended on the subjective choice of regressors.

In order to avoid subjectivity in this respect, SDM proposed the following algorithm, being the starting point of the BACE approach. First, a prior probability of relevance was assigned to each possible model – i.e. each possible set of regressors selected from the initial list considered in the analysis. This can be done in several ways. For example, one can assume that the prior probability of each model is the same. This, however, would seem inconsistent to claim that the model with 100 regressors would be adequate with the same probability as a model with one regressor. SDM proposed the use of so-called Bernoulli priors, which consists in assuming that the probability of relevance of each possible regressor is the same across their set and is equal to the ratio of the number of regressors that the scholar expects in the correct model divided by the number of regressors that are analysed. In consequence, the prior probability of relevance is computed for each possible model basing on Bernoulli's probability scheme. However, if the number of regressors is excessively high, making estimation of all possible models infeasible, the probabilities need to be computed for a random sample of analysed models and not for all of them. These are then corrected using the Bayes formula, thus yielding posterior probabilities of relevance for each of the considered models.

Kim (2002) proposed how to compute the posterior probabilities in the case of models estimated with GMM: while the SDM's BACE yielded usually no bigger computational problems, with the general BMA algorithm the computations were much more complicated. We summarize the key points of the BMA procedure while the interested reader could refer to a number of source articles such as those mentioned above: Kim (2002); Sala-i-Martin, Doppelhofer, and Miller (2004); or Próchniak and Witkowski (2013).

As suggested by Kim, let n be the number of observations for every object (in our case "object" stands for a given country). Let us denote the number of the considered potential regressors – the variables considered as potentially relevant growth factors – by K. Let $Q(\theta_j)$ be the GMM loss function that is minimized while estimating model M_j with $j = 1,..., J$ and let D be the dataset used, while $P(M_j \mid D)$ shall denote the probabilities of the relevance of each M_j – i.e. the prior probabilities "corrected" by to which extent D supports the hypothesis that M_j is the true model. As long as all the possible models (with all the possible subsets of the considered set of potential regressors) are considered, $J = 2^K$. However, as it has been stated, this number increases very fast in K; thus, in numerous research not all the possible models are considered and only a sample of J possible M_js are considered (with $J < 2^K$).

We then obtain

$$\ln P(D \mid M_j) = -0.5nQ\left(\hat{\theta}_j\right) - 0.5K'_j \tag{4.5}$$

with K'_j being the (total) number of parameters of M_j and $Q\left(\hat{\theta}_j\right)$ being the minimized value of $Q(\theta_j)$ which is the limited information likelihood analogue to Schwarz's BIC. That, after the proper substitution, allows writing the posterior probability of M_j as follows:

$$P(M_j \mid D) = \frac{P(M_j) n^{-K'_j/2} \exp[-0.5nQ\left(\hat{\theta}_j\right)]}{\sum_{i=1}^{J} P(M_i) n^{-K'_i/2} \exp[-0.5nQ\left(\hat{\theta}_i\right)]}. \tag{4.6}$$

The final estimates of the regression parameters are obtained as weighted estimates of the parameters from each estimated model, while posterior probabilities (4.6) are treated as weights. A similar method is applied to obtain the standard errors of estimates. Let $\hat{\beta}_{r,\,j}$ be the estimator of a parameter standing by the variable r in model M_j. Let $\hat{\beta}_r$ be the "final" estimator of parameter r, being the result of the total BMA process. Let us denote their variances as $\mathrm{Var}\left(\hat{\beta}_{r,\,j}\right)$ and $\mathrm{Var}\left(\hat{\beta}_r\right)$, respectively. Then,

$$\hat{\beta}_r = \sum_{j=1}^{2^K} P(M_j \mid D)\hat{\beta}_{r,j}, \tag{4.7}$$

$$\mathrm{Var}\left(\hat{\beta}_r\right) = \sum_{j=1}^{2^K} P(M_j \mid D) \cdot \mathrm{Var}\left(\hat{\beta}_{r,j}\right) + \sum_{j=1}^{2^K} P(M_j \mid D) \cdot (\hat{\beta}_{r,j} - \hat{\beta}_r)^2. \tag{4.8}$$

The last issue is the validation of the relevance or significance of the particular regressors. One possible approach that is used frequently is to compute the posterior probabilities (4.6) and use the sum of posterior probabilities for models in which a given regressor was present as a proxy for the posterior probability of relevance of the given regressor. Such a posterior probability is then compared with the prior probability and the variable is considered relevant if the posterior probability is no lower than the prior one. However, such an approach might be problematic if the number of regressors is too high to estimate all the possible models and, in particular, cannot be used if some of the variables are believed to be relevant and included in all of the models – in their case the posterior probability of relevance would obviously be equal to 1. In consequence in this study, we use the pseudo t because we include the lagged log GDP per capita in each equation: this reflects the strong belief in the existence of β convergence. Specifically, we compute a p-value for the test of significance of each variable in each model separately and average the obtained p-values over the models for each x'_{it} applying posterior probabilities (4.6) as weights and then using the final average to validate the relevance of each x'_{it}.

4.3 Empirical evidence for different country groups: dynamic panel data approach

The results of the examination of β convergence for the distinguished groups of countries using single models are presented in Tables 4.2–4.11. The data show estimated panel data regressions using Blundell and Bond's GMM system estimator. In each case, models (1) and (2) present the estimates of absolute and conditional convergence for the whole analysed period (1995–2019); models (3) and (4) are estimated for the years before 2008 (i.e. the pre-crisis period); and models (5) and (6) refer to the period after 2008 (i.e. the post-crisis period).

The following explanatory variables are used in the analysis:

- investment rate (% of GDP) [inv],
- general government total expenditure (% of GDP) [gov_exp],
- general government balance (% of GDP) [gov_bal],
- CPI inflation rate (%) [inf],
- exports of goods and services (% of GDP) [exp],
- current account balance (% of GDP) [cab].

These are the typical economic growth factors with a low number of missing observations in official statistics. GDP per capita time series are expressed at PPP constant 2011 international dollars. The abbreviation lnGDP(−1) used in the tables refers to a one-year lagged natural logarithm of GDP per capita, while _cons means a constant term. The data are taken from the IMF (World Economic Outlook) and the World Bank (World Development Indicators) databases. It should be emphasized that the choice of the regressors is limited not only by their economic meaning but also by the data availability for the complete sample which in many cases is a serious limitation.

Since the analysis is based on annual data, the growth factors are primarily those variables that affect economic growth from a short-run demand-side perspective. The supply-side economic growth determinants, i.e. the variables influencing medium- or long-run GDP dynamics (like human capital or institutional factors), are omitted here because their capability of describing yearly fluctuations in GDP per capita is limited.

Applying the system GMM estimator requires a couple of assumptions and some technical details to be decided beforehand. The first issue is the assumptions regarding the relation of the regressors with the error term. The BB estimation technique gives the freedom to treat them as strictly exogeneous, predetermined, or endogenous which has its consequences for the applied set of instruments in the GMM framework. It should be observed that all the considered growth factors are of macroeconomic character and all but one are expressed as a share of the GDP. We thus allow for their endogeneity which seems natural in this case and safest for the consistency of the estimator under the condition of no autocorrelation of the error term (specifically, no AR(2) autocorrelation). The latter can be verified with the Arellano and Bond test (Arellano and Bond, 1991), which we perform for each of the models presented in this chapter concluding no reasons to reject the null hypothesis which states that no autocorrelation is observed.

The technical details regarding the estimation process include one more important decision regarding the set of instruments. Technically, it is possible to use all the available lags (by at least two periods) of the regressors as instruments. However, further lags are likely to be weak instruments and cause the problem of proliferation. It is thus advisable to limit the set of instruments which we do, limiting them to at most three lags (as long as those are available).

Table 4.2 shows the estimates for the EU28 countries. Throughout the whole 1995–2019 period, the EU countries have been growing in line with the β convergence hypothesis. The catching-up of these countries is confirmed by both the absolute and conditional convergence models. The parameter β amounts to 7.7% (absolute convergence) and 5.1% (a conditional one), pointing to a moderate pace of catching-up process among the EU28 countries. The obtained results are consistent with the other studies on the subject. Many of them also confirm the prevalence of convergence in the European Union, although the exact definition of catching-up, the econometric methodology, period, and sample of countries may be different in individual studies. A detailed review of the latest empirical research on convergence in the EU is presented by Matkowski, Próchniak, and Rapacki (2016). Próchniak (2020) shows the newest analysis of absolute β and σ convergence in the EU[2]. The books by Malaga (2004), Michałek, Siwiński, and Socha (2007), Liberda (2009), Batóg (2010), and Jóźwik (2017) are entirely or largely devoted to the phenomenon of convergence.

Important studies on convergence are also published in the papers by Sarajevs (2001), Kaitila (2004), Polanec (2004), Growiec (2005), Varblane and Vahter (2005), Rogut and Roszkowska (2006), Rapacki and Próchniak (2007, 2010, 2012, 2014, 2019), Borys, Polgár, and Zlate (2008), Lein, León-Ledesma, and Nerlich (2008), Markowska and Sobczak (2008), Vojinovic and Oplotnik (2008), Čihák and Fonteyne (2009), Kutan and Yigit (2009), Niebuhr and Schlitte (2009), Vamvakidis (2009), Wolszczak-Derlacz (2009), Adamczyk-Łojewska (2010, 2011), Halmai and Vásáry (2010), Herrmann and

Table 4.2 Estimates of β convergence regressions: EU28 countries

	(1)	(2)	(3)	(4)	(5)	(6)
	lnGDP	*lnGDP*	*lnGDP*	*lnGDP*	*lnGDP*	*lnGDP*
lnGDP(−1)	0.926[***]	0.950[***]	0.942[***]	0.953[***]	0.941	0.961[***]
	(−7.52)	(−8.41)	(−6.22)	(−5.15)	(−1.57)	(−2.99)
inv		0.00376[***]		0.00315[***]		0.00376[***]
		(5.99)		(3.65)		(3.82)
gov_exp		0.000107		−0.000438		−0.0000797
		(0.25)		(−0.76)		(−0.17)
gov_bal		0.00478[**]		0.00460[**]		0.00423[*]
		(3.10)		(3.03)		(2.28)
inf		−0.000957[***]		−0.00116[***]		−0.00338[***]
		(−3.94)		(−3.99)		(−4.94)
exp		0.000237[*]		0.0000659		0.000418[*]
		(2.43)		(0.64)		(2.06)
cab		0.00102		0.00154[*]		0.000694
		(1.13)		(2.11)		(0.43)
_cons	0.782[***]	0.452[***]	0.620[***]	0.465[***]	0.628	0.334[**]
	(7.66)	(7.66)	(6.49)	(5.35)	(1.60)	(2.88)
N	672	636	364	356	308	280
β	7.7%	5.1%	6.0%	4.8%	6.1%	4.0%

Source: Own calculations.
t-statistics in parentheses; for the lagged ln GDP the convergence hypotheses tested, i.e. H0: $\beta = 1$.
[*] $p < 0.05$, [**] $p < 0.01$, [***] $p < 0.001$.

Winkler (2010), Marelli and Signorelli (2010), Puziak and Gazda (2010), Szeles and Marinescu (2010), Tatomir and Alexe (2011), Alexe (2012), Czasonis and Quinn (2012), Duro (2012), Kulhánek (2012), Mucha (2012), Staňisić (2012), Walczak (2012), Crespo Cuaresma, Havettová, and Lábaj (2013), Grzelak and Kujaczyńska (2013), Monfort, Cuestas, and Ordóñez (2013), Borsi and Metiu (2015), Głodowska (2017), Bolea, Duarte, and Chóliz (2018), Cabral and Castellanos-Sosa (2019), Siljak and Nagy (2019), and Borowiec (2020). The above list shows only the examples of studies devoted to convergence. In the economic literature, there is a huge number of such analyses. For the sake of conciseness, we are not going to describe the quoted studies. The interested reader should look at the cited sources.

Table 4.2 indicates that the pace of convergence in the pre-crisis period was similar to that in the post-crisis period (although for absolute convergence model estimated for the post-crisis period the coefficient on initial income level is not statistically significantly different from 1). In terms of absolute convergence, the respective β parameters amounted to 6.0% and

6.1% (although the latter one is not statistically significantly different from 1), while for the conditional convergence they stood at 4.8% and 4.0%, respectively. These results show that as time passes, the temporary violation of convergence trends during the global crisis has been offset by further developments so the current study demonstrates that the coefficients β for both subperiods are relatively similar.

The convergence for the European countries has been also largely confirmed by the analysis. In Table 4.3, all the coefficients standing on initial income are significantly less than 1. These results support the earlier outcomes for the European Union (with the difference that pseudo t-statistics reported in Table 4.3 for model (5) gives statistical significance at the 5% significance level and the analogous pseudo t-statistics reported in Table 4.2 does not yield statistically significant outcomes at the 5% significance level). As we can see, the catching-up process occurs not only within the EU countries but also in a wider group encompassing the Western and Central-Eastern European countries which are not EU members.

The β parameter in the absolute convergence model estimated for the whole period amounts to 6.2% for the 40 European countries. The β

Table 4.3 Estimates of β convergence regressions: Europe

	(1)	(2)	(3)	(4)	(5)	(6)
	lnGDP	*lnGDP*	*lnGDP*	*lnGDP*	*lnGDP*	*lnGDP*
lnGDP(−1)	0.940***	0.958***	0.948***	0.964***	0.970*	0.964***
	(−7.15)	(−6.13)	(−5.41)	(−5.04)	(−1.72)	(4.57)
inv		0.00411***		0.00308***		0.00402***
		(7.37)		(3.89)		(4.38)
gov_exp		0.000222		−0.0000244		0.0000376
		(0.42)		(−0.03)		(0.06)
gov_bal		0.00431***		0.00308**		0.00468**
		(4.61)		(2.81)		(2.84)
inf		−0.000604*		−0.000659**		−0.00206**
		(−2.25)		(−3.02)		(−3.10)
exp		0.000340**		0.000266*		0.000589**
		(2.82)		(2.27)		(2.62)
cab		0.00138**		0.00114*		0.000663
		(2.74)		(2.19)		(0.55)
_cons	0.630***	0.344***	0.550***	0.327***	0.321	0.273***
	(7.38)	(4.90)	(5.74)	(4.74)	(1.81)	(3.67)
N	958	865	518	475	440	390
β	6.2%	4.3%	5.3%	3.7%	3.0%	3.7%

Source: Own calculations.
t-statistics in parentheses; for the lagged ln GDP the convergence hypotheses tested, i.e.
H0: $\beta = 1$.
* $p < 0.05$, ** $p < 0.01$, *** $p < 0.001$.

parameter for the conditional convergence model and the whole period equals 4.3%. The analogous parameters for only the EU28 countries (presented in Table 4.2) were equal to 7.7% (absolute convergence) and 5.1% (conditional convergence).

As we can see, the convergence in the whole of Europe is slower than in the EU countries. It can be interpreted as the beneficial effects of EU membership. The EU policy aimed at implementing institutional reforms promoting economic freedom and the development of the market economy as well as the direct actions in the form of EU aid funds played a positive role in diminishing the income gap between richer and poorer countries. The inclusion of the countries which are not EU members (mainly the Balkan states and the former CIS countries) causes a deceleration of the pace of convergence. However, even in the whole of Europe, the convergence is relatively fast and driven by the imitation of technology, flows of factors of production, the inflow of remittances, and the institutional reforms.

As regards the time stability of convergence over time, the absolute convergence model indicates a more rapid pace of convergence prior to the global crisis (the β parameter for the period till 2008 equals 5.3% versus the value of 3.0% for the period after 2008). The global crisis slowed down the convergence tendencies in Europe. This result is confirmed by some other studies which indicated the temporary emergence of divergence tendencies in Europe during the global crisis (e.g. Próchniak, 2020).

The North African and Middle East countries were also growing in line with the convergence hypothesis (Table 4.4). Poorer countries of this group grew on average faster than more developed ones. The β parameter for the whole period is relatively high (6.4% in the case of absolute convergence and 6.0% in the case of conditional convergence; the latter one is, however, statistically insignificant assuming the 5% significance level).

The convergence in this group of countries is fuelled by the fact that this group is relatively homogenous in some respects. Mainly, the majority of countries belong to the Arab world. They have the same or similar religion, norms of living, and the organization of the economy. Their cooperation and international trade as well as the flow of people between them are relatively large. As a result, the group as a whole exhibited significant convergence tendencies.

Some examples of the good economic performance of selected Arab countries are the developments of Dubai and Qatar; Saudi Arabia is also growing rapidly as confirmed, among others, by the construction of the tallest building in the world (Jeddah Tower with its height planned to exceed 1000 m). Some poorer countries, like Morocco, invest a lot in infrastructure networks (e.g. the development of a modern railway system); Tunisia and Egypt earn a lot from the tourist sector. Nevertheless, the potential risk for further development is the uncertain future and political instability. The tensions related to the Arab Spring and the collapse of governments in Libya and Egypt, the still existing war in Syria, the Qatar diplomatic crisis

Table 4.4 Estimates of β convergence regressions: North Africa and the Middle East

	(1)	(2)	(3)	(4)	(5)	(6)
	lnGDP	*lnGDP*	*lnGDP*	*lnGDP*	*lnGDP*	*lnGDP*
lnGDP(−1)	0.938*	0.942	0.968**	0.975***	0.894	0.862
	(−1.649)	(−1.53)	(−2.21)	(−3.03)	(−1.26)	(−1.25)
inv		0.00183		−0.000644		0.00489
		(1.87)		(−0.86)		(1.64)
gov_exp		−0.00262**		−0.000105		−0.00334***
		(−3.19)		(−0.14)		(−3.45)
gov_bal		−0.00180*		0.0000113		−0.00236*
		(−1.97)		(0.01)		(−2.24)
inf		−0.00162		−0.00300		−0.00353
		(−1.09)		(−1.39)		(−1.03)
exp		0.000351		0.000427		0.00151
		(0.86)		(0.61)		(0.91)
cab		0.00386*		0.000200		0.00642***
		(2.37)		(0.19)		(3.32)
_cons	0.615	0.598	0.332*	0.264**	1.042	1.293
	(1.64)	(1.65)	(2.29)	(2.85)	(1.24)	(1.30)
N	360	260	195	144	165	116
β	6.4%	6.0%	3.3%	2.5%	11.2%	14.9%

Source: Own calculations.
t-statistics in parentheses; for the lagged ln GDP the convergence hypotheses tested, i.e. H0: β = 1.
* $p < 0.05$, ** $p < 0.01$, *** $p < 0.001$.

and the Qatar blockade by Saudi Arabia, the danger from Iran (whose president threatened to destroy Israel, and recently to attack Dubai), and so on. Hence, unlike the European countries, in the North African and Middle East countries the future is much more uncertain.

The convergence process in the region of North Africa and the Middle East was not stable over time. Before the global crisis, the catching-up process was relatively slow (β parameters standing at 3.3% and 2.5%). β parameters rose to 11.2% and 14.9%, respectively, after 2008, suggesting a more rapid convergence, but the models lost their statistical significance in terms of the coefficient standing on initial GDP per capita. If the current growth paths are maintained, the perspective for the future is supposed to be beneficial and we may expect the poorer countries of this region to catch up with the richer ones.

The growth paths for sub-Saharan Africa were different compared to the previously analysed groups of countries. In the 1995–2019 period as a whole, the sub-Saharan African countries were not growing in line with the absolute convergence hypothesis. In model (1) of Table 4.5, the coefficient

Table 4.5 Estimates of β convergence regressions: sub-Saharan Africa

	(1)	(2)	(3)	(4)	(5)	(6)
	lnGDP	*lnGDP*	*lnGDP*	*lnGDP*	*lnGDP*	*lnGDP*
lnGDP(−1)	1.000	0.981**	1.082***	0.993	0.940***	0.964***
	(0.00)	(−2.21)	(4.20)	(−0.60)	(−2.69)	(−4.35)
inv		0.000867		0.000794		0.00110
		(1.52)		(0.85)		(1.83)
gov_exp		0.000603		0.000772		−0.000548
		(1.05)		(1.24)		(−0.76)
gov_bal		0.00207**		0.00215**		0.000567
		(2.73)		(2.76)		(0.50)
inf		−0.000208***		−0.000183***		−0.00106**
		(−5.85)		(−4.69)		(−2.72)
exp		0.000214		−0.000000781		0.000629
		(0.52)		(−0.00)		(1.55)
cab		0.000227		−0.0000441		0.000774
		(0.52)		(−0.07)		(1.40)
_cons	0.0217	0.136*	−0.618***	0.0405	0.493**	0.287***
	(0.43)	(2.30)	(−4.02)	(0.55)	(2.75)	(4.41)
N	1104	861	598	461	506	400
β	–	1.9%	–	0.7%	6.2%	3.7%

Source: Own calculations.
t-statistics in parentheses; for the lagged ln GDP the convergence hypotheses tested, i.e. H0: $\beta = 1$.
* $p < 0.05$, ** $p < 0.01$, *** $p < 0.001$.

standing on initial income is 1.000, meaning that in the untransformed convergence model (where the growth rate is the explained variable), the coefficient on initial GDP per capita is zero. Thus, the GDP per capita growth rate was independent of the initial per capita income level.

Such an outcome results from the fact that sub-Saharan Africa is a very heterogeneous region. The countries involved have different economic institutions. Some of them have been engaged in civil wars or any other local or regional tensions for many years. In many countries, the level of institutional development is very low, the authorities are highly corrupted, and it is difficult for them to achieve rapid economic growth. For example, the least developed countries of this group are Burundi, the Central African Republic, and the Democratic Republic of Congo. Kinshasa, the capital of the latter, with its population of more than 10 million, is treated as the most dangerous city in the whole of Africa. The level of crime is very high. Many citizens (including children) in Kinshasa are homeless. Under such circumstances, it is very difficult to expect rapid economic growth for the whole country. It is also necessary to emphasize that the current situation is the result of history. For example, the Democratic Republic of Congo, former Zair, was the private property of Leopold II, the King of Belgium, during many years in the 19th century when many local citizens died due to disease and exploitation. As we can see, even a 100-year period is not enough to eliminate the negative effects of "path dependence".

On the other hand, this group includes island countries, such as Seychelles and Mauritius, where the standard of living is much higher due to, among others, large income from the tourist sector. In general, richer sub-Saharan African countries are the states which are located in the Southern part of the continent. Their prospects for further development are relatively optimistic due to good historical situations (like South Africa) or favourable international cooperation (e.g. Equatorial Guinea or Gabon). In 2019, Equatorial Guinea and Gabon ranked third and fourth, respectively, in terms of GDP per capita at PPP among the sub-Saharan African countries (after Seychelles and Mauritius). Their prospects for future growth are good due to, among others, China's interest in the exploration of oil and gas and other minerals (in the case of Equatorial Guinea) or in building the hydropower plant to produce energy (Gabon). At the end of the Apartheid era (at the beginning of the 1990s), the South African development level was very good and this tendency has been maintained till now (although the rising levels of crime and income inequalities in this country).

Despite ambiguous results in terms of absolute convergence or divergence, sub-Saharan African countries converged in conditional terms (with the β parameter at the level of 1.9%). This convergence was, however, very slow. The catching-up process in sub-Saharan Africa was unstable over time. Before the global crisis, the convergence did not take place (in absolute terms there was statistically significant divergence). It started after the global crisis. However, due to the heterogeneous sample of countries, there is no guarantee to maintain convergence trends in the future.

The South American countries confirmed the tendency towards conditional convergence throughout the whole 1995–2019 period (Table 4.6). In model (2), the coefficient for initial GDP per capita was statistically significantly lower than 1. The respective β parameter was equal to 2.1%. Compared with the European countries, convergence was slow. The time stability of the catching-up process in South America was very differentiated and our calculations give mixed results. Before the global crisis, absolute convergence did not take place. Convergence in absolute terms appeared after 2008 with quite a high β parameter (9.8%).

The Caribbean countries recorded a moderate pace of convergence during the 1995–2019 period at the level of 2.5% in absolute terms (Table 4.7). Before the global crisis, these countries did not converge in both absolute and conditional terms (the coefficient on initial GDP per capita was greater than 1 and – in the case of absolute convergence model – statistically significantly different from 1). After 2008, at the first view convergence started to appear at the level of 3.4% in absolute terms and only 0.3% in conditional terms but

Table 4.6 Estimates of β convergence regressions: South America

	(1)	(2)	(3)	(4)	(5)	(6)
	lnGDP	*lnGDP*	*lnGDP*	*lnGDP*	*lnGDP*	*lnGDP*
lnGDP(−1)	0.977	0.979**	1.071***	0.961*	0.907**	0.999
	(−0.98)	(−2.50)	(3.00)	(−1.72)	(−2.09)	(−0.10)
inv		0.00312**		0.00423***		0.00221*
		(2.64)		(3.63)		(2.33)
gov_exp		0.00113*		0.00213*		0.000883
		(1.97)		(2.49)		(1.66)
gov_bal		0.00498**		0.00634**		0.00400***
		(3.20)		(2.65)		(3.71)
inf		−0.000627*		−0.000738*		−0.000544
		(−2.17)		(−2.53)		(−1.36)
exp		−0.000156		−0.000332		0.000897*
		(−1.56)		(−1.60)		(2.04)
cab		−0.000127		0.000477		−0.00162*
		(−0.12)		(0.46)		(−2.04)
_cons	0.230	0.135*	−0.632**	0.256	0.883*	−0.0582
	(1.07)	(2.26)	(−2.87)	(1.41)	(2.11)	(−0.52)
N	288	222	156	123	132	99
β	2.3%	2.1%	–	4.0%	9.8%	0.1%

Source: Own calculations.
t-statistics in parentheses; for the lagged ln GDP the convergence hypotheses tested, i.e.
H0: $\beta = 1$.
* $p < 0.05$, ** $p < 0.01$, *** $p < 0.001$.

taking into account the lack of statistical significance of the respective coefficients the results are rather ambiguous. Such mixed and unstable outcomes for both South American and Caribbean countries are likely to be caused by the fact that these groups of countries are to some extent heterogeneous and driven by a completely different institutional system. But some common characteristics can also be noted which strengthens the impact of factors fuelling convergence tendencies.

On the one hand, the South American group includes Venezuela, which is a very poor country with a non-market economic system where institutions recently collapsed and the internal stability is violated. On the other hand, we can distinguish Chile with a large scope of economic freedom and a modern pension system. Another good example of completely different countries is the small Caribbean island divided between two countries: Haiti and the Dominican Republic. These two small countries located on one island have a completely different institutional, political, and economic system, and – as a result – their income per capita gap is enormous (the Dominican

Table 4.7 Estimates of β convergence regressions: Caribbean

	(1)	(2)	(3)	(4)	(5)	(6)
	lnGDP	*lnGDP*	*lnGDP*	*lnGDP*	*lnGDP*	*lnGDP*
lnGDP(−1)	0.975**	0.999	1.027**	1.002	0.967	0.997
	(−1.97)	(−0.15)	(2.16)	(0.27)	(−1.37)	(−0.43)
inv		0.00133***		0.00141**		0.00142*
		(3.35)		(2.90)		(2.11)
gov_exp		−0.00180**		−0.00139		−0.00232**
		(−2.84)		(−1.65)		(−2.87)
gov_bal		0.000757		−0.000301		0.00148**
		(1.20)		(−0.21)		(2.94)
inf		−0.000887*		−0.000721		−0.00155**
		(−2.47)		(−1.89)		(−2.86)
exp		0.000620***		0.000550***		0.000563**
		(4.14)		(3.72)		(3.03)
cab		−0.000919		−0.000915		−0.00114
		(−1.66)		(−1.88)		(−1.35)
_cons	0.247*	0.0160	−0.228*	−0.0229	0.313	0.0502
	(2.03)	(0.28)	(−1.96)	(−0.38)	(1.36)	(0.79)
N	528	309	286	163	242	146
β	2.5%	0.1%	–	–	3.4%	0.3%

Source: Own calculations.
t-statistics in parentheses; for the lagged ln GDP the convergence hypotheses tested, i.e. H0: $\beta = 1$.
* $p < 0.05$, ** $p < 0.01$, *** $p < 0.001$.

Republic was about ten times richer than Haiti in 2019). These examples show that it is almost impossible for the two above-mentioned pairs of countries (Venezuela and Chile as well as Haiti and the Dominican Republic) to converge. Moreover, the income differences between these countries are likely to widen in the future.

However, there are also factors stimulating convergence in South America and the Caribbean. For example, many Caribbean countries are growing rapidly due to the development of the tourism sector. In the case of income from tourism, the law of diminishing returns is likely to be satisfied, so it is much easier to increase income at the first stages of tourism development. The economic growth of many countries can be also fuelled by close links with the USA (e.g. Mexico where many Mexicans live in the USA and send remittances to their families living in Mexico) or to the fact that the European Union has its overseas territories in Latin America (French Guyana, and Martinique and Guadeloupe are the regions of France). All in all, the further paths of economic growth of the Latin American countries will depend on the continuation of their institutional reforms. In other words, the further paths much depend on whether these countries imitate Uruguay or Brazil (which are ones of the best performers) or rather Salvador and Haiti (which lag behind in terms of the institutional system, political stability, and economic freedom).

South-East Asian countries recorded stable moderate convergence in the whole 1995–2019 period as well as in the two shorter subperiods (Table 4.8). The pace of absolute convergence was 1.6% during 1995–2019. It accelerated from 1.1% before 2008 (this coefficient is however statistically insignificant) to 2.3% after 2008. As regards conditional convergence, its pace during the 1995–2019 period amounted to 2.1%. When estimated for the shorter subperiods, it equalled 1.8% during both the before-crisis and post-crisis periods.

Quite similar results for the South-East Asian countries in all the distinguished periods indicate that their economic growth paths were relatively stable and predictable over time. Indeed, except for some outliers (e.g. Iran), this group includes countries with stable institutional architectures and well-established political and economic systems. The quality of education and the level of human capital in South-East Asian nations are relatively high. All these factors strengthened the tendency towards convergence in

Table 4.8 Estimates of β convergence regressions: South-East Asia

	(1)	*(2)*	*(3)*	*(4)*	*(5)*	*(6)*
	lnGDP	*lnGDP*	*lnGDP*	*lnGDP*	*lnGDP*	*lnGDP*
lnGDP(−1)	0.984***	0.979***	0.989	0.982**	0.977***	0.982***
	(−2.77)	(−4.65)	(−1.48)	(−2.40)	(−2.94)	(−2.87)
inv		0.000400		0.0000338		0.000922
		(1.02)		(0.07)		(1.91)
gov_exp		−0.000445		−0.000133		−0.00135*
		(−0.69)		(−0.15)		(−2.24)
gov_bal		0.00160		0.00139		0.00115
		(1.86)		(1.35)		(1.69)
inf		−0.000843		−0.000796		−0.00177*
		(−1.04)		(−0.92)		(−2.07)
exp		0.000252***		0.000212		0.000224*
		(4.41)		(1.64)		(2.49)
cab		−0.000628		−0.000637		−0.000767
		(−1.36)		(−0.88)		(−1.57)
_cons	0.182***	0.219***	0.134*	0.196***	0.245***	0.208***
	(3.44)	(5.51)	(1.99)	(3.30)	(3.39)	(3.53)
N	576	480	312	265	264	215
β	1.6%	2.1%	1.1%	1.8%	2.3%	1.8%

Source: Own calculations.
t-statistics in parentheses; for the lagged ln GDP the convergence hypotheses tested, i.e. H0: $\beta = 1$.
* $p < 0.05$, ** $p < 0.01$, *** $p < 0.001$.

this group. The future development of South-East Asia will depend to a large extent on the future growth of the Chinese economy as the whole region is largely dependent on China. Till now, China has been growing very rapidly which stimulated convergence tendencies in the whole group. An important factor from the point of view of the future development of this region is also the political situation in North Korea. The unpredictable decisions made by the North Korean leader may negatively influence the economic growth of some countries in the region.

Unlike the previous groups, the countries from Australia and Oceania recorded slightly different economic growth paths. Throughout the whole 1995–2019 period, they did not reveal convergence tendencies. Moreover, divergence trends are the most likely outcome. As data in Table 4.9 indicate, the coefficient on initial income level was greater than 1 in models (1) and (2) but it wasn't statistically significantly different from 1.

Such an outcome results from the fact that the considered group of countries is very heterogeneous. On the one hand, there are two big economies (Australia and New Zealand) with the Anglo-Saxon capitalist model. Their institutional environment resembles to a large extent that prevailing in the

Table 4.9 Estimates of β convergence regressions: Australia and Oceania

	(1)	(2)	(3)	(4)	(5)	(6)
	lnGDP	*lnGDP*	*lnGDP*	*lnGDP*	*lnGDP*	*lnGDP*
lnGDP(−1)	1.025	1.001	1.022	0.984***	1.038**	1.023***
	(1.46)	(0.37)	(1.10)	(−3.67)	(1.97)	(5.51)
inv		0.00298*		0.00310**		0.00255*
		(2.05)		(2.75)		(2.52)
gov_exp		0.00111**		0.00327***		0.000688
		(2.84)		(19.09)		(1.80)
gov_bal		0.00340***		0.00426***		0.00227*
		(3.52)		(4.66)		(2.42)
inf		0.00254		−0.00139		0.00209
		(0.88)		(−0.64)		(1.77)
exp		0.000275		0.00103		0.00215***
		(1.05)		(1.60)		(7.61)
cab		0.00261*		0.00295***		0.00138
		(2.03)		(5.11)		(1.76)
_cons	−0.199	−0.106*	−0.175	−0.0268	−0.310	−0.371***
	(−1.40)	(−2.20)	(−1.05)	(−0.41)	(−1.68)	(−12.94)
N	264	77	143	45	121	32
β	–	–	–	1.6%	–	–

Source: Own calculations.
t-statistics in parentheses; for the lagged ln GDP the convergence hypotheses tested, i.e. H0: $\beta = 1$.
* $p < 0.05$, ** $p < 0.01$, *** $p < 0.001$.

UK leading to a very high income per capita level in these countries. On the other hand, there are small island countries from the Oceania region which are located far away from the mainland whose economies are based primarily on agriculture and fisheries, with underdeveloped industry and tourist sector (the latter makes them different compared to the Caribbean region). As a result, the income level in countries such as Kiribati, Solomon Islands, Vanuatu, Micronesia, and Papua New Guinea is very low. Moreover, Papua New Guinea is an unsafe country with a high level of crime making the whole economy difficult to grow. Hence, the whole region diverged. For example, in 1995, GDP per capita in Australia (the richest country) was 1749% higher than in Kiribati (the poorest country), while the GDP per capita in New Zealand (the second richest one) exceeded by 1118% income per capita in Solomon Island (the second rank from the bottom). In 2019, the percentage differences between these countries were higher and amounted to 2397% (between Australia and Kiribati) and 1678% (between New Zealand and the Solomon Islands).

Post-socialist countries grew in line with the concept of β convergence throughout the whole 1995–2019 period (Table 4.10). The β parameter for

Table 4.10 Estimates of β convergence regressions: post-socialist countries

	(1)	(2)	(3)	(4)	(5)	(6)
	lnGDP	*lnGDP*	*lnGDP*	*lnGDP*	*lnGDP*	*lnGDP*
lnGDP(−1)	0.965***	0.967***	1.050**	1.001	1.003	0.975*
	(−4.64)	(−3.96)	(2.24)	(0.09)	(0.15)	(−1.87)
inv		0.00422***		0.00321***		0.00234**
		(7.45)		(4.55)		(3.09)
gov_exp		−0.000585		−0.00169		−0.00108
		(−0.98)		(−1.86)		(−1.91)
gov_bal		0.00218		−0.000175		0.00452***
		(1.38)		(−0.12)		(4.63)
inf		−0.000461		−0.000807**		−0.00163***
		(−1.68)		(−3.17)		(−3.96)
exp		0.000640**		0.000349		0.00135***
		(2.60)		(1.21)		(3.66)
cab		0.00151*		0.00201*		−0.000838
		(2.17)		(2.12)		(−1.53)
_cons	0.363***	0.249***	−0.398*	0.0325	−0.00292	0.193
	(5.06)	(3.91)	(−1.97)	(0.44)	(−0.02)	(1.78)
N	670	553	362	295	308	258
β	3,6%	3,4%	–	–	–	2,5%

Source: Own calculations.
t-statistics in parentheses; for the lagged ln GDP the convergence hypotheses tested, i.e. H0: $\beta = 1$.
* $p < 0.05$, ** $p < 0.01$, *** $p < 0.001$.

the absolute convergence model equals 3.6% while that for the conditional one amounts to 3.4%. The results for the shorter subperiods indicate that convergence occurred only after the global crisis and in conditional terms. Before 2008 and in absolute terms after 2008, the catching-up process did not take place.

These outcomes result from the fact that the group of post-socialist countries includes many underdeveloped countries being part of the Soviet Union in the socialist era (e.g. the South-Caucasian and Central-Asian economies). These countries suffered a deep and long transformation recession which did not necessarily finish before the mid-1990s. As a result, in the second part of the 1990s, these countries' rate of economic growth was very low or even negative despite their low initial income level. These factors weakened convergence tendencies in the whole group. Even in the second part of the analysed period, the convergence is not so clearly visible as in the case of some other groups of countries due to the same factors.

In the post-socialist world, we can distinguish two clusters of countries: the first one encompassing the EU member states and some other countries where the process of market transformation is advanced; the second one includes the countries in which institutions are far away from those existing in Western Europe. Moreover, many countries of the region suffered from wars and other conflicts (internal and international) that weakened convergence tendencies. The good examples are the conflicts between Russia and Ukraine since 2014 or between Russia and Georgia in 2008. Many countries are not internally stable. For example, the Nagorno-Karabakh Republic is a part of Azerbaijan according to international law but de facto it is populated and controlled by Armenians. Abkhazia and South Ossetia are internationally recognized as part of Georgia; however, they are actually independent states (recognized by only a few countries of the world, including Russia). Under such circumstances, it is quite difficult for many less developed post-socialist countries to grow rapidly and to catch up with the richer ones.

Table 4.11 shows the results for the OECD countries. This group differs compared to the previous ones as it is heterogeneous in terms of both geographical and economic criteria. On the one hand, OECD consists of countries from different continents except for Africa. On the other hand, it also includes less developed countries such as Mexico and Turkey. The results for OECD confirm the prevalence of convergence in all the model specifications. For the whole 1995–2019 period, OECD members caught up at a rate of 8.2% (absolute convergence) and 5.4% (conditional convergence). In the case of subperiods, the results are ambiguous. It is largely caused by a relatively high heterogeneity of this group and the different effects of the global crisis in individual countries.

After the examination of the convergence models based on single equations, it is worth analysing the robustness of the results. It is important to check whether the results are stable and can be treated as a certain feature of the economic growth paths of the respective groups of countries. Bayesian

Table 4.11 Estimates of β convergence regressions: OECD countries

	(1)	(2)	(3)	(4)	(5)	(6)
	lnGDP	*lnGDP*	*lnGDP*	*lnGDP*	*lnGDP*	*lnGDP*
lnGDP(−1)	0.921***	0.947***	0.935***	0.944***	0.891***	0.954***
	(−8.32)	(−7.16)	(−6.53)	(−8.07)	(−2.74)	(−2.89)
inv		0.00317***		0.00147*		0.00372***
		(5.20)		(2.02)		(4.64)
gov_exp		0.000451		0.000859*		−0.000368
		(1.36)		(2.46)		(−0.70)
gov_bal		0.00396***		0.00451***		0.00334*
		(4.74)		(4.39)		(2.47)
inf		−0.000903		−0.000971		−0.00495***
		(−1.67)		(−1.86)		(−6.51)
exp		0.000344***		0.000340***		0.000479***
		(3.80)		(3.31)		(4.21)
cab		0.000177		−0.000236		−0.00107
		(0.23)		(−0.36)		(−0.65)
_cons	0.838***	0.469***	0.699***	0.525***	1.155**	0.422**
	(8.48)	(7.03)	(6.83)	(8.53)	(2.78)	(2.75)
N	864	809	468	453	396	356
β	8.2%	5.4%	6.7%	5.8%	11.5%	4.7%

Source: Own calculations.
t-statistics in parentheses; for the lagged ln GDP the convergence hypotheses tested, i.e. H0: $\beta = 1$.
* $p < 0.05$, ** $p < 0.01$, *** $p < 0.001$.

model averaging framework, presented in the next section, allows us to verify the robustness of these outcomes.

4.4 Empirical evidence for different country groups: Bayesian model averaging

As stated in the previous chapter, the estimates of a single dynamic panel data model are generally not robust to the choice of its specification in the sense of the set of regressors. The sensitivity of the GMM estimates to even minor changes of the set of regressors or the sample used is not a secret. Thus, it seems vital to provide proper estimates which could ensure the robustness of the presented results. As a solution to the problem of the lack of unambiguously correct functional form of the model and its potential sensitivity to its choice, we use the BMA procedure averaging the output across a number of different functional forms with the different choice of regressors. Tables 4.12–4.21 show Bayesian model averaging estimates of the model based on the whole period as well as the models based on the two pre- and post-crisis shorter subperiods.

Table 4.12 Estimates of β convergence regressions using the Bayesian model averaging: EU28

	The whole 1995–2019 period	The pre-crisis period	The post-crisis period
lnGDP(−1)	0.955620	0.957513	0.972464
	0.000	0.000	0.012
inv	0.004403	0.003386	0.004152
	0.000	0.000	0.002
gov_exp	−0.001601	−0.001155	−0.002104
	0.120	0.168	0.126
gov_bal	0.006250	0.006872	0.005372
	0.000	0.000	0.000
inf	−0.000666	−0.000884	−0.002388
	0.001	0.000	0.100
exp	0.000302	0.000204	0.000530
	0.067	0.077	0.002
cab	0.000703	0.000752	0.002006
	0.015	0.098	0.119
β	4.5%	4.3%	2.8%

Source: Own calculations.
Weighed t-significance p-value in parentheses; for the lagged ln GDP the convergence hypotheses tested, i.e. H0: $\beta = 1$.

Table 4.13 Estimates of β convergence regressions using the Bayesian model averaging: Europe

	The whole 1995–2019 period	The pre-crisis period	The post-crisis period
lnGDP(−1)	0.962625	0.966156	0.977840
	0.003	0.004	0.011
inv	0.004370	0.003427	0.003998
	0.000	0.000	0.000
gov_exp	−0.001892	−0.001165	−0.002929
	0.211	0.199	0.069
gov_bal	0.005795	0.004331	0.005809
	0.000	0.000	0.000
inf	−0.000554	−0.000713	−0.001630
	0.022	0.008	0.000
exp	0.000364	0.000379	0.000601
	0.022	0.001	0.001
cab	0.000546	0.000398	0.000635
	0.000	0.002	0.171
β	3.8%	3.4%	2.2%

Source: Own calculations.
Weighed t-significance p-value in parentheses; for the lagged ln GDP the convergence hypotheses tested, i.e. H0: $\beta = 1$.

Table 4.14 Estimates of β convergence regressions using the Bayesian model averaging: North Africa and the Middle East

	The whole 1995–2019 period	*The pre-crisis period*	*The post-crisis period*
lnGDP(−1)	0.941684	0.979039	0.881725
	0.035	0.062	0.044
inv	0.001192	−0.000859	0.004458
	0.148	0.057	0.024
gov_exp	−0.002149	−0.000274	−0.002657
	0.003	0.640	0.086
gov_bal	0.000806	0.000147	0.001022
	0.113	0.425	0.190
inf	−0.000839	−0.002083	−0.001851
	0.392	0.050	0.338
exp	0.000517	0.000454	0.001590
	0.299	0.265	0.220
cab	0.003301	−0.000194	0.005928
	0.000	0.233	0.000
β	6.0%	2.1%	12.6%

Source: Own calculations.
Weighed *t*-significance *p*-value in parentheses; for the lagged ln GDP the convergence hypotheses tested, i.e. H0: β = 1.

Table 4.15 Estimates of β convergence regressions using the Bayesian model averaging: sub-Saharan Africa

	The whole 1995–2019 period	*The pre-crisis period*	*The post-crisis period*
lnGDP(−1)	0.985438	1.014255	0.960124
	0.241	0.064	0.022
inv	0.001924	0.002143	0.000826
	0.000	0.003	0.061
gov_exp	−0.000245	−0.000386	0.000135
	0.161	0.212	0.371
gov_bal	0.002164	0.001764	0.001869
	0.000	0.012	0.076
inf	−0.000122	−0.000098	−0.001342
	0.161	0.155	0.013
exp	0.000501	0.000017	0.000796
	0.259	0.416	0.039
cab	−0.000166	−0.000508	0.000168
	0.160	0.265	0.386
β	1.5%	–	4.1%

Source: Own calculations.
Weighed *t*-significance *p*-value in parentheses; for the lagged ln GDP the convergence hypotheses tested, i.e. H0: β = 1.

Table 4.16 Estimates of β convergence regressions using the Bayesian model averaging: South America

	The whole 1995–2019 period	The pre-crisis period	The post-crisis period
lnGDP(−1)	0.985119	0.992356	0.979875
	0.0132	0.254	0.061
inv	0.004762	0.005560	0.004020
	0.000	0.000	0.001
gov_exp	0.000462	0.001235	0.000168
	0.094	0.294	0.184
gov_bal	0.005834	0.006872	0.005079
	0.000	0.000	0.000
inf	−0.000360	−0.000784	−0.000347
	0.028	0.000	0.128
exp	0.000183	0.000106	0.001186
	0.329	0.243	0.014
cab	0.000363	0.000875	−0.000967
	0.143	0.151	0.256
β	1.5%	0.8%	2.0%

Source: Own calculations.
Weighed *t*-significance *p*-value in parentheses; for the lagged ln GDP the convergence hypotheses tested, i.e. H0: $\beta = 1$.

Table 4.17 Estimates of β convergence regressions using the Bayesian model averaging: Caribbean

	The whole 1995–2019 period	The pre-crisis period	The post-crisis period
lnGDP(−1)	0.994649	1.001276	0.993864
	0.756	0.647	0.802
inv	0.002103	0.002136	0.002069
	0.000	0.000	0.003
gov_exp	−0.001813	−0.000189	−0.002498
	0.000	0.290	0.000
gov_bal	0.001579	0.001056	0.001911
	0.013	0.214	0.016
inf	−0.000521	−0.000879	−0.000756
	0.153	0.001	0.376
exp	0.000658	0.000269	0.000811
	0.006	0.253	0.019
cab	−0.000761	−0.000339	−0.001340
	0.130	0.208	0.091
β	0.5%	−	0.6%

Source: Own calculations.
Weighed *t*-significance *p*-value in parentheses; for the lagged ln GDP the convergence hypotheses tested, i.e. H0: $\beta = 1$.

Table 4.18 Estimates of β convergence regressions using the Bayesian model averaging: South-East Asia

	The whole 1995– 2019 period	The pre-crisis period	The post-crisis period
lnGDP(−1)	0.979912	0.982222	0.980700
	0.132	0.097	0.103
inv	0.000360	0.000012	0.000922
	0.127	0.515	0.054
gov_exp	−0.000878	−0.001059	−0.000837
	0.157	0.216	0.195
gov_bal	0.001804	0.001541	0.001622
	0.000	0.004	0.003
inf	−0.000887	−0.000683	−0.001701
	0.003	0.035	0.003
exp	0.000327	0.000318	0.000294
	0.000	0.002	0.002
cab	−0.000750	−0.000665	−0.001071
	0.005	0.136	0.020
β	2.0%	1.8%	1.9%

Source: Own calculations.
Weighed t-significance p-value in parentheses; for the lagged ln GDP the convergence hypotheses tested, i.e.H0: $\beta = 1$.

Table 4.19 Estimates of β convergence regressions using the Bayesian model averaging: Australia and Oceania

	The whole 1995– 2019 period	The pre-crisis period	The post-crisis period
lnGDP(−1)	1.005671	1.002223	1.009987
	0.804	0.876	0.783
inv	0.002255	0.003219	0.001609
	0.000	0.000	0.011
gov_exp	0.000550	0.001637	0.000253
	0.022	0.004	0.497
gov_bal	0.002045	0.002842	0.001530
	0.000	0.026	0.027
inf	0.000458	−0.000184	0.000199
	0.352	0.459	0.339
exp	0.000713	0.001068	0.001668
	0.081	0.117	0.271
cab	0.000851	0.001579	0.000259
	0.179	0.098	0.287
β	–	–	–

Source: Own calculations.
Weighed t-significance p-value in parentheses; for the lagged ln GDP the convergence hypotheses tested, i.e. H0: $\beta = 1$.

Table 4.20 Estimates of β convergence regressions using the Bayesian model averaging: post-socialist countries

	The whole 1995–2019 period	*The pre-crisis period*	*The post-crisis period*
lnGDP(−1)	0.967414	1.013029	0.978209
	0.043	0.469	0.064
inv	0.004123	0.002832	0.002812
	0.000	0.000	0.001
gov_exp	−0.001958	−0.003215	−0.001874
	0.008	0.000	0.173
gov_bal	0.004297	0.001532	0.005943
	0.000	0.307	0.000
inf	−0.000535	−0.000918	−0.001259
	0.000	0.000	0.009
exp	0.000831	0.000715	0.001864
	0.000	0.006	0.000
cab	0.000993	0.001706	−0.000504
	0.182	0.001	0.169
β	3.3%	−	2.2%

Source: Own calculations.
Weighed t-significance p-value in parentheses; for the lagged ln GDP the convergence hypotheses tested, i.e. H0: $\beta = 1$.

Table 4.21 Estimates of β convergence regressions using the Bayesian model averaging: OECD countries

	The whole 1995–2019 period	*The pre-crisis period*	*The post-crisis period*
lnGDP(−1)	0.948016	0.948489	0.947013
	0.000	0.000	0.000
inv	0.004157	0.002518	0.004756
	0.000	0.015	0.000
gov_exp	−0.000915	−0.000101	−0.001754
	0.160	0.055	0.068
gov_bal	0.004901	0.005327	0.004396
	0.000	0.000	0.000
inf	−0.001014	−0.001175	−0.004172
	0.000	0.000	0.007
exp	0.000414	0.000406	0.000578
	0.000	0.000	0.000
cab	0.000175	−0.000088	0.001110
	0.126	0.103	0.153
β	5.3%	5.3%	5.4%

Source: Own calculations.
Weighed t-significance p-value in parentheses; for the lagged ln GDP the convergence hypotheses tested, i.e. H0: $\beta = 1$.

In the majority of cases, the BMA estimates confirm the validity of the single models and the earlier interpretation of the results. In some cases, however, the BMA approach specifies better the nature of economic growth paths of the countries under study. If a given relationship is confirmed by BMA estimates, we can infer that it undoubtedly exists in the real economy.

It turns out that conditional convergence exists. The confirmation of conditional catching-up has been validated for the majority of examined groups in the whole 1995–2019 period as well as in the shorter subperiods. The only exceptions which did not grow in line with the conditional convergence hypothesis are sub-Saharan African, Caribbean, and post-socialist countries before the global crisis as well as Australia and Oceania group in all the periods. For these groups in given periods the neoclassical growth theory, presented at the beginning of the book, does not apply. The lack of conditional convergence is, however, something atypical and refers to the minority of countries.

It is necessary to think about what are the causes of the lack of even conditional convergence. The most obvious answer can be found for Australia and Oceania. The countries included in this group are, on the one hand, Australia and New Zealand which are relatively big (Australia is the sixth largest country in terms of surface area in the world) and achieve good records in terms of economic development. On the other hand, this continent includes many island countries that are relatively less developed, have a different history, and have a separate political and economic system; it is not possible for them to catch up with the leaders. The examples of large discrepancies in terms of income level and large heterogeneity of this group have been presented in the previous section. The results of the lack of convergence based on the BMA approach are consistent with the earlier outcomes achieved based on single regression models. In such a case, we can undoubtedly state that the countries from Australia and Oceania diverged in the last years. This outcome has an important policy implication. Namely, it is very difficult to expect the change of past trends in the future. Regardless of the efforts and adopted policies, Australia and New Zealand are expected to widen the income gap against the other island countries in Oceania.

The lack of convergence in the post-socialist countries before 2008 can be explained primarily based on history and different paths of economic transformation. Post-socialist countries adopted completely different models of market transformation and the transformation to a capitalist economy. On the one hand, some countries are EU members. They were relatively highly developed at the end of the socialist era and due to the "integration anchor", they suffered only minor transformation recession and adopted market institutions which led them to achieve rapid economic growth. EU funds were one of the important drivers of fast GDP growth which started in the 1990s and continued to fuel the economies of these countries in the 2000s. On the other hand, the post-socialist group includes less advanced countries that suffer enormous obstacles to achieve rapid growth. The obstacles may be political (Russia, Belarus, Turkmenistan, i.e. the countries which are *de facto* not democratic and governed by authoritarian presidents).[3] Other obstacles come from internal problems (e.g. in Ukraine and Moldova) where the lack of unitary society and a huge Russian minority in the Eastern parts of these countries make it difficult to achieve stable political and economic institutions. Armenia is stuck between enemy countries (Azerbaijan and Turkey), making it almost impossible to develop freely and promote international trade. Georgia is another case with Abkhazia and South Ossetia being recognized internationally as parts of Georgia but de facto governed by separatist governors.[4] All these things caused that post-socialist countries as the whole group was diverging in terms of income level.

The relative heterogeneity of the countries, different political and institutional system, different history, internal problems, and different prospects for the future are also the factors explaining the lack of convergence in the Caribbean world and sub-Sahara Africa.

All in all, the majority of groups were growing in line with the conditional convergence hypothesis. It means that the neoclassical growth theory turns out to be valid. Despite some shortcomings and simplifications of the neoclassical models, one of their main implications about the existence of conditional convergence is valid. The world countries have been developing in line with the conditional convergence hypothesis. It is necessary to emphasize that the conditional catching-up process does not necessarily mean a decrease in income inequalities. Under a conditional convergence model, the countries tend to the individual steady states, and the higher the distance from the individual steady state, the faster the growth. Steady states may be, however, completely different for various countries – some of them may be characterized by steady states with high income levels, in the others a steady state may correspond to a low level of economic development. The confirmation of conditional convergence does not thus mean that policymakers have nothing to do and that income disparities between nations will disappear. The income gap in official GDP statistics refers to absolute convergence which is not verified under the BMA approach presented in this section. Policymakers should still make decisions to bridge the income gap between the leaders and the laggers. Such a process is not automatic. It requires a lot of effort and careful decisions and it is beyond the scope of this study to indicate the actions needed to achieve this goal.

The economic validity of the models estimated in this chapter can also be confirmed based on the coefficients standing for the other explanatory variables. In the majority of cases, the coefficients are in line with the theoretical structural model. When the economic theory is ambiguous, the sign of coefficients gives us an interesting interpretation as to the nature of the relationship between a given variable and GDP dynamics.

The coefficient standing on the investment rate [inv] in the majority of cases is positive and statistically significant. It indicates that the accumulation of physical capital stock is important from the point of view of rapid GDP dynamics. However, it is necessary to notice that from the economic point of view, the impact of investments on economic growth is twofold. On the one hand, it is of a short-run demand-side nature. Investment spending is part of aggregate demand and is included in the GDP equation (according to the expenditure method, one of the components of GDP is investment expenditure). This case does not say much about the efficiency of investments and it is necessary to take this fact into account when interpreting the results. It is possible to invest a lot but if money is not properly allocated the rate of return will be zero and investments will not contribute to physical capital accumulation. On the other hand, the relationship may be of a long-run supply-side nature. Investments lead to physical capital accumulation, i.e. one of the factors of production. With more inputs, potential output rises and the economy can produce more. Such a relationship can be verified on the basis of data averaged over a longer time span.

As regards fiscal policy, our models suggest that a good fiscal stance is favourable to economic growth. In the majority of cases, the sign for the general government balance variable [gov_bal] is positive and statistically significant. It means that excessively high public spending leading to high budget deficit (and as a result high public debt) is not good from the point of view of output dynamics. Policymakers should conduct careful fiscal policies aiming at achieving low budget deficits (or even budget surpluses).

It turns out that in many cases the size of government matters as well. The coefficient standing on the variable measuring general government total expenditure (as % of GDP) [gov_exp] is negative. It means that the large size of the public sector hampers economic growth. From the point of view of long-run GDP growth, policymakers should decrease the level of fiscalism. An argument for such an outcome is the fact that in many countries under study governments are corrupted and money which is collected and spent by the government is not efficiently allocated and does not lead to a higher level of economic development and a better standard of living.

The study gives also interesting implications as regards the impact of inflation on economic growth. The majority of BMA models indicate that the sign of the coefficient standing on the inflation rate [inf] is negative and statistically significant. It means that high inflation negatively affects output growth. This outcome is important for monetary policymakers. Namely, central banks should conduct monetary policy aiming at low inflation; if inflation jumps, they should take action to decrease it.

Last but not least, the variables related to international trade also matter from the point of view of output dynamics. Exports rate [exp] usually is positively related to economic growth. It means that the greater the openness of the country towards international trade, the more rapid the GDP growth. Hence, some actions made by authoritarian regimes that prevail in some countries and introduce a variety of barriers in international trade do not accelerate economic growth. To achieve rapid GDP growth, high foreign trade openness should co-exist with external equilibrium as indicated by a positive sign of the coefficient standing on current account balance [cab].

Notes

1 The EU28 group includes the UK which has not been the EU member since 1 February 2020.
2 The σ convergence exists if income differences between countries (measured e.g. by standard deviation of log GDP per capita levels) decrease over time.
3 It is necessary to distinguish between two important concepts existing in the law sciences: *de iure* and *de facto*. The Russian political system is *de iure* democratic; however, it is *de facto* authoritarian and it is almost impossible to become the president for a person from opposition. The same refers to Belarus, governed by President Alaksandr Łukaszenka since 1994. The 2020 presidential elections and massive protests in the streets of Belarusian cities, especially in the capital city Minsk, showed that it is hardly believable for the system to be democratic.
4 See Suska (2021) for an interesting study of the economies of Abkhazia and South Ossetia.

References

Adamczyk-Łojewska, G. (2010). Procesy konwergencji i dywergencji ekonomicznej. *Studia i Materiały Polskiego Stowarzyszenia Zarządzania Wiedzą*, 27, pp. 17–27.

Adamczyk-Łojewska, G. (2011). Problemy konwergencji i dywergencji ekonomicznej na przykładzie krajów Unii Europejskiej, w tym Polski. *Prace Naukowe Uniwersytetu Ekonomicznego we Wrocławiu. Ekonomia*, 211, pp. 57–76.

Alexe, I. (2012). How Does Economic Crisis Change the Landscape of Real Convergence for Central and Eastern Europe?. *Romanian Journal of Fiscal Policy*, 3, pp. 1–8.

Arellano, M. and Bond, S. (1991). Some Tests of Specification for Panel Data: Monte Carlo Evidence and an Application to Employment Equations. *Review of Economic Studies*, 58(2), pp. 277–297, doi: 10.2307/2297968.

Batóg, J. (2010). *Konwergencja dochodowa w krajach Unii Europejskiej*. Szczecin: Wydawnictwo Naukowe Uniwersytetu Szczecińskiego.

Blundell, R. and Bond, S. (1998). Initial Conditions and Moment Restrictions in Dynamic Panel Data Models. *Journal of Econometrics*, 87(1), pp. 115–143, doi: 10.1016/s0304–4076(98)00009-8.

Bolea, L., Duarte, R. and Chóliz, J.S. (2018). From Convergence to Divergence? Some New Insights into the Evolution of the European Union. *Structural Change and Economic Dynamics*, 47, pp. 82–95, doi: 10.1016/j.strueco.2018.07.006.

Borowiec, J. (2020). The Convergence and Synchronization of Business Cycles in the European Union and the European Monetary Union. *Prace Naukowe Uniwersytetu Ekonomicznego we Wrocławiu*, 64(3), pp. 7–20.

Borsi, M.T. and Metiu, N. (2015), The Evolution of Economic Convergence in the European Union. *Empirical Economics*, 48, pp. 657–681, doi: 10.1007/s00181-014-0801-2.

Borys, M.M., Polgár, É.K. and Zlate, A. (2008). Real Convergence and the Determinants of Growth in EU Candidate and Potential Candidate Countries: A Panel Data Approach. *European Central Bank Occasional Paper Series*, 86, Frankfurt am Main.

Cabral, R. and Castellanos-Sosa, F.A. (2019). Europe's Income Convergence and the Latest Global Financial Crisis. *Research in Economics*, 73(1), pp. 23–34, doi: 10.1016/j.rie.2019.01.003.

Čihák, M. and Fonteyne, W. (2009). Five Years After: European Union Membership and Macro-Financial Stability in the New Member States. *IMF Working Paper*, 2009/68, Washington, DC, doi: 10.5089/9781451872156.001.

Crespo Cuaresma, J., Havettová, M. and Lábaj, M. (2013). Income Convergence Prospects in Europe: Assessing the Role of Human Capital Dynamics. *Economic Systems*, 37(4), pp. 493–507, doi: 10.1016/j.ecosys.2013.02.004.

Czasonis, M. and Quinn, M.A. (2012). Income Convergence in Europe: Catching Up or Falling Behind?. *Acta Oeconomica*, 62(2), pp. 183–204, doi: 10.1556/aoecon.62.2012.2.3.

Duro, E. (2012). Speed of Convergence. CEE and Western Balkans Countries. *International Journal of Scientific & Engineering Research*, 3(4), pp. 88–94.

Głodowska, A. (2017). Business Environment and Economic Growth in the European Union Countries: What Can Be Explained for the Convergence? *Entrepreneurial Business and Economics Review*, 5(4), pp. 189–204, doi: 10.15678/eber.2017.050409.

Growiec, J. (2005). Dynamika konwergencji Polski z Unią Europejską. *Gospodarka Narodowa*, 5–6, pp. 101–118, doi: 10.33119/gn/101548.

Grzelak, A. and Kujaczyńska, M. (2013). Real Convergence of the European Union Members States – Evaluation Attempt. *Management*, 17(1), pp. 393–404, doi: 10.2478/manment-2013–0028.

Halmai, P. and Vásáry, V. (2010). Real Convergence in the New Member States of the European Union (Shorter and Longer Term Prospects). *European Journal of Comparative Economics*, 7(1), pp. 229–253.

Herrmann, S. and Winkler, A. (2010). Real Convergence, Financial Markets, and the Current Account: Emerging Europe versus Emerging Asia. In: F. Keereman, I. Szekely, eds., *Five Years of an Enlarged EU. A Positive Sum Game*. Berlin, Heidelberg: Springer-Verlag, pp. 123–152.

Jóźwik, B. (2017). *Realna konwergencja gospodarcza państw członkowskich Unii Europejskiej z Europy Środkowej i Wschodniej. Transformacja, integracja i polityka spójności*. Warszawa: Wydawnictwo Naukowe PWN.

Kaitila, V. (2004). Convergence of Real GDP Per Capita in the EU15. How Do the Accession Countries Fit In? *ENEPRI Working Paper*, 25.

Kim, J.-Y. (2002). Limited Information Likelihood and Bayesian Analysis. *Journal of Econometrics*, 107(1–2), pp. 175–193, doi: 10.1016/s0304–4076(01)00119-1.

Kulhánek, L. (2012). Real Convergence in Central European EU Member States. In: I. Honová, L. Melecký, M. Staníčková, eds., *Proceedings of the 1st International Conference on European Integration 2012, ICEI 2012*. 1st International Conference on European Integration, Ostrava, Czech Republic, May 17–18, VŠB – Technical University of Ostrava, Department of European Integration, Faculty of Economics, pp. 161–170.

Kutan, A.M. and Yigit, T.M. (2009). European Integration, Productivity Growth and Real Convergence: Evidence from the New Member States. *Economic Systems*, 33(2), pp. 127–137, doi: 10.1016/j.ecosys.2009.03.002.

Leamer, E. (1978). *Specification Searches: Ad Hoc Inference with Non Experimental Data*. New York: John Wiley & Sons.

Lein, S.M., León-Ledesma, M.A. and Nerlich, C. (2008). How Is Real Convergence Driving Nominal Convergence in the New EU Member States?. *Journal of International Money and Finance*, 27(2), pp. 227–248, doi: 10.1016/j.jimonfin.2007.12.004.

Liberda, Z.B. (2009). *Konwergencja gospodarcza Polski*. VIII Congress of Polish Economists. Warszawa: Polskie Towarzystwo Ekonomiczne.

Malaga, K. (2004). *Konwergencja gospodarcza w krajach OECD w świetle zagregowanych modeli wzrostu*. Poznań: Wydawnictwo Akademii Ekonomicznej.

Marelli, E. and Signorelli, M. (2010). Institutional, Nominal and Real Convergence in Europe. *Banks and Bank Systems*, 5(2), pp. 140–155.

Markowska, M. and Sobczak, E. (2008). Problematyka konwergencji gospodarczej krajów i regionów. *Prace Naukowe Akademii Ekonomicznej we Wrocławiu. Ekonometria*, 1195, pp. 127–138.

Matkowski, Z., Próchniak, M. and Rapacki, R. (2016). Real Income Convergence between Central Eastern and Western Europe: Past, Present, and Prospects. *Ekonomista*, 6, pp. 853–892.

Michałek, J.J., Siwiński, W. and Socha, M. (2007). *Polska w Unii Europejskiej – dynamika konwergencji ekonomicznej*. Warszawa: Wydawnictwo Naukowe PWN.

Monfort, M., Cuestas, J.C. and Ordóñez, J. (2013). Real Convergence in Europe: A Cluster Analysis. *Economic Modelling*, 33, pp. 689–694, doi: 10.1016/j.econmod.2013.05.015.

Mucha, M. (2012). Mechanizm dywergencji gospodarczej w strefie euro. *Ekonomista*, 4, pp. 487–498.

Niebuhr, A. and Schlitte, F. (2009). EU Enlargement and Convergence: Does Market Access Matter?. *Eastern European Economics*, 47(3), pp. 28–56, doi: 10.2753/eee0012-8775470302.

Polanec, S. (2004). Convergence at Last? Evidence from Transition Countries. *Eastern European Economics*, 42(4), pp. 55–80, doi: 10.1080/00128775.2004.11041081.

Próchniak, M. (2020). Income Convergence of Poland to the Average EU Level. In: A.M. Kowalski, M.A. Weresa, eds., *Poland. Competitiveness Report 2020. Focus on Service Sector*. Warsaw: World Economy Research Institute, SGH Warsaw School of Economics, pp. 67–79.

Próchniak, M. and Witkowski, B. (2013). Time Stability of the Beta Convergence among EU Countries: Bayesian Model Averaging Perspective. *Economic Modelling*, 30, pp. 322–333, doi: 10.1016/j.econmod.2012.08.031.

Puziak, M. and Gazda, J. (2010). Realna konwergencja gospodarek nadbałtyckich w świetle dekompozycji wzrostu gospodarczego. *Zeszyty Naukowe Uniwersytetu Ekonomicznego w Poznaniu*, 132, pp. 162–172.

Rapacki, R. and Próchniak, M. (2007). Konwergencja beta i sigma w krajach postsocjalistycznych w latach 1990–2005. *Bank i Kredyt*, 8–9, pp. 42–60.

Rapacki, R. and Próchniak, M. (2010). Wpływ rozszerzenia Unii Europejskiej na wzrost gospodarczy i realną konwergencję krajów Europy Środkowo-Wschodniej. *Ekonomista*, 4, pp. 523–546.

Rapacki, R. and Próchniak, M. (2012). Wzrost gospodarczy w krajach Europy Środkowo-Wschodniej na tle wybranych krajów wschodzących. *Gospodarka Narodowa*, 1–2, pp. 65–96, doi: 10.33119/gn/101018.

Rapacki, R. and Próchniak, M. (2014). Wpływ członkostwa w Unii Europejskiej na wzrost gospodarczy i realną konwergencję krajów Europy Środkowo-Wschodniej. *Ekonomia*, 39, pp. 87–122.

Rapacki, R. and Próchniak, M. (2019). EU Membership and Economic Growth: Empirical Evidence for the CEE Countries. *European Journal of Comparative Economics*, 16(1), pp. 3–40, doi: 10.25428/1824-2979/201901-3-40.

Rogut, A. and Roszkowska, S. (2006). Konwergencja warunkowa w krajach trans-formacji. *Gospodarka Narodowa*, 9, pp. 35–55, doi: 10.33119/gn/101447.

Sala-i-Martin, X., Doppelhofer, G. and Miller, R. (2004). Determinants of Long-Term Growth: A Bayesian Averaging of Classical Estimates (BACE) Approach. *American Economic Review*, 94(4), pp. 813–835, doi: 10.1257/0002828042002570.

Sarajevs, V. (2001). Convergence of European Transition Economies and the EU: What Do the Data Show. *BOFIT Discussion Paper*, 13, Helsinki.

Siljak, D. and Nagy, S.G. (2019). Do Transition Countries Converge towards the European Union?. *TalTech Journal of European Studies*, 9(1), pp. 115–139, doi: 10.1515/bjes-2019-0007.

Stanišić, N. (2012). The Effects of the Economic Crisis on Income Convergence in the European Union. *Acta Oeconomica*, 62(2), pp. 161–182, doi: 10.1556/aoecon.62.2012.2.2.

Suska, M. (2021). *Handel towarami jednostek nieuznawanych - przypadek Abchazji i Osetii Południowej*. Warszawa: Szkoła Główna Handlowa w Warszawie.

Szeles, M.R. and Marinescu, N. (2010). Real Convergence in the CEECs, Euro Area Accession and the Role of Romania. *European Journal of Comparative Economics*, 7(1), pp. 181–202.

Tatomir, C.F. and Alexe, I. (2011). Laggards or Performers? CEE vs. PIIGS Countries' Catch-up with the Euro Area in the Last Ten Years. *MPRA Paper*, 35715, Munich.

Vamvakidis, A. (2009). Convergence in Emerging Europe: Sustainability and Vulnerabilities. *Eastern European Economics*, 47(3), pp. 5–27, doi: 10.2753/eee0012-8775470301.

Varblane, U. and Vahter, P. (2005). An Analysis of the Economic Convergence Process in the Transition Countries. *University of Tartu Economics and Business Working Paper*, 37-2005, doi: 10.2139/ssrn.757204.

Vojinovic, B. and Oplotnik, J. (2008). Real Convergence of GDP Per Capita in the New EU Member States. *Transformations in Business & Economics*, 7, pp. 89–103.

Walczak, E. (2012). Czynniki wzrostu gospodarczego w krajach Unii Europejskiej. *Wiadomości Statystyczne*, 4, pp. 65–84.

Wolszczak-Derlacz, J. (2009). Does Migration Lead to Economic Convergence in an Enlarged European Market? *Bank i Kredyt*, 40, pp. 73–90.

5 Application of the hidden Markov models in convergence studies

A worldwide perspective

5.1 Introduction

In this chapter, we use the concept of HMM described in Chapter 2 to validate the convergence hypothesis in wider groups of the world countries divided into the particular regions. The analysed time series of GDP per capita cover the period from 1995 to 2019. A limited number of years determines the maximum number of HMM states which can be considered in the convergence analysis. The two-state hidden Markov chain gives just the blurred information about the convergence for the considered group of countries because in most cases just one turning point was identified. This is mainly due to time constant direction of the process in the whole period (either convergence or divergence) at the national level, while the two-state approach does not allow us to observe the changes in the rate of convergence itself over time. This is why the three-state hidden Markov model was adopted in this analysis and all the results in this chapter are given on a three-state basis.

In this context, state 0 on the Viterbi path means that in this particular year a group of countries was getting closer to the (hypothetical) leader. On the contrary, state 1 indicates a discrepancy between the reference time series and other countries. State ½ corresponds to the transition period and should be interpreted as years with neither convergence nor divergence. On a relative basis, state ½ can be interpreted as a state when the speed of convergence or divergence decelerated compared with the previously observed convergence (state 0) or divergence (state 1).

It should be emphasized that the results obtained by the HMM convergence are relative to the investigated period. It means that e.g. divergence in the second part of the period should be interpreted as a statistically significant greater difference in the GDPs per capita between pairs of analysed countries in relation to the data from the first part, which in this context should be considered in terms of the convergence process. When we restrict our analysis only to the second period, the optimal sequence of HMM states would change. Results in this shortened period would indicate other years in which countries would be considered more similar (convergence) or rather different (divergent) – all relative to the values given in this particular period.

Figures showing HMM convergence, selected from the hundreds of pairs of countries, that are presented in the remaining part of this chapter carry a variety of information. First of all, with the solid line, the difference in the GDPs per capita between pairs of countries is marked. Second, the Viterbi path is given using the dotted line. The values of the states on the Viterbi path are marked on the first (left-hand side) vertical axis and are taken from the set {0, ½, 1} which represents the states from the three-state HMM space. The interpretation of those states was given at the beginning of this section. To better visualize the changes between phases corresponding to different rates of convergence/divergence, grey background with different shades was added. Following the example of visualization for early warning signalling used with Markov-switching models, which harmonizes with the concept of the Ifo business cycle traffic lights (Abberger and Nierhaus, 2010), the phases in dark grey coincide with state 1, in light grey coincide with state 0, and in middle grey corresponds with the transition period denoted by state ½.

5.2 Empirical results of the HMM-based study

In this part of the chapter, we present the results of the analyses regarding the different regions of the world. As in the case of the β convergence analysis described in Chapter 4, the conclusions differ across regions which we outline in the particular subsections.

In each group, the reference country is the country which recorded the highest GDP per capita at the end of the analysed period, i.e. in 2019. If such a country was the richest country in a given group throughout the whole analysed period, the reference point is just the GDP per capita time series for this country (multiplier = 1). If such a country wasn't the richest economy during all the years covered by the analysis, it is necessary to apply a multiplier to obtain the hypothetical time series of GDP per capita which is the actual GDP per capita time series for the reference country multiplied by a specified multiplier to obtain the time series with the values greater than GDP per capita figures for all the remaining countries in all years (see also Chapter 2).

Computed multipliers for each group of countries are given in Table 5.1.

5.2.1 European Union

We follow the approach described in Chapter 2 and begin with identifying the leader. In the EU28 group, the richest country is Luxembourg. Hence, convergence to the richest country means the convergence of individual countries to per capita income level prevailing in Luxembourg. Figure 5.1 shows GDP per capita time series in Luxembourg and selected EU28 countries, namely new EU member states from Central and Eastern Europe (CEE): Bulgaria, Croatia, Czech Republic, Estonia, Hungary, Latvia,

Table 5.1 The reference countries and multipliers

Group of countries	Reference country	Multiplier
European Union (EU28)	Luxembourg	1.000000
Europe	Luxembourg	1.000000
North Africa and the Middle East	Qatar	1.335624
Sub-Saharan Africa	Seychelles	2.038441
South America	Chile	1.293020
Caribbean	Aruba	1.043105
South-East Asia	Singapore	1.955350
Australia and Oceania	Australia	1.000000
Post-socialist countries	Czech Republic	1.091504
OECD countries	Luxembourg	1.000000

Source: Own calculations.

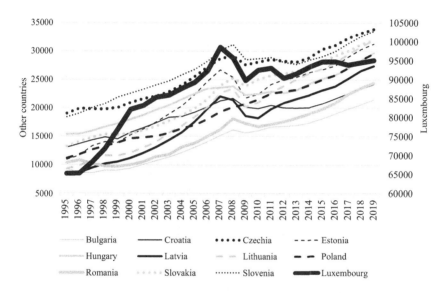

Figure 5.1 GDP per capita time series for the reference country (Luxembourg) and the other selected economies from the EU28 group (at purchasing power parity, constant prices, 2011 international dollars).

Lithuania, Poland, Romania, Slovakia, and Slovenia.[1] Results of the three-state HMM approach applied to Luxembourg and each of these countries separately are presented in Figures 5.2–5.12 in forms of graphs showing the convergence or divergence over the years.

Figure 5.1 indicates that the income gap between the CEE countries and Luxembourg is enormous. The new EU member states lag behind in terms of the per capita income level. Statistics for Luxembourg show that GDP per capita in Luxembourg was rising relatively fast till the global crisis and

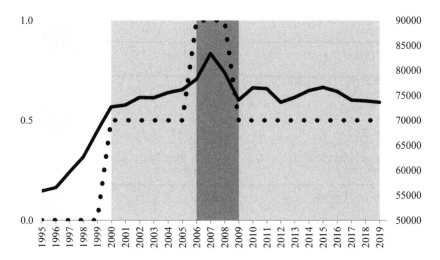

Figure 5.2 Per capita income gap (solid line) and the Viterbi path (dotted line) for Bulgaria against Luxembourg.

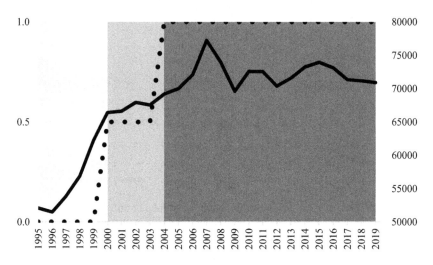

Figure 5.3 Per capita income gap (solid line) and the Viterbi path (dotted line) for Croatia against Luxembourg.

income differences between Luxembourg and CEE countries rose. However, during the global crisis Luxembourg faced a deep recession as reflected by a sharp drop in income level followed by its moderate increase – the pattern followed by many highly developed regions with the financial sector being an engine of their economies.

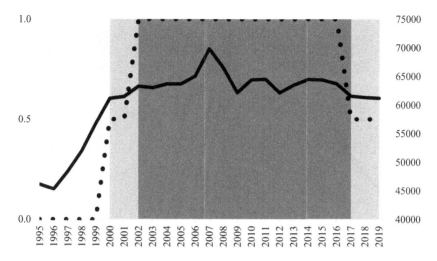

Figure 5.4 Per capita income gap (solid line) and the Viterbi path (dotted line) for Czechia against Luxembourg.

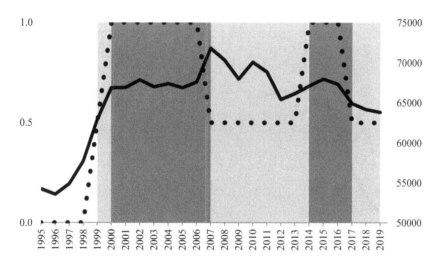

Figure 5.5 Per capita income gap (solid line) and the Viterbi path (dotted line) for Estonia against Luxembourg.

When analysing convergence for Bulgaria (Figure 5.2), the HMM approach indicates divergence in income level till 2008 – states on the Viterbi path rose from 0 during 1995–1999 to 0.5 during 2000–2005 and 1 during 2006–2008. It means that just before the global crisis the Bulgarian GDP growth path diverged from that in Luxembourg. From 2009 onwards, states

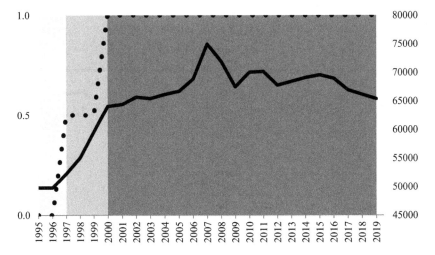

Figure 5.6 Per capita income gap (solid line) and the Viterbi path (dotted line) for Hungary against Luxembourg.

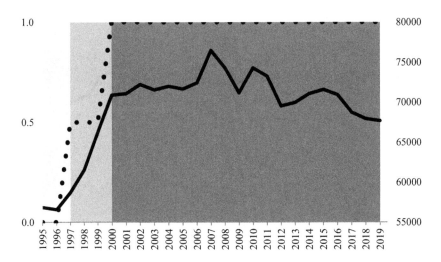

Figure 5.7 Per capita income gap (solid line) and the Viterbi path (dotted line) for Latvia against Luxembourg.

on the Viterbi path take the value of 0.5 again meaning that divergence trends strongly weakened, but the statistics do not allow to infer about convergence. In terms of this graph, state 0.5 can be interpreted as an ambiguous outcome – neither divergence nor convergence.

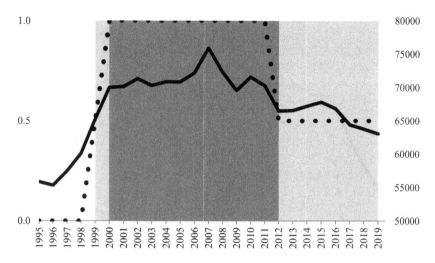

Figure 5.8 Per capita income gap (solid line) and the Viterbi path (dotted line) for Lithuania against Luxembourg.

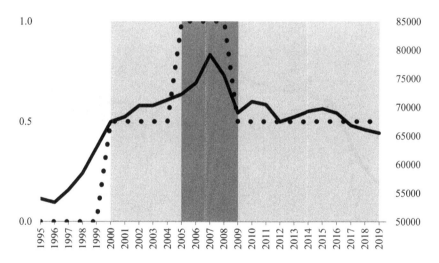

Figure 5.9 Per capita income gap (solid line) and the Viterbi path (dotted line) for Poland against Luxembourg.

The application of the HMM approach to the analysis of convergence can be easily explained when comparing Bulgaria with Croatia. In the initial part of the analysed period, income per capita differences between Croatia and Luxembourg were rising (Figure 5.3). Such divergence trends are evidenced by the behaviour of the Viterbi path whose states changed from 0 (till 1999)

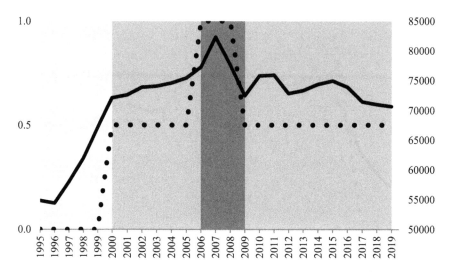

Figure 5.10 Per capita income gap (solid line) and the Viterbi path (dotted line) for Romania against Luxembourg.

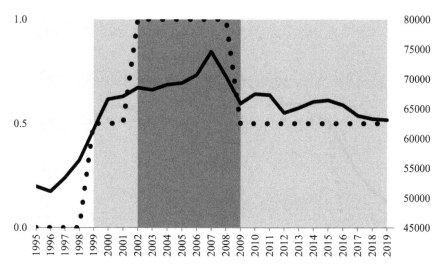

Figure 5.11 Per capita income gap (solid line) and the Viterbi path (dotted line) for Slovakia against Luxembourg.

to 0.5 (during 2000–2003) and 1 (from 2004 onwards). The behaviour in the initial years is similar to that in Bulgaria. However, unlike Bulgaria, Croatia remained at the divergent path till 2019: after the global crisis income differences between Croatia and Luxembourg remained high and did not notice a considerable drop as in the case of Bulgaria. That is why the Viterbi path

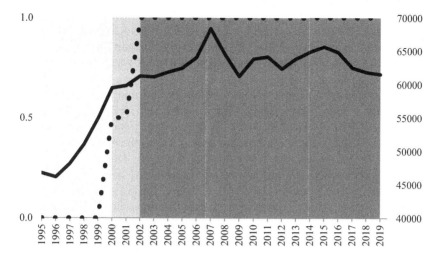

Figure 5.12 Per capita income gap (solid line) and the Viterbi path (dotted line) for Slovenia against Luxembourg.

for Croatia did not change in the 2010s and state 1 was evidenced until the end of the analysed period. A change in the state on the Viterbi path can be treated as the turning point in the process of convergence. Hence, after full convergence, Bulgaria recorded a turning point towards neither divergence nor convergence, whereas Croatia has stayed on the divergent path due to slower growth of per capita income during the 2010s.

The behaviour of the Czech Republic is similar to that of Bulgaria but with different turning points. At the beginning of the analysed period, the economy of the Czech Republic revealed divergent trends against Luxembourg as reflected by changes in the states from 0 to 1 around 2000 (Figure 5.4). According to the HMM approach, state 1 prevailed till 2016 followed by the change of the state to 0.5. This last turning point which took place in 2017 shows that the Czech economy changed its path towards convergence trends; however, full convergence (state 0) did not appear till 2019; hence, the Czech growth path during 2017–2019 can be classified as neither convergence nor divergence.

The results obtained using the HMM-based analysis suggest that the behaviour of Estonia is slightly different compared to the previously examined countries, but some similarities exist as well. There was a rapid divergence before 2000 which was maintained until 2006 (Figure 5.5). Afterwards, the states on the Viterbi path take the values of 0.5 and 1, pointing to the variable behaviour of time series and indicating that the income gap between Estonia and Luxembourg fluctuated in different directions. In some years there was a tendency towards convergence as state 0.5 suggests (but full convergence according to HMM was not evidenced); this process was however skewed towards divergence as indicated by states 1 during 2014–2016. It is

worth mentioning that the HMM method takes into account the whole behaviour of the time series. In the other words, it indicates turning points
and individual states in a smart way. For example, a local peak in 2010 was
not classified as divergence (despite a higher income gap than in 2015 when
divergence was recorded). It is because the 2010 peak was a short-run deviation of a downward trend in time series involved.

A smart way of indicating turning points and optimal sequence of states
can be shown based on Hungary which is presented in Figure 5.6. According to the HMM method, the fully divergent state 1 was achieved already
in 2000 and the economy remained in this state till the end of the analysed
period. The time series plotted in the figure shows a slight decrease in income disparities between Hungary and Luxembourg after 2007; however,
the HMM approach did not classify it as a trend towards convergence and a
turning point was not recorded. Despite a fall in income differences, Hungary should be treated as a still divergent country against Luxembourg.

The Viterbi path for Latvia is the same as that for Hungary (Figure 5.7).
Till 2000, the HMM method indicated a rapid movement from convergence
to divergence. After 2000, state 1 was evidenced meaning that according
to the HMM algorithm the Latvian economy exhibited a divergent trend
against Luxembourg despite a decrease in the income gap between these
countries. The results for Latvia and Hungary are worth comparing with
those for Lithuania (Figure 5.8). Lithuania again showed a rapid movement
from convergence to divergence till 2000. Unlike Hungary and Latvia, however, a fall in income differences between Lithuania and Luxembourg after
2007 was significant enough to exert the impact on the order in the sequence
of states of the hidden Markov chain. Indeed, in 2012, a turning point was
recorded and from 2012 onwards, state 0.5 has been evidenced on the Viterbi
path. This outcome demonstrates that Lithuania succeeded in abandoning
divergence tendencies. A decrease in income gap towards Luxembourg, although greater than in the case of Hungary and Latvia, was too small for
the Viterbi path to evidence state 0, i.e. full convergence.

Compared to the previously examined countries, Poland recorded quite
good outcomes in terms of the convergence process. This is confirmed by
the Viterbi path for Poland presented in Figure 5.9. The HMM method indicates that divergence in GDP per capita between Poland and Luxembourg
occurred only during 2005–2008. In the remaining years, convergence or
ambiguous outcome (meaning neither convergence nor divergence) was
recorded. After 2007, the differences in income level between Poland and
Luxembourg started to decrease and the sharpest drop occurred during
2007–2009. Such an outcome stems from the fact that Poland was the only
EU country that avoided recession during the global crisis. Such a rapid
fall in the income gap between Poland and Luxembourg influenced the Viterbi path whose smart algorithm found a turning point in the catching-up
process. The turning point was evidenced in 2009 and after this year the
Viterbi path for Poland assumed state 0.5 indicating the lack of divergence

or convergence. Although state 0 has not appeared since 2009 (due to the fact that a decreasing trend in income differences weakened in the 2010s), the behaviour of the Polish economy was different than that of the majority of the other CEE countries where state 1 was evidenced till 2019 indicating continuous divergence.

Figure 5.10 shows the Viterbi path for Romania. It turns out that the convergence/divergence process between Romania and Luxembourg was very similar to that for Poland. The full divergence between Romania and Luxembourg was recorded during a very short period. After 2009 the HMM method points to neither convergence nor divergence which is the same outcome as in the case of Poland. For both countries, it was the global financial crisis, which triggered the changes in the rate of divergence.

Quite similar is also the behaviour of Slovakia (Figure 5.11). The main difference compared to Poland is that in Slovakia the HMM approach suggests the appearance of full divergence three years earlier (in 2002 instead of 2005). Both the 2009 turning point and state 0.5 afterwards observed for Poland were also confirmed in the case of Slovakia implying high similarities between these two neighbouring countries from Central and Eastern Europe.

Unlike Bulgaria, Czech Republic, Estonia, Lithuania, Poland, Romania, and Slovakia, the Slovenian economy recorded full divergence throughout the major part of the analysed period (Figure 5.12). The HMM method suggests that full divergence between per capita income in Slovenia and Luxembourg started already in 2002 and has lasted till now. This outcome makes Slovenia similar to Croatia, Hungary, and Latvia, although these countries differ in terms of the turning point dating when the process of full divergence begun.

* * *

For the sake of completeness, we provide additional results for the entire group of Europe. As Luxembourg exhibits the highest GDP also in this wider group, it is used as a reference country as well. As a result, the most interesting results described above remain valid.

Different outcomes for the individual CEE countries can be explained on the basis of some differences in their institutional systems. As a result, the individual countries react differently to external shocks, e.g. the global financial crisis. One of the ways of explanation of the differences between single countries is the nature of the model of capitalism. According to the study by Rapacki (2019), the CEE countries did not create their own model of capitalism nor fully adopted one of the models of capitalism prevailing in Western Europe (continental model, Anglo-Saxon model, Nordic model, or Mediterranean model). In contrast, they copied a mix of solutions from Western European countries, and the institutional system prevailing in the CEE countries can be dubbed as patchwork capitalism. This concept reflects the fact that the individual countries adopted different institutions from different economic and political systems and the complementarity of institutions was often violated. This is one of the reasons for the lack of coherent behaviour in terms of the Viterbi path.

5.2.2 North Africa and the Middle East

In the remaining distinguished groups, we select and show the results for only three selected countries (though the complete calculations for all the countries included in a given group were conducted). The selected countries usually are large or important countries of a given region.

In the case of North Africa and the Middle East, the selected countries are Egypt, Israel, and the United Arab Emirates (UAE) whom we report in detail in this book. The reference point is Qatar, i.e. the country with the highest GDP per capita level in 2019. Figure 5.13 shows GDP per capita time series for Qatar, Egypt, Israel, and the UAE. As we can see, the income gap between Qatar and the remaining three countries has widened since 1995.

The detailed results for Egypt, Israel, and the UAE are presented in Figures 5.14–5.16. Instead of describing the figures in detail, we will focus on conclusions. Namely, all these three countries exhibited a tendency from convergence towards divergence during the 1995–2019 period. They started with state 0 on the Viterbi path and at the end of the period, their Viterbi paths switched towards full divergence (state 1) or an ambiguous outcome

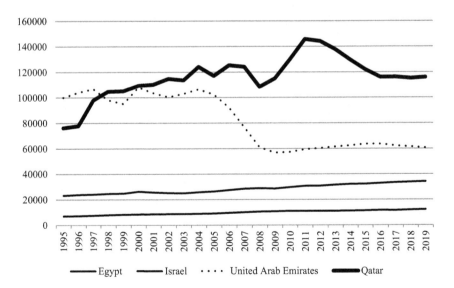

Figure 5.13 GDP per capita time series for the reference country (Qatar) and the other selected economies from North Africa and the Middle East (at purchasing power parity, constant prices, 2011 international dollars).

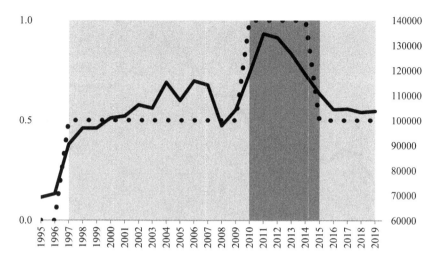

Figure 5.14 Per capita income gap (solid line) and the Viterbi path (dotted line) for Egypt against Qatar.

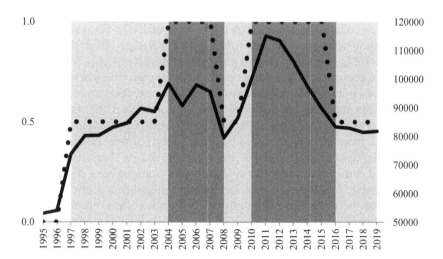

Figure 5.15 Per capita income gap (solid line) and the Viterbi path (dotted line) for Israel against Qatar.

(state 0.5). The latter state, compared with state 0, indicates the movement from the catching-up towards an increase in income-level differences. When analysing the other countries from the region, the figures for which are not presented in this book, it turns out that a similar path (state 0 in 1995 and state 0.5 or 1 in 2019) was recorded for all of them. This conclusion means

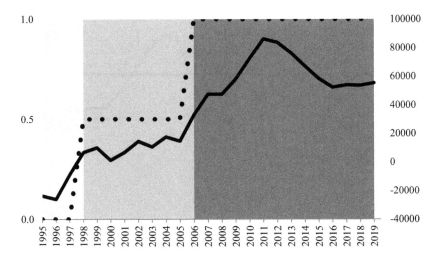

Figure 5.16 Per capita income gap (solid line) and the Viterbi path (dotted line) for United Arab Emirates against Qatar.

that the richest country exhibited quite a different growth mechanism and evidently diverged from all the other countries of the region.

A similar conclusion was drawn in the case of EU28 countries. In that case, the reference point was Luxembourg and it diverged from the majority of the other EU countries. Such an outcome suggests high polarization in the level of economic development within country groups when individual countries are compared with the most developed one. Rich countries earn a lot of income and they are following their own growth paths. Income does not tend to be equally distributed. There may be different factors responsible for high income levels recorded by the outliers, i.e. most developed countries. In the case of Luxembourg, it is tax regulations that attract foreign capital and cause that many transnational corporations have headquarters or are registered in Luxembourg. In the case of Qatar, it is gas and oil resources and their efficient exploitation which makes this country relatively richer compared to its neighbours from the Middle East and North Africa.[2]

5.2.3 Sub-Saharan Africa

The group of sub-Saharan African countries does not have an obvious leader in terms of GDP per capita as Luxembourg or Qatar in the case of two previous groups of countries. For sub-Saharan Africa the reference country is Seychelles which has been the richest country in this region since 2016. In the earlier years, Equatorial Guinea (during 2001–2015) or Gabon (during 1995–2000) were the leaders in terms of per capita income level. Equatorial Guinea noticed a large drop in GDP per capita in the last years and that is why Seychelles has appeared to be the most developed country in sub-Saharan Africa.[3] In this group, we provide the detailed results for Kenya, Nigeria, and South Africa which we believe are important players in the considered region. GDP per capita time series of these three countries and Seychelles are presented in Figure 5.17.

Seychelles significantly increased the distance from the remaining countries. Such a growth path is caused, *inter alia*, by the high development of the tourism sector in Seychelles. This allows Seychelles to earn a considerable amount of money from foreign visitors travelling to this country. Other sub-Saharan African countries do not have this scale of possibilities compared to the size of the country.

Figures 5.18–5.20 present the Viterbi paths for Kenya, Nigeria, and South Africa. Kenya was selected because of the developed tourism sector which makes this country similar to Seychelles. Nigeria is the most intensively populated African country. South Africa was selected due to the relatively high level of economic development and atypical history compared with the other African countries linked with the prevalence of the Apartheid era. Unlike in the previously considered groups, the three countries examined here recorded full convergence towards the reference country during a relatively long period, i.e. in the 1990s and early 2000s. In Kenya, state 0 on the Viterbi path (which indicates full convergence) has been identified from 1995 to 2005, in Nigeria – from 1995 to 2006 and in South Africa – from 1995 to 2010. Divergence tendencies started to appear in the last years which is the

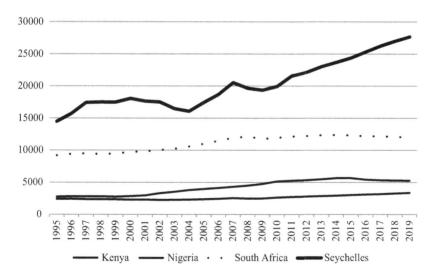

Figure 5.17 GDP per capita time series for the reference country (Seychelles) and the other selected economies from sub-Saharan Africa (at purchasing power parity, constant prices, 2011 international dollars).

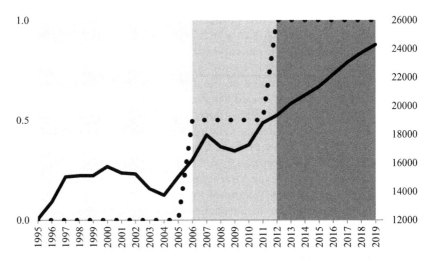

Figure 5.18 Per capita income gap (solid line) and the Viterbi path (dotted line) for Kenya against Seychelles.

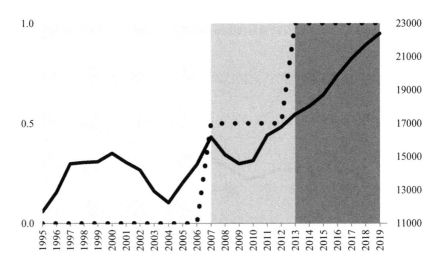

Figure 5.19 Per capita income gap (solid line) and the Viterbi path (dotted line) for Nigeria against Seychelles.

result of a relatively rapid economic growth in Seychelles. It is worth noting that in the last years all 45 sub-Saharan African countries examined in this book have recorded state 1 on their Viterbi paths indicating that all of them have recently diverged from Seychelles.[4]

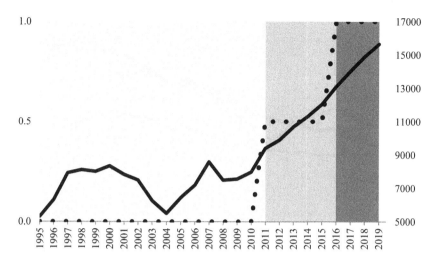

Figure 5.20 Per capita income gap (solid line) and the Viterbi path (dotted line) for South Africa against Seychelles.

5.2.4 South America

In the case of South America, the three selected countries for the detailed analysis of convergence are Argentina, Brazil, and Venezuela. The first two choices result from the fact that Argentina and Brazil are countries with a large surface area and large economic potential. Venezuela was chosen due to atypical growth paths caused by the lack of economic freedom, political instability, and internal tensions prevailing in this country leading to an economic crisis. The reference country in South America is Chile, which was the country with the highest GDP per capita in 2019.

Figure 5.21 shows that GDP per capita time series for Argentina, Brazil, and Venezuela diverge from that for Chile. Hence, the detailed results should indicate divergence tendencies in this group of countries. An interesting country is Venezuela which has recorded a sharp drop in per capita income since 2013.

The Viterbi paths for Argentina, Brazil, and Venezuela are presented in Figures 5.22–5.24. They are very similar. All of them begin with state 0, indicating convergence. Then, state 0.5 was noted, followed by state 1 meaning full divergence. The individual countries differ (although not very much) in terms of the exact dating of turning points. The first turning point (the switch of the state from 0 to 0.5) occurred in 2002 in Argentina and Venezuela and 2005 in Brazil. The second turning point took place in 2010 in Venezuela and in 2012 in Argentina and Brazil.

We can raise the following conclusions for South America. First, the states on Viterbi paths indicate only whether convergence or divergence exists but

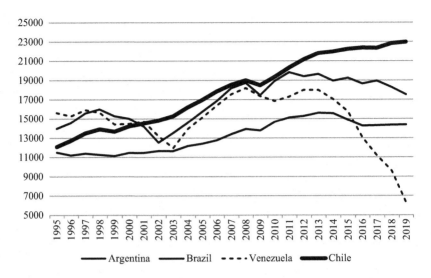

Figure 5.21 GDP per capita time series for the reference country (Chile) and the other selected economies from South America (at purchasing power parity, constant prices, 2011 international dollars).

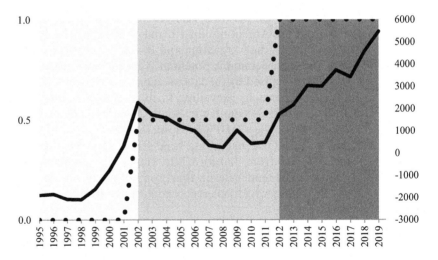

Figure 5.22 Per capita income gap (solid line) and the Viterbi path (dotted line) for Argentina against Chile.

they do not say anything about the strength of this process. All the three countries (Argentina, Brazil, and Venezuela) exhibited divergence at the end of the analysed period, but Figure 5.21 shows that the magnitude of the process was completely different. Venezuela diverged to a much greater extent

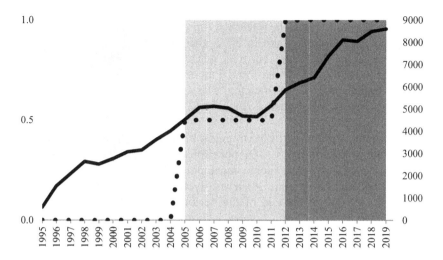

Figure 5.23 Per capita income gap (solid line) and the Viterbi path (dotted line) for Brazil against Chile.

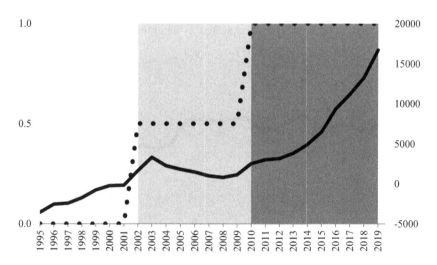

Figure 5.24 Per capita income gap (solid line) and the Viterbi path (dotted line) for Venezuela against Chile.

than Argentina and Brazil. Second, according to the HMM-based analysis, full divergence in Venezuela started relatively early compared to all the 11 South American countries (also those which are not presented in the figures in this chapter) – only Uruguay noted an earlier divergence (that begun already in 2004) but with a temporary break during 2009–2010.

5.2.5 The Caribbean

In the Caribbean region, the reference country is Aruba. It was the country with highest GDP per capita in 2019, although Puerto Rico ranked very close to Aruba. The three countries selected for detailed analysis are the Dominican Republic, Mexico, and Panama due to their important economic and/or political significance. The GDP per capita time series are plotted in Figure 5.25, whereas Figures 5.26–5.28 show the results for the individual countries.

It turns out that the Caribbean region behaved differently from the previously examined countries. GDP per capita in Aruba was declining during 1995–2019 along with the increasing income level in the Dominican Republic, Mexico, and Panama. As a result, these countries initially diverged against Aruba but at the end of the period their GDP per capita growth paths caught up with Aruba. Figure 5.27 for Mexico shows the Viterbi path with only two states (0 and 1) because the change in GDP per capita differences between countries in 2008–2009 was so rapid that the HMM algorithm made an immediate shift between states 1 and 0 omitting middle state 0.5. It is worth noting that similar behaviour to that for Dominican Republic, Mexico, and Panama was also noted for the remaining 18 Caribbean countries whose growth paths showed generally the switch from divergence to convergence during the 1995–2019 period. In countries other than Mexico the change was not so instant, and state 0.5 was identified. Mexico behaved

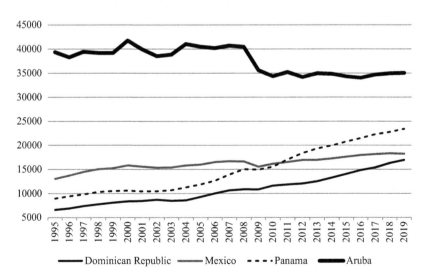

Figure 5.25 GDP per capita time series for the reference country (Aruba) and the other selected economies from the Caribbean region (at purchasing power parity, constant prices, 2011 international dollars).

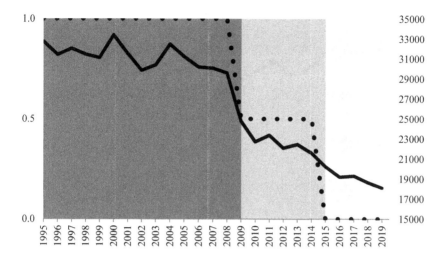

Figure 5.26 Per capita income gap (solid line) and the Viterbi path (dotted line) for Dominican Republic against Aruba.

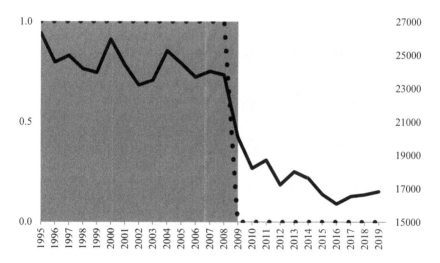

Figure 5.27 Per capita income gap (solid line) and the Viterbi path (dotted line) for Mexico against Aruba.

differently due to a different economic and political environment caused, *inter alia*, by its close links with the USA, large territory, and huge economic potential making this country much different compared with all the other states which are relatively small (in terms of total GDP, surface area, and the population number).

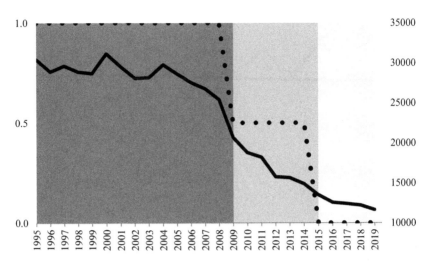

Figure 5.28 Per capita income gap (solid line) and the Viterbi path (dotted line) for Panama against Aruba.

5.2.6 South-East Asia

For South-East Asian countries, the catching-up process is analysed against Singapore. It was the richest country in 2019. Moreover, as Figure 5.29 demonstrates, GDP per capita in Singapore was rising significantly during the last years. As a result, we can expect a huge divergence in income levels between the South-East Asian nations and the benchmark.

Figures 5.30–5.32 show the Viterbi paths for China, Japan, and Korea (South), which are key players in the region with (especially in the case of Japan and Korea) very high level of economic development. Despite the systematic growth of GDP per capita in these three countries, Singapore experienced a more rapid economic growth. As a result, China, Japan, and Korea recorded divergence against Singapore. For all these three countries, the Viterbi paths begun with state 0, followed by state 0.5, and ending with state 1. In the other words, economic growth paths tended from convergence to divergence. The individual countries also behaved almost identically in terms of the dating of turning points. The first turning point (the switch from state 0 to 0.5) occurred in 2004 in China, Japan, and Korea. The second turning point (the switch from state 0.5 to 1) took place in 2010 in Japan and in 2011 in China and Korea. For the sake of completeness, let's add that the remaining 20 South-East Asian nations also exhibited very similar Viterbi paths in terms of both the sequence of states and the dating of turning points. Such an outcome means that the group of South-East Asian countries is relatively homogenous from the

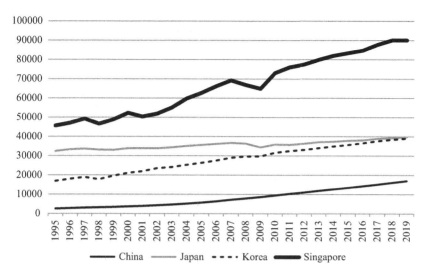

Figure 5.29 GDP per capita time series for the reference country (Singapore) and the other selected economies from South-East Asia (at purchasing power parity, constant prices, 2011 international dollars).

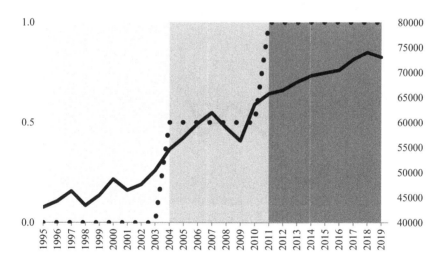

Figure 5.30 Per capita income gap (solid line) and the Viterbi path (dotted line) for China against Singapore.

point of view of the behaviour of GDP per capita compared with the most advanced country. It is a conclusion that would be difficult to draw without the application of HMM.

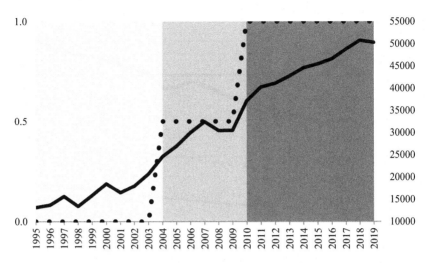

Figure 5.31 Per capita income gap (solid line) and the Viterbi path (dotted line) for Japan against Singapore.

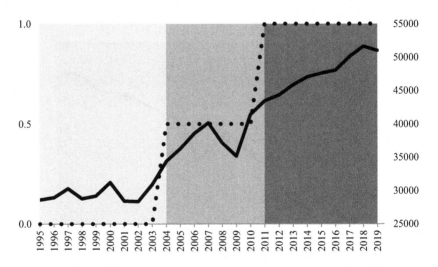

Figure 5.32 Per capita income gap (solid line) and the Viterbi path (dotted line) for Korea against Singapore.

5.2.7 *Australia and Oceania*

Figures 5.33–5.36 refer to Australia and Oceania. For this group, convergence is analysed towards Australia. Three countries were chosen for detailed analysis: New Zealand, Fiji, and Kiribati.

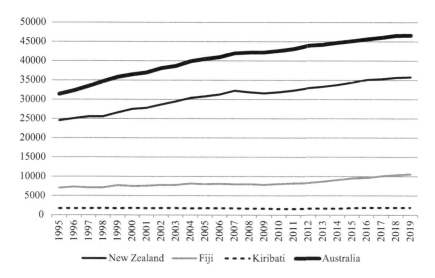

Figure 5.33 GDP per capita time series for the reference country (Australia) and the other selected economies from the Australia and Oceania group (at purchasing power parity, constant prices, 2011 international dollars).

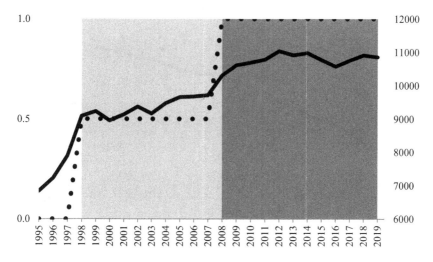

Figure 5.34 Per capita income gap (solid line) and the Viterbi path (dotted line) for New Zealand against Australia.

Data in Figure 5.33 indicate that GDP per capita in Australia revealed an increasing tendency which was more rapid than that for New Zealand, Fiji, and Kiribati. We may thus expect divergence trends in this group of countries. Such an expectation is confirmed by the Viterbi paths presented in Figures 5.34–5.36. In the case of New Zealand, the period of full convergence

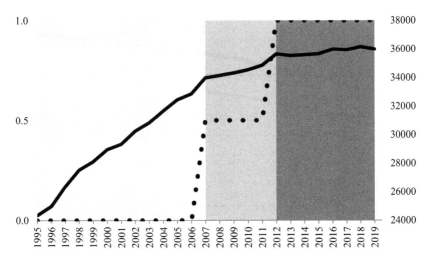

Figure 5.35 Per capita income gap (solid line) and the Viterbi path (dotted line) for Fiji against Australia.

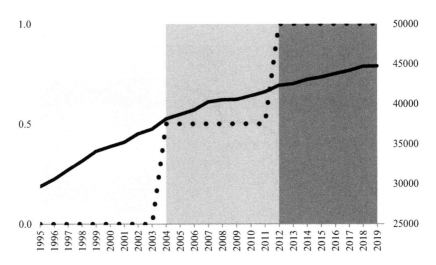

Figure 5.36 Per capita income gap (solid line) and the Viterbi path (dotted line) for Kiribati against Australia.

was only evidenced at the beginning – during 1995–1997. Afterwards, the Viterbi path for New Zealand recorded state 0.5, followed by state 1 from 2008. As we can see, according to the HMM algorithm New Zealand has been diverging from Australia in terms of per capita income level for the last decade. Despite the fact that many people may think that these two countries (Australia and New Zealand) are very similar, it turns out that the mechanisms driving their economies are different, making these countries diverging. Fiji and Kiribati noted a longer period of convergence at the beginning and started the period of divergence (according to the HMM algorithm) later. However, the sequence of states on the Viterbi paths is the same for all the three countries despite different dating of turning points.

5.2.8 Post-socialist countries

The next considered group includes post-socialist countries. In this group, the richest country in 2019 in terms of the GDP per capita was the Czech Republic. Three others were chosen for detailed analysis: Armenia, Russia, and Ukraine. Here, we decided not to analyse in detail the new EU members because these countries have already been examined in the case of the EU28 group. Moreover, from the economic point of view, the convergence within the EU countries should be analysed towards Western Europe. That is why three countries being former parts of the Soviet Union where two of them (Armenia and Russia) belong also to the Commonwealth of Independent States were chosen. In their case, convergence towards a more advanced CEE country is economically justified.

Figure 5.37 shows the time series of GDP per capita for the Czech Republic, Armenia, Russia, and Ukraine. The Viterbi paths are presented in Figures 5.38–5.40. The results show that the behaviour of Armenia and Ukraine in terms of the catching-up process is relatively similar. The

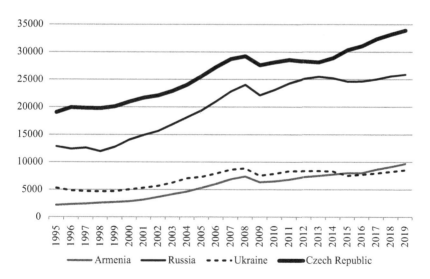

Figure 5.37 GDP per capita time series for the reference country (Czechia) and the other selected economies from the group of post-socialist countries (at purchasing power parity, constant prices, 2011 international dollars).

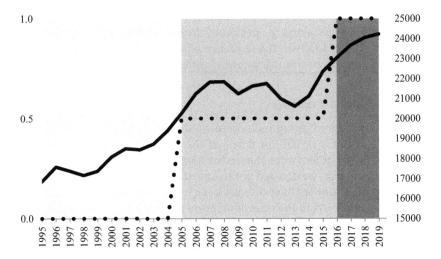

Figure 5.38 Per capita income gap (solid line) and the Viterbi path (dotted line) for Armenia against Czechia.

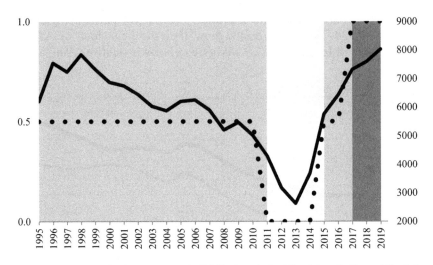

Figure 5.39 Per capita income gap (solid line) and the Viterbi path (dotted line) for Russia against Czechia.

increase in GDP per capita of these two countries throughout the whole period was not so large as in the case of the Czech Republic (moreover, Ukraine did not record an increase in output in the last decade – its 2019 GDP per capita was less than in 2008, i.e. before the global crisis). Due to such growth trajectories, the Viterbi paths for Armenia and Ukraine started with state 0 and then switched to states 0.5 and 1. From the economic point

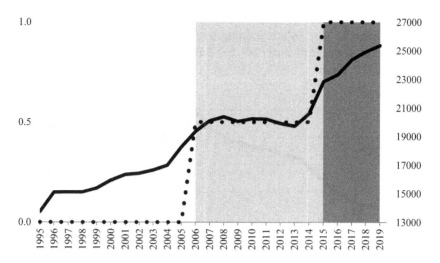

Figure 5.40 Per capita income gap (solid line) and the Viterbi path (dotted line) for Ukraine against Czechia.

of view, such a sequence of states indicates diverging tendencies between these countries and the Czech Republic.

Unlike Armenia and Ukraine, Russia exhibited a different behaviour (see Figure 5.39). During 1995–2009, the Russian Viterbi path noted state 0.5 leading to an ambiguous conclusion in terms of the catching-up process compared to the rest of the considered period. Such an outcome results from the fact that GDP per capita in Russia and the Czech Republic was rising at a similar rate during this period (see Figure 5.37). After the global crisis, GDP per capita in the Czech Republic exhibited a slower recovery than in Russia implying that during 2011–2014 the Russian Viterbi path indicated state 0, i.e. full convergence. Since 2014, the tendencies have reversed. Russia noted a slowdown and a moderate growth while the Czech Republic returned to its rapid growth observed prior to the global crisis. As a result, the Viterbi path changed the state to 0.5 in the years 2015–2016 and 1 during 2017–2019. Hence, the HMM algorithm demonstrates that Russia was diverging from the Czech Republic in the last three years. Such a result is not surprising, given the very unfavourable actions of Russia on the international arena and internal changes in the law being in contrast with the standards of the democratic society.

5.2.9 OECD countries

The last analysed group is OECD. The reference point is Luxembourg as in the EU28 group. That is why the selection of three countries includes the countries from outside the CEE region to avoid data redundancy: Australia,

Germany, and the USA. The respective time series and Viterbi paths are presented in Figures 5.41–5.44.

Differences in per capita income level between Australia and Luxembourg increased significantly till 2007. Afterwards, they were constant or

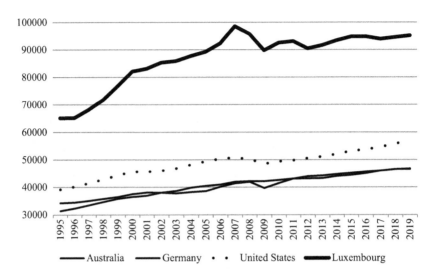

Figure 5.41 GDP per capita time series for the reference country (Luxembourg) and the other selected economies from the OECD group (at purchasing power parity, constant prices, 2011 international dollars).

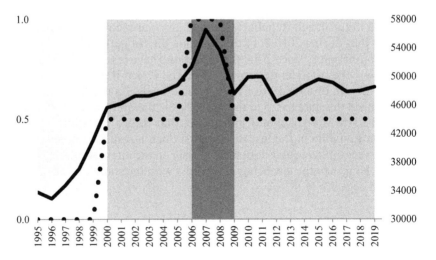

Figure 5.42 Per capita income gap (solid line) and the Viterbi path (dotted line) for Australia against Luxembourg.

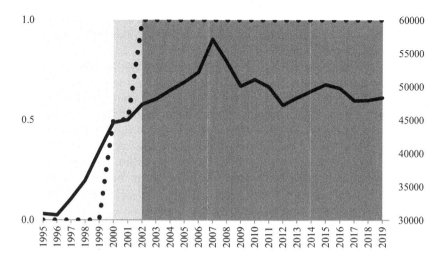

Figure 5.43 Per capita income gap (solid line) and the Viterbi path (dotted line) for Germany against Luxembourg.

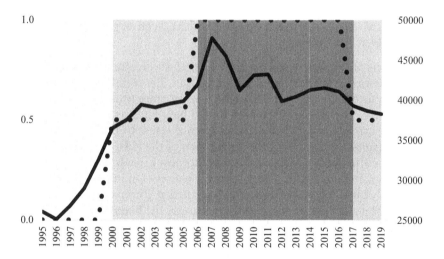

Figure 5.44 Per capita income gap (solid line) and the Viterbi path (dotted line) for the USA against Luxembourg.

even decreasing. This behaviour is well reflected by the Viterbi path for Australia: state 0 at the beginning till 1999, state 0.5 during the years 2000–2005, state 1 (full divergence) during 2006–2008, followed by state 0.5 from 2009 till the end of the analysed period. As we can see, in the last decade the HMM approach has not confirmed full convergence or full divergence between Australia and Luxembourg.

In the case of Germany, state 1 achieved already in 2002 was maintained until 2019. Hence, according to the HMM algorithm Germany, unlike Australia, has revealed divergence tendencies against Luxembourg during almost the last two decades.

The behaviour of the USA is akin to that for Australia and Germany; however, some dissimilarities exist as well. Differences in income per capita between the USA and Luxembourg were rising till 2007, then they started to fall. As a result, the sequence of states on the Viterbi path is such that the movement from convergence to divergence was observed at the beginning (turning point from state 0 to 0.5 occurred in 2000 and the one from state 0.5 to 1 took place in 2006). Hence, according to the HMM algorithm, divergence tendencies started already in 2006. However, the fall in the income gap between the USA and Luxembourg in the last years caused that the HMM method found another turning point in 2017 when the Viterbi path changed the state from 1 to 0.5. As a result, in the last year, the behaviour of the American economy is ambiguous from the point of view of confirmation or negation of convergence tendencies. It partly results from the fact that deep determinants of economic growth in Luxembourg and the USA are completely different, taking into account, e.g., the role these two countries play in the international arena.

5.3 HMM-based approach versus classical β convergence analysis – a summary

The results of HMM-based convergence analysis give an interesting picture of the economic growth paths compared with the standard approaches to the analysis of convergence – like the β convergence presented in the previous chapter. The results given here should be treated as complementary to those described earlier. The main difference refers to the fact that basing on the results obtained with the application of the HMM, the convergence is analysed towards a single country. Moreover, each country is treated separately. In contrast, in the β convergence regressions, all the countries are jointly included in model estimations; hence, β convergence results can be interpreted as giving the average picture of the behaviour of individual economies. In the HMM approach presented in this chapter, the countries are treated individually and the results are valid for a given pair of countries. Hence, they are not mean figures for the whole sample.

It is possible to average the results obtained for the individual countries with the HMM method and hence to analyse the convergence for the whole group. This approach has been assumed in Chapter 3 with regional convergence. However, due to a large number of analysed countries and the lack of possibility or doubtful sense of presenting the results for each of them separately, it was decided to omit the graphs and the analysis of the convergence process for the entire group of countries under study against the reference country.

Similarly, it is also possible to verify convergence not towards the most developed (or richest) country, but towards a given benchmark value (which may be the income level for the subgroup of countries, like Western Europe) (see, e.g., Bernardelli, Próchniak, and Witkowski, 2017, 2018). However, the idea of the HMM approach is still the same: states on the Viterbi path are found based on the examination of the single time series which – in the case of real income-level convergence – is the difference between per capita income in the two countries, regions, or their groups.

Compared to the conventional, econometric methods, an approach based on HMM has by far the advantage that it does not require many assumptions of a statistical or asymptotic nature. HMM convergence is also quite flexible and gives the possibility of easy generalizations, e.g. subgroup of countries, different time series (not only GDP), or use in averaging of weights related to the number of inhabitants. However, this method allows only for historical study, without – obvious for econometric models – forecasting feature. The last, but not least difference between these two approaches is the matter of time dependence and expressions of quantitative relationships. In the β convergence we have explicit value measuring the strength of the dependence, and in each time point, it is possible to estimate the value of the phenomenon under study. Meanwhile, in the HMM approach, we have blurred information in terms of the most probable state only. On this basis, we are unable to identify potential differences between the various years. We can, however, determine the moment when the change turned out to be so significant that it was reflected in the change of states. Taking into account the averaged results for many countries, compared to β convergence, there is, therefore, no need to study the stability of parameters, because the convergence function can be easily traced. If we limit ourselves to one pair of countries, the convergence function is simply the Viterbi path and the changes made by leaps and bounds, which gives much less information than the econometric model.

The comparison of β convergence and HMM convergence presented in this book, and most of all the results of empirical analysis, proves that each of approaches receives a valuable contribution to the analysis of the convergence process for a selected group of countries or regions. Convergence research should not be limited to any of the available methods, as the use of several of them at the same time may give a broader picture of the phenomenon under study. Moreover, research on convergence should be repeated along with the incoming macroeconomic data to be able to validate the previously obtained results, improve the methods used, and, above all, give arguments to politicians and economists as to the accuracy of their decisions affecting the regional, national, and world economy.

Notes

1 Since the GDP per capita values for Luxembourg are incomparably higher than the corresponding data for the CEE countries, the time series for Luxembourg is plotted on the right-hand side vertical axis of Figure 5.1, while the left-hand side vertical axis refers only to the CEE countries. If we were to plot the time series for all countries on one axis, the graph would be unreadable.

2 North Africa and the Middle East is a quite heterogeneous group. For example, the study by Hadizadeh (2019) suggests that there were two converging clubs in the group of 15 MENA (Middle East and North African) countries during the 1990–2015 period.
3 It has to be noted that Seychelles is not the typical Sub-Saharan African state. It is the island country located relatively far away from mainland Africa (the capital city of Victoria lies about 1,500 km from the mainland Africa). However, in some classifications this country is treated as Sub-Saharan African country. Such an approach was also adopted in this book. As a result, the convergence of Sub-Saharan African countries is analysed towards Seychelles.
4 See also the study by Ndao, Nenovsky, and Tochkov (2019) who analyse income convergence among the 14 African countries belonging to the CFA (*Communauté Financière Africaine*) monetary area using, among others, Markov models.

References

Abberger, K. and Nierhaus, W. (2010). Markov-Switching and the Ifo Business Climate: the Ifo Business Cycle Traffic Lights. *OECD Journal: Journal of Business Cycle Measurement and Analysis*, 2, pp. 1–13, doi: 10.1787/jbcma-2010–5km4gzqtx248.

Bernardelli, M., Próchniak, M. and Witkowski, B. (2017). The Application of Hidden Markov Models to the Analysis of Real Convergence. *Dynamic Econometric Models*, 17, pp. 59–80, doi: 10.12775/DEM.2017.004.

Bernardelli, M., Próchniak, M. and Witkowski, B. (2018). Przydatność ukrytych modeli Markowa do oceny podobieństwa krajów w zakresie synchronizacji wahań cyklicznych i wyrównywania się poziomów dochodu. *Roczniki Kolegium Analiz Ekonomicznych SGH*, 53, pp. 77–96.

Hadizadeh, A. (2019). Testing the Convergence Clubs Hypothesis among MENA Countries. *Iranian Economic Review*, 23(2), pp. 437–449, doi: 10.22059/ier.2019.70304.

Ndao, S., Nenovsky, N. and Tochkov, K. (2019). Does Monetary Integration Lead to Income Convergence in Africa? A Study of the CFA Monetary Area. *Portuguese Economic Journal*, 18, pp. 67–85, doi: 10.1007/s10258-018-0150-8.

Rapacki, R., ed. (2019). *Diversity of Patchwork Capitalism in Central and Eastern Europe*. London: Routledge.

Index

Note: **Bold** page numbers refer to tables; *italic* page numbers refer to figures and page numbers followed by "n" denote endnotes.

Printed in the United States
by Baker & Taylor Publisher Services